*Acknowledgments*

For special assistance to the editor during the compilation of the texts contained in this book, profoundest thanks to Greg Boyd, Jordan Jones, and P. R. Perkins, Esqs., to Drs. Guy Bennett, Geoff Hargreaves, and Gary Kern, and to the Hon. Imogen Wurzbach, Baroness von Tannenberg, scholars and gentlepersons, one and all.

# Pipe Dreams

## The Drug Experience in Literature

*Also by Gilbert Alter-Gilbert*

Anthologies

*Life and Limb: Selected Tales of Peril, Predicament, and Dire Distress*

Fictive Histories

*Poets Ranked by Beard Weight*

*The Desktop Digest of Despots and Dictators: An A to Z of Tyranny*

Translations

*The Mirror of Lida Sal: Tales Based on Mayan Myths and Guatemalan Legends* by Miguel Angel Asturias

*Manifestos Manifest* by Vicente Huidobro

*Strange Forces* by Leopoldo Lugones

*Scarecrow & Other Anomalies* by Oliverio Girondo

*Streetcorners: Prose Poems of the Demi-Monde* by Francis Carco

*Dead Man and Company: Poems* by Marie Redonnet

*On A Locomotive & Other Runaway Tales* by Massimo Bontempelli

# Pipe Dreams

## The Drug Experience in Literature

---

*Edited and with an Introduction by*
*Gilbert Alter-Gilbert*

COYOTE ARTS

Albuquerque, New Mexico

Cover photo: "Portrait of Charles Baudelaire," circa 1862, by Étienne Carjat.

"Circle Game" by Michael Stephans appeared previously in *The Color of Stones* (1997) Red Dancefloor Press.



**ISBN**

Paper: 978-1-58775-026-7

E-Book: 978-1-58775-038-0

LCCN 2021942506

10 9 8 7 6 5 4 3

Coyote Arts LLC

PO Box 6690

Albuquerque, New Mexico 87197-6690

www.coyote-arts.com

# Contents

# Introduction

*Gilbert Alter-Gilbert*

There are two histories of drug use: the social history and the secret history of subjective experience.

The social history is venerable and vast. Production of alcohol by fermentation was known to the Egyptians by 6,400 BCE, and alcohol was probably in general use as early as 10,000 BCE. In antiquity, Scythians threw cannabis onto bonfires or heated stones and inhaled the smoke; the effects of this "sacred grass" were known in India and China as early as 3,000 BCE. Sumerians were using opium, which they called their "joy plant," as early as 4,000 BCE. In 340 BCE there were 30,000 betel shops in Persia. Psychedelics have been in continuous use in Mexico for the past 5,000 years. Mushroom and cactus cults flourished not only in ancient Mesoamerica, but also in ancient Greece, China, and Mesopotamia.

Ataraxia, the ideal state of well-being in which the mind is balanced and free from care, was considered by the ancient Epicurean philosophers as the highest good. "To the extent that drugs exert these effects," one observer has noted, "they have long been endowed with a halo of divinity by the people who used them. The peyotyl was sacred to the Aztecs, the coca to the Incas. The gods in the *Vedas* drank soma, those of the Greeks ambrosia." It is not known whether certain drugs of which the ancients spoke are mythical or real. Nepenthe and lethe, gifts of Somnus, god of sleep, are as fabled as the "hundred-headed narkissus" and the story of the "lotos-eaters." Mang and soma are named in the *Avesta* and the *Rig Veda.* In Græco-Roman lore, phytochemical tickets to paradise are proffered by the poppy goddess, Demeter, while another taste of the infinite is offered by Dionysus and Bacchus, gods of wine. Drug experiences have been recorded by every culture in the world. In pagan Greece, the "Pythia" or priestess of the Oracle at Delphi, seated on a tripod in an ecstatic trance, pronounced predictions for the future after chewing laurel leaves and inhaling ecstatic fumes emitted from a fissure in the floor of the temple. Also, in Greece, the Mysteries of Demeter performed each autumn involved the holy drug kykeon, which engendered illumination. Yet another drug, which was probably ergot, a mold containing LSD, precipitated momentous spiritual experiences during the Eleusinian Mysteries, when it was administered to initiates by precinct hierophants. At the Incan Temple of the Sun in Cuzco, Peru, worshipers could enter only after having partaken of coca leaf. Incan artisans depicted their gods as crowned with coca wreaths. The sacred water lily associated with the ancient Egyptian god Osiris is the narcotic species Nymphæa cærulea. At Minoan archæological sites, clubs have been found carved in the shape of opium poppy capsules. Toltec and Mixtec civilizations of Guatemala and other sections of the Gulf of Mexico have left totemic sculptures representing psilocybin mushroom caps. Wherever men have found psychoactive plants, they have incorporated them into their religious beliefs, and preserved interpretive images of them in their art. Some scientists and social anthropologists have postulated that plants and man have undergone a process of biochemical co-evolution, an interaction involving not just food plants but also drug plants, including psychoactive ones. According to this theory, pastoral protohominids inhabiting East African grassland savannas ate the wild psilocybin mushrooms which sprouted there, and the resulting cognitive experience was the triggering event that set mankind on the road toward language, consciousness, and the concept of God.

Throughout the ages man has turned to drugs in a quest for release from his cares, mystical union with the godhead, or gateways to higher worlds. But despite the uniquely seductive powers of drugs, and the fascination they hold over the human imagination, man is yet earthbound, after all, and subject, as such, to the exigencies of mundane occupation. Thus it is that commerce in drugs such as coffee, tea, tobacco, chocolate, opium, hemp, and cocaine, has not only busied untold legions of men, but changed the course of nations. During the Opium Wars of 1839–1842, Britain forced opium consumption upon its defeated enemy, China, and millions of Chinese were addicted. Mandrake was used by Hannibal and Julius Cæsar to neutralize their foes. Vikings took fly-agaric to enter the "berserker" state for battle. BZ, a substance supposedly much more toxic than LSD, is part of the current U. S. Army chemical warfare arsenal. Narcotic incense was known during the Middle Ages, as was the administration of "sleep sponges" to induce surgical anæsthesia. Nevertheless, Raymond Lully, discoverer of anæsthetic properties of ether in 1290, Paracelsus, who prescribed the "Anodyne Specific" laudanum, or liquid opium, in the 16th century, and Joseph Priestly, who extolled nitrous oxide as an anæsthetic during the early 1700s, were all persecuted, sometimes unto death. Statues of the Father of Medicine, Æsculapius, show him crowned with poppy flowers. Hippocrates and Galen both advocated the liberal use of opium, which was dispensed and administered in the form of plasters, ointments, colloidal suspensions, and suppositories. By 1700, Venice Treacle, Sydenham's Laudanum, and Dr. Bates's Pacific Pill, all laced with opium, were prescribed for all sorts of aches and pains as well as "refreshment of the spirits." In the first decades of the twentieth century, medicine shows toured rural America, vending doped-up cure-alls. Even the most potent drugs were available by mail order, when door-to-door traveling salesmen weren't around. Belladonna was once a leading ingredient of the sleeping aid Sominex. Heroin and Cocaine were, at one time, trade names for patent medicines purchasable over the counter. Bayer, the German pharmaceutical firm famous for analgesics, created Heroin as a sort of super-aspirin. Marijuana wasn't made illegal until 1937. "Ether frolics" and "chloroform jags" were once widespread fads and, during the mid-nineteenth century, there was an ether-drinking epidemic in Ulster, Ireland, involving no fewer than 50,000 miscreants. In the 1960s, there was a phenacetin craze in Sweden. America's drug epidemics, which have sometimes been so severe as to have been regarded as national emergencies, have come in several waves, beginning with the period immediately following the War Between the States and continuing, of course, into the present epoch, with its smugglers and cartels inescapable items on the nightly news. At the opposite end of the scale from sybaritic indulgence in drugs for idle amusement, there is punitive psychiatry, in which medical drug abuse is performed by licensed physicians for purposes of mind control; a practice which was adopted in the "treatment" of political dissidents placed in Soviet "mental health" institutions and, some would argue, perpetuated even in certain U. S. sanitaria where "human warehousing" takes place. Whether drugs are the milk of paradise or the assassin of youth, man has put them to purposes both sacred and profane, and the controversy over the glories and dangers of both vogue drugs of the past and the most up-to-date, clandestinely synthesized "designer drugs" of the present, continues to rage.

Today, fine jewelry stores market platinum cocaine spoons which can be worn as pendants. At the beginning of the last century, morphine was perfectly legal and so fashionable that New York socialites custom-ordered jeweled syringes from Tiffany's for their morphine parties. Contemporary "discomania" and the "rave scene" have direct antecedents in the Parisian masked balls frequented by ether-fiends like Jean Lorrain. In the Belle Epoque, Alphonse Mucha painted advertising posters for absinthe distillers. Today, connoisseurs collect LSD "blotter" art, with hits intact. According to the Shaefer Commission report of 1973, "sixty to seventy per cent of the population are at least occasional medical users of psychoactive drugs"; people have even tried such alternative non-chemical methods of altering consciousness as chanting and the recitation of mantras, meditation, prolonged observation, manual phosphene stimulation, voluntary silence, self-hypnosis, prolonged isolation, fasting, sleep deprivation, the encouragement of hypnagogic phenomena, corybantic dancing, rolfing, concentration on mandalas, and the use of the Zen power yell, and stroboscopes. Among the substances on the contemporary scene which alter mood or consciousness or are used to get high are: meprobamate, methanol, methylphenidate, naloxone, oxycodone, phencyclidine, pentazocine, phenothiazine, paramethoxyamphetamine, propoxyphene, tricyclic antidepressants, amyl nitrite, anileridine, atropine, scopolamine and related alkaloids, chloral hydrate, diphenoxlate, ephedrine, ethchlorvynol, fenfluramine, haloperidol, harmaline and harmine, hydrocodone, levallorphan, lithium carbonate, methyprylon, MAO inhibitors, phenmetrazine, phentermine, STP, DOM, trimethoxyamphetamine, benzodiazepine, chlordiazepoxide, diazepam, oxazepam, flurazepam, triazolam, diethylpropion, disulfiram, glutethimide, hyrdromorphone, isopropanol, meperidine, Dilaudid, methadone, ketamine hydrochloride, and methaqualone.

No wonder that pharmacolatry has been called the religion of the present age.

Physicians, chemists, psychologists and sociologists, theologists and anthropologists, religious devotees, adventurers, journalists, philosophers and artists, street people and socialites have written about their exploits with drugs. The relationship between drugs and literature has been a long and fruitful one. Homer, Vergil, Chaucer, Shakespeare, and Milton, all allude to intoxicating drugs. Magical pills, potions, and elixirs even crop up in fairy tales. Whether watching their words being chiseled in clay tablets, or while energetically puffing on long-stemmed clay pipes, hoisting tankards, and driving long quills over sheets of parchment, or while pounding the keys of an aged typewriter, glugging coffee, and smoking chains of cigarettes, writers have cursed and solemnized, damned and glorified, denigrated and immortalized, deprecated and apotheosized, opprobriated and panegyrized drugs, and debated the virtues and vices of the states of mind they bring about. French playwright Antonin Artaud authored ferocious polemical texts defending freedom of drug use while Anaïs Nin wrote a memoir concerning an experiment with LSD, which she dismissed as unproductive. Sigmund Freud championed cocaine, then rejected it. Other scientists have written about drugs sheerly from a standpoint of neurochemical interest. Many anthropological treatises by and about members of the Native American Church and the "Peyote Road" they follow have inspired readers to seek their own visions. Confessions of junkies have done little or nothing to curtail morphinism or to dissuade newcomers from taking it up. Drug writings run the gamut from diary to diatribe, from straight science to loopy speculation and wild fantasy. But the spiritual history of drug use—the personal, direct, intimate history of drug use—is the subjective history of the drug experience itself. Drugs have often had a life-changing impact on those who've used them, and writers have not escaped this axiom. German novelist Ernst Jünger, a much-decorated professional soldier who died in 1998 at the age of 102, had many experiences with psychedelics, authored *A Mushroom Symposium* and other writings about drugs, and coined the term "psychonaut," to refer to those bound on drug-propelled voyages of spiritual discovery. Aldous Huxley's seminal exploratory essays, *Doors of Perception* and *Heaven and Hell,* ultimately present drugs as the salvation of society and the renewer of religion. During the 1950s and 1960s Huxley and Gordon Wasson, a banker who became convinced that psilocybin mushrooms were at the root of mankind's conception of God, published articles about psychedelics not only in scholarly journals but in popular, mass-circulation magazines the likes of *Life* and *The Saturday Evening Post.* In more recent years, Truman Capote and Tennessee Williams had much-publicized problems with drugs. Other writers, such as Ken Kesey and Hunter S. Thompson, celebrated them.

Drugs have exerted an influence on literature since the beginning. Roman poet Petronius, Chinese poet Li Po, and Persian poet Omar Khayyam were celebrants of wine. Nostradamus is said to have received his prophetic revelations while in a narcotic trance. English poet Thomas Chatterton committed suicide with poison at the age of seventeen. Upon the publication of Charles Dickens's *The Mystery of Edwin Drood,* with its atmospheric evocation of an East London opium den, many journalistic portraits of hophouses followed and, in fiction, opium use was conducted by such characters as Lord Henry Wotton in Oscar Wilde's *The Picture of Dorian Gray.* There is a scene in *Villette* by Charlotte Bronte, in which the character Lucy Snowe wanders about the streets of Brussels at night, high on opium. Victorian poets Dante Gabriel Rossetti and Algernon Charles Swinburne were chloral hydrate habituées. In fact, Rossetti suffered, on occasion, from chloral delirium, a delirum tremens–like condition involving persecution mania precipitated by excessive chloral use. Rossetti's wife Elizabeth Siddall was addicted to laudanum; Edgar Allan Poe had a lady friend who was given to inhaling from her ever-present ether-soaked handkerchief. Jean Lorrain and Guy de Maupassant were ether addicts. Ether and chloroform stories include "Dreams" by Guy de Maupassant; "Possessed" by Jean Lorrain; "Under the Knife" by H. G. Wells; and "Under Chloroform" by Maurice Level. Lafcadio Hearn used drugs; Artaud was addicted to morphine. Fitz Hugh Ludlow was a friend of Fitz-James O'Brien and turned on Thoreau and Melville to hashish. Algernon Blackwood and Sax Rohmer both used drugs at one time; Marcel Scwob smoked cigarettes mixed with opium; Ernest Dowson was an absinthist; Georg Trakl was a drug addict; Charles Nodier is said to have been an opium user; and it is probable that Laurent Tailhade was, too. French writers who took ether, opium, or hashish and wrote about it are: Latouche, Musset, Alphonse Karr, Balzac, Dumas, Gautier, Nerval, Baudelaire, Lorrain, Merimee, Farrerre, Michaux, Artaud, Boissard, Pierre MacOrlan, and Francis Carco. Drug stories by French authors include "Dark Angel" by Gaston Danville; *Journey to the Orient* by Gérard de Nerval; "The Drug" by Leon-Paul Fargue; and *Affidavits of an Ether-Drinker* by Jean Lorrain.

Anti-marijuana scare literature of the 1930s, 1940s, 1950s, such as *Growth of the Marijuana Habit Among Our Youth* and *On the Trail of Marijuana, the Weed of Madness,* are notable modern pieces, as is Herbert Huncke's *A Brief Oral History of Benzedrine Use in the U.S.*, dating from the same period. Pulp novels of the 1950s and 1960s such as *Reefer Girl* and *Drugged Into Sin* evolved into Ryū Murakami's hedonist-nihilist *Almost Transparent Blue* of the 1970s, then the "hip urban novels" such as Tama Janowitz's *Slaves of New York;* Brett Easton Ellis's *Less Than Zero,* and Jay McInerney's *Bright Lights, Big City* of the 1980s. Cocaine peppers the pages of these books, and cough syrup dribbles across them. McInerney calls cocaine "Bolivian marching powder"; other drugs of fashion in these novels are Valium, Xanax, Ritalin, crystal methedrine, Celestone, Decadron, Desoxyn, Actifed, Thorazine, Nembutal, Seconal, lithium, amyl nitrite, codeine, and Nyquil. *Almost Transparent Blue,* an import from Japan, is an exemplar of the contemporary drug novel, with its Nibrole pill parties, promiscuous sex, and pools of brown vomit. In its wake, appeared such exercises as *'Ludes* by Benjamin Stein, and *Spidertown* by Abraham Rodriguez, Jr. Perpetuating the bloodline is the current brood of more-decadent-than-thou compositions by Scotland's Irvine Welsh: *Ecstasy; The Acid House*; and *Trainspotting,* in which the reckless excesses extend to just about everything short of mainlining formaldehyde. All this pop fiction had its precedents. Of all the paperback potboilers aimed at the topical market, an indisputable standout is Jacqueline Susann's *The Valley of the Dolls,* with its beautiful losers, ridiculous plot, utter lack of literary value, and profligate use of Seconal and Demerol, the original "trashy novel."

Miscellaneous drug-themed literary works of the 1950s and 1960s range from Aldous Huxley's *Island*, with its mystical drug, "moksha"; to Anthony Burgess's *A Clockwork Orange*, with its Droogs who frequent the Korova Milk Bar, availing themselves of such psychedelic beverages as "Molokko Plus" seasoned with "Synthemesc," "Vellocet," or "Drencrom"; to the single, sustained opium fantasy of Sadegh Hedayat's *The Blind Owl*; to Terry Southern's *The Blood of a Wig*, which embroiders on the idea of deriving a psychedelic-style trip via blood transfusions taken from a schizophrenic; to Nelson Algren's *The Man With the Golden Arm* and William S. Burroughs's *Junkie*—realist portraits of morphinism as a social problem.

Lighter fare in the same vein finds expression in such endeavors as Robin Cook's *Acceptable Risk*, in which a neuroscientist synthesizes a vial of antidepressant alkaloid from a drug linked to the Salem Witch Trials; and in the perpetual lineup of detective fiction featuring "knock-out drops" slipped into cocktails, and substances such as curare, "tasteless, odorless, untraceable"—clichés of murder mysteries utilized by malefactors to perpetrate the "perfect crime."

The long tradition of confessional and cautionary literature, usually luridly sensationalizing the more prurient aspects of drug use—the "anonymous jaws and hairy machines" of bad trips, and the pitfalls of addiction—is represented by such novels and autobiographies as Michael Chaplin's *I Couldn't Smoke the Grass on My Father's Lawn*; Nina Bawden's *The Birds on the Trees*; *I Was a Drug Addict* by Leroy Street; and Nathan McCall's *Makes Me Wanna Holler.* Whether it's a memoir of taking the sleep cure for morphinism in Switzerland, or nostalgia for the bad old days of ample dope and wanton companions, these books run the gamut. *Opium: Diary of a Cure* by Jean Cocteau is written in the spirit of contrition and affliction; *The Diaries of Harry Crosby* are straightforward and matter-of-fact. *Hashish* by Horacio Quiroga outlines, step-by-step, what happened when a strong oral dose of hashish "put him near death." Quiroga, having ingested the drug in pill form, after procuring it from a friend who worked at a pharmacy, grossly overdosed, and thought he was going to die. Quiroga also tried opium (without effect), saturated himself with ether (which resulted in nausea and headache), and dosed himself with chloroform in "brutal quantities," which proved so effective, that he didn't have time to stopper the flask before blacking out; he slept with 100 grams spilled on his pillow. "At first," he writes, "it gently hallucinated me, later it idiotized me, so I decided to leave it alone ... but hashish was, by far, the worst." Also of note are Reuben Eubank's 1903 *Twenty Years in Hell,* which recounts his "two decades on the needle"; D. F. McMartin's 1923 autobiography *Thirty Years in Hell, or the Confessions of a Drug Fiend,* concerning his morphinism; and the anonymous *Confessions of a Young Lady Laudanum-Drinker,* circa 1889.

Drug-themed sociological literature assumes a broad range of expressions. *Smack* by Arup Kumar Datta, is an unashamedly propagandistic children's book from India, where heroin addiction is a problem among early teens and sub-teens; *Addicted: Kids Talking About Drugs in Their*

*Own Words* by Joel Engele and *The Negative Scream* by Sally O'Brien are comprised of interviews, patient profiles, and case histories of persons who took drug overdoses. *Heroin: The Myths and the Facts* by Richard Ashley and *The Addict* by Dan Wakefield are standard "day in the life of a junkie" portraits. Besides the accident report and the fatigue inquest, another subgenre is the study, clinical or fictional, of the psychology of addiction. Of this subtype, may be cited *Dope: The Story of the Living Dead* by Winifred Black, and *Dope* by Sax Rohmer. Some habituées who have kicked the hard drug habit by means of the "writing cure," have left gripping vintage accounts of cold turkey withdrawal sickness from severe addiction at such institutions as the gothic and draconian Lexington Drug Rehabilitation Facility in Kentucky. Other remedies for the scourge of addiction prescribed by the vintage literature are the "hyoscine cure" and the "sleep cure."

A sizable body of standard scholarly treatises by criminologists and sociologists offers a general overview of the properties and effects of recreational drugs and patterns of use, while morbidly observing the rituals of the drug culture in minute detail. In these books, the hophead's paraphernalia is carefully listed, and esoteric terminology is explained. Thus the reader learns that "joy-popper" is a weekend drug user, and a "safety pin shot" is an injection of drugs squirted from an eye dropper into a puncture made by the point of a safety pin. A "yen tsiang," the reader is advised, is an opium pipe or "smoke pistol"; "hop toy" is a buffalo horn box to keep opium in; "yen hauck" is a kit consisting of a needle, a small glass lamp with a glass cover, and a pair of tweezers. Glossaries are often appended to these tomes, by way of elucidating drug culture's peculiar nomenclature. Here, terms such as "uppers," "downers," "nickel bag," "dime bag," "THC," "hash oil," and "mood elevators" are defined. Some works, like *Street of Joy* by Henry de Leeuw, while finding no offense in the moral faiblesse of dope fiends, wallow in the sordid particulars of drug preparation, harvesting, preparation, use and consequences. With books of this sort, aimed at optimal titillation, the reader glimpses hashish salons in Beirut, where almond-eyed Arab girls "toast the brownish syrupy drug over dim lamps" and hopjoints in Shanghai, where Mandarins "use yen-hooks to stab wads of opium for toasting a bolus of green paste over a hissing fire." At least they are free of anecdotes such as that in *Blackwoods Magazine* of 1853, which stated that users of opium blew smoke out their ears.

Inspired by Charles Dickens's *Mystery of Edwin Drood*, a host of European and American yellow journalists began to look for opium dens in their own back yards and, in major port cities, invariably found them. "Opium's Varied Dreams" by Stephen Crane is a good example of one such journalistic exposé. Another is "Dissipation of New York Belles: Interior of a Hasheesh Hell," an article which appeared in the *Illustrated Police News* of December 2, 1876. Perhaps the best of them, H. H. Kane's article "A Hashish House in New York," was published in *Harper's New Monthly Magazine* in 1883. Beneath glaring headlines, these articles sniff out hemp retreats and other domdaniels of dissolution and despair like terriers sniffing out rats. Corroborating the master-slave paradigm of drug addiction, they run riot with moral outrage among "diabolical drug undergrounds," "laboratories manufacturing death," and "dumping grounds for forfeit souls."

Temperance tracts warning of the evils of alcohol and other drugs have always shadowed the conventional forms of literature concerned with the subject. Perusing these writings conjures visions of sanctimonious tub-thumpers with their harangues and imprecations against vice triumphant imploring dazed cocainomaniacs to forgo their execrable rations, urging all persons of conscience to join in the effort to rid respectable society of pushers, panders, and all affiliated scum, and calling on sad, "infatuated beings" addled by illicit drugs to desist and repent, in a dither of reprimands, recriminations, regrets and illusions. A special target of disapproval in the United States in the 1930s was marijuana. Officially labeled "the killer weed" and "destroyer of youth," this bringer of "reefer madness" was said to foment murder and suicide. In more recent years, truly destructive drugs have come to the fore. The "crack house" has become a major subject of study, and reports of PCP frenzies often grab the headlines. PCP, also known as "angel dust," is the drug Sernyl which, like "crack," seems particularly prone to promoting toxic psychosis and transforming its votives into vicious degenerates. Demon Rum, of course, has occasioned any number of classic caveats to depraved dipsomaniacs to "steer clear of the liquid venom," and warning the degenerate "drunkard, his brain aflame with glory, hideously splashing in the gutter's filth" that, before he quaffs his next cup of cheer, he should consider that what awaits him is Warnicke's syndrome, Korsakoff's psychosis, and the formication and hallucinosis of delirium tremens.

In addition to *The Hasheesh Eater: Passages from the Life of a Pythagorean,* Fitz Hugh Ludlow authored a cautionary tract titled "What Shall They Do To Be Saved?" which Louis Bragman called an "impassioned indictment against the treacherous poppy seed." In this article Ludlow writes "God seems to help a man in getting out of every difficulty but opium. There you have to CLAW your way out over red hot coals on your hands and knees and drag yourself by main strength through the burning dungeon bars." Cloyingly melodramatic, Ludlow's tract advises the application of chloroform as a last resort to alleviate symptoms of opium withdrawal. Ludlow posits that a doctor might tell an opium user of ten years standing: "Sir, the chances are entirely against you ... You have either suffered a disorganization of irreproducible membranes, or you have deposited so much improper material in your tissues that your life is not consistent with the protracted pain of removing it ... All this time you continued to absorb an agent which directly acts for what, by a *paradox,* may be called fatal conservation of the tissue. Whether through its complexly burned nitrogen, carbon or both ... the drug has starved the fires of your whole system.... You have sealed up all but one excretory passage—the pores of the skin, and when that gives out, your body shall be shut up like an entirely choked chimney.... The rest of your life must be spent in keeping comfortable, not in being happy."

Where drugs are concerned, medical literature has concentrated on matters of dosage, adulterants and impurities, side effects and adverse reactions, and risks of anæsthetic accidents. Encyclopedic drug compendia such as Dioscorides's *Materia Medica,* the Chinese *Pen Ts'ao,* and the Indian *Rajvallabha,* have been around since antiquity. Important successors to them include the *Pharmacopoea Persica* by Père Ange; the *Complete English Dispensatory; The Medicines of the Egyptians* by Propser Alpini; and *Colloquies on the Simples and Drugs of India* by Garcia da Orta. Apart from frequently maudlin case histories, most medical writing tends to take the form of logbooks and records of experiments. From Æsculapius forward, physicians have acted as human guinea pigs, first testing the therapeutic potential of drugs on themselves. Many medical men historically experimented in the quest to find effective surgical anæsthesia, and medical psychologists Sigmund Freud, Havelock Ellis, Weir Mitchell, and William James, all tried various psychoactive drugs in an attempt to understand their mechanisms and harness their medicinal benefits. Occasionally, their reports show flashes of startling insight, but all too often they are inaccessibly insulated by elaborate but dry titles such as *On the Comparative Ethnopharmacology of Myristaceous and Malpighiaceous Hallucinogens,* or are merely quaintly amusing, as in the case of the phrase "faradic and galvanic electrical shocks are applied to boost the Autotoxin's general convulsant properties."

A considerable body of anthropological literature examines the use of naturally occurring hallucinogenic substances among "primitive" peoples and the brujos, shamans, and curanderos who dispense plant medicines and mediate during drug-taking rites. Typical of the genre is R.

Gordon Wasson's *The Hallucinogenic Fungi of Mexico,* which assumes religious and philosophical overtones. Antonin Artaud's *The Peyote Dance* details the peyote rituals of the Tarahumara Indians of Northern Mexico, whom Artaud called "the race of lost men." *The Yage Letters* of Beat poet Allen Ginsberg and gentleman junkie William S. Burroughs consist of letters they exchanged while touring the jungles of Bolivia in search of "the vine of souls." Terence and Dennis McKenna's entertaining books recapture their colorful exploits in Ecuador in search of wild psilocybin. Paddy Chayevsky's *Altered States* begins in this familiar way, with a field expedition to the fastnesses of the Mexican high sierra: "The Hinchi Indians weren't in San Luis Potosi but in Zapatecus Province, a tribe of pre-Aztecs living amid the brutal barrancas of central Mexico. They were descendants of the Chichimec Toltecs, but the local brujo turned out to be a Tarahumara Indian who had married into the tribe." As the novel proceeds, the Hinchis are seen to be gathering a plant they call the "First Flower," because it "invokes ancient memories." Then, after the return from the sacred fields, the ground roots, buds, leaves, and petals are mixed with crumbled mushrooms and "stored away for a year in sealed gourds to become sufficiently moldy." Later, they are broken out, melted into "a sludgelike yellow substance" made from "boiled mushroom caps, which had been calcinating for two days now," and ingested. The user of this drug returns to the "First Soul," which the Indians call "Unborn Stuff." Chayevsky delivers up rich descriptions of the "caking calx" which forms the basis for a psychedelic admixture consisting of "three parts of the dried mushroom residue to one part sinicuiche powder and one part the powder of some third plant with a Toltec name." And his dialog, exemplified by such lines as, "I didn't turn into a molten mass of neural substance, did I?" is priceless. Carlos Castaneda's Teachings of *Don Juan; A Separate Reality*; and *A Yaqui Way of Knowledge* concern the lessons imparted by the probably fictitious "plant teacher" Don Juan Matus, a Mexican herbalist who instructs the author in the art of "seeing," using peyote buttons and a "smoking mixture" compounded from psychotropic plants. Don Juan, who calls peyote "mescalito," explains the plants as being vehicles that conduct a man to an understanding of the "units of meaning" of certain impersonal forces or "powers," with which a sorcerer has "meetings" in order to gain control over them. According to Castaneda's purported field notes, "a man of knowledge perceives the 'essence' of the things of the world." Most drug-related anthropological literature is reportorial in tone, and tends to approach its subject as a mystico-religious phenomenon, as in the case of mesoamerican mycolatry, devotion to the "Peyote Road," or in worship of any of various other forms of vegetation, whether among the Huichol roadmen, Putamayo, Hindu sadhus, or African Bwiti cults. The anthropological literature also acknowledges the fact that for thousands of years, the "sorcery" practiced by native Americans has been a legitimate science, and its stews, brews, unguents, electuaries, collations, and distillations form a folk pharmacopeia from whose bitter charms many secrets may be gleaned. Anthropologists note, for example, that peyotists and ayahuasceros exhibit confirmed instances of psychopharmacognosy: the drug-facilitated faculty of peering into the future.

Drugs abound in science fiction and fantasy literature, with some of the earliest examples focusing on immortality draughts. Nathaniel Hawthorne's "Dr. Heidegger's Experiment" concerns the water of the Fountain of Youth, while his stories "The Birthmark" and "The Dolliver Romance" center on the elixir of immortality, as does Balzac's "Elixir of Life." Other early specimens are *Dr. Jekyll and Mr. Hyde* by Robert Louis Stevenson, a story revolving around the effects of a personality-transformation potion, while Lewis Carroll's *Through the Looking Glass* and *Alice in Wonderland* refer to pills which gigantize or miniaturize those who swallow them. Among the many invented drug stories are Frank Belknap Long's "The Hounds of Tindalos," which features pellets of the ancient Chinese preparation "Liao," intended to aid travel through time; H. G. Wells's "The New Accelerator," which explores the social implications of a synthetic superstimulant, and Marcel Ayme's "The Walker-Through-Walls," in which a man named Dutilleul, a third-grade clerk in the Ministry of Registration, suddenly finds himself, thanks to an invisibility pill, able to walk through walls, undetected by all around him, until he takes the antidote, a cachet of "tetravalent reintegration powder," which not only renders him visible once again but results in his finding himself imprisoned in an apartment building partition. In Felisberto Hernandez's "Lovebird Furniture," a drummer for a furniture manufacturer boards a municipal trolley and, as a "promotional stunt," accosts a passenger, rubs alcohol on his bare arm, and injects him with a hypodermic syringe. The passenger then begins to hear in his head a radio program sponsored by "Lovebird Furniture," detectable only by those "sensitized" to the broadcasts, and that can be turned off only by taking a "lovebird" pill. "The Chaser," perhaps the most celebrated story in John Collier's collection *Fancies and Goodnights*, has to do with the murderous use of a certain "glove cleaner," which becomes imperative after the all-too-successful effects of a love potion prove intolerable. In "The Underdevelopment Pharmacy" by Turkish author Nazli Eray, the "Antamericana" pill, which costs 10,000 liras for a 31 day cure, helps the inhabitants of third-world countries to forget the benefits of advanced civilization. The use of drugs for social control or hedonic engineering is a frequent theme in such science fiction as "The Opium Eater" by David H. Keller; *The Valley of Silent Men* by C. E. Vivian; "The Phantom Drug" by A. W. Kapfer; *Dr. Orpheus* by Ian Wallace; "The Plutonian Drug" by Clark Ashton Smith; *The Sacred Mushroom* by Andrija Pukarich; *Pausodyne* by G. Allen; "The Strange Drug of Dr. Caber" by Lord Dunsany; "The Diabolical Drug" by Claire Winger Harris; and *The Unsleep* by Diana Gillon. William S. Burroughs's drug-glutted *Naked Lunch* veers into fantasy, as does Santiago Dabove's "To Be Dust," a tale of a man who falls off his horse after dosing himself with painkillers, and gradually begins to take root in the earth, like a plant.

The historical impact of nicotine and caffeine on literary production is not inconsequential. The earliest European observation of tobacco use occurred in Brazil in 1555. By 1600, tobacco use had spread around the world. By 1614, 7,000 shops in London purveyed tobacco and the "stinking and infectious breath" of smokers had already become a problem. By 1921, 14 states in the USA prohibited smoking; in 1927, this prohibition was repealed. About tobacco Robert Ingersoll penned the prose-poem "The Sacred Leaves," while Alfred Dunhill mustered such efforts as *The Gentle Art of Smoking* and *The Pipe Book.*

The flower of the tea plant, Camellia thea, has inspired many a poet. The Chinese bard Lu Wuh authored a three-volume book about tea during the Tang Period; afternoon tea has become a tradition in England, and is the setting for innumerable scenes in drawing room comedies and Edwardian novels. Cocoa, also known as cacao, cacahuatl, or chocolate, and whose scientific name is theobroma, comes from the seeds of a tree, and was served in the court of Montezuma. The African kola nut, which also comes from a tree, is made into a stimulant beverage. Kava-kava, as it is called in Fiji and Tonga, is derived from a pepper plant rhizome, and is used as a matinal pick-me-up throughout Polynesia. Guarana, a morning beverage which comes from the Amazon region, is another drug dependent for its action on caffeine. It contains two and a half times as much of the stuff as coffee or kola. When first introduced in Egypt, coffee was condemned as the Devil's beverage, its use was suppressed, and inventories of coffee, whenever found, were burned by the authorities. Today, coffee is an economic staple in almost every country in the Tropics. Sufi dervishes in mid-15th century Ethiopia were the first to use coffee, which they employed to lengthen their religious devotions. Coffee quickly caught on, and its use in the Arabian Peninsula spread throughout Europe, where the coffee house, a novelty imported from the lands of the Prophet, soon found its niche, and became a casual literary forum. From the time The Angel, the first coffee house in England, opened in Oxford in 1651, and provided a cozy haven for Samuel Pepys and John Aubrey, the "penny universities," as they were called, because a cup of coffee cost a penny, became a regular fixture in the European cultural landscape, and gave birth to the "Bohemian" conviviality which was to be their hallmark ever after. Coffee was called the wine of Islam and, from the 1600s on, was enjoyed in cities from Berlin and Vienna to Seville and Buenos Aires, and from Rome and Naples to Zurich and Prague. Brother Coffee was considered a stimulant to thought. Alexander Pope and Jonathan Swift were coffee fanatics; Voltaire is said to have put away 80 cups per day! Preeminent among the Old English coffee houses was Will's, on Russell Street, in the Covent Garden district of London, an establishment frequented by Dryden, Pope, Congreve, Wycherly, and Addison during the Augustan Age. At Button's Coffee House, Richard Steele and Ambrose Phillips hung out with Opoe and Swift. At Parisian coffee houses such as The Pomme de Pin, François Villon, Rabelais, Mathurin Regnier, Guillaume Colletet, Bensarade, and Faret sipped java. Saint-Amont took his aromatic refections at Le Petit Muare. The Mouton Blanc was where La Fontaine, Molière, and Boileau could be seen. But the premier literary café in Paris in the late 17th and early 18th centuries was the Procope, where the preparation of coffee was said to be a science, and where, because of its proximity to the Comédie-Française, many actors and playwrights congregated. The Procope was a pageant of glory for 100 years, eventually playing host to Diderot, D'Alembert and the Encyclopedists and to such other writers as Beaumarchais, Saint-Ange, Pierre Roy, Guyot de Merville, Moncrif, Nivelle de la Chausée Richer, Saint-Ange, Buyrette du Belloy, Lemiere, Grimm, Buffon, Boindin-Duclos, Lagrange-Chancel, Danchet, Baron, Regnard, Crébillon père and Crébillon fils, Rousseau, l'abbé Alary, Houdard de la Motte, Fontenelle, l'abbé Pellegrin, Fréret, Prion, and Dumarsais.

In time, the traditional coffee house evolved into the modern café, and continued to serve as a natural meeting place for writers and artists of all stripes. But before the Futurists, Dadaists, Vorticists, and Surrealists convened their cabals at La Closerie des Lilas or Les Deux Magots in Paris, Théophile Gautier patronized the Café de Constantinople; Huysmans, Paul Fort, Jules Laforgue, and Edouard Dujardin patronized the Café Voltaire; and admirers of Greek poet Jean Moreas flocked to sit at his feet at the Dead Rat. Yet another colorfully named establishment was The Fountain of Grammar, where poet Émile Goudeau formed the literary circle known as the Hydropaths, who were succeeded, in turn, by the Hirsutes, who gathered at the Café du Commerce. Brillat-Savarin hung out at the Café de Foy; at the Momus and Brasserie des Martyrs, writers such as Henry Murger and Gérard de Nerval hung their hats. The brothers Goncourt, Dumas père, and Balzac preferred Tortoni's, as did Musset, Vigny, and Champfleury. The Café Guerbois was Zola's favorite. During the Mauve Decade of the 1890s, the Domino Room of London's Café Royal hosted a rogues' congress of literary fauna: Frank

Harris, Max Beerbohm, George Moore, Walter Pater, and Algernon Charles Swinburne spent as much time there as Stephen Spender and Christopher Isherwood were to do 50 years later. Described as a "halfway house between Soho and Mayfair," The Café Royal was where Oscar Wilde held court. Augustan London had 2,000 coffeehouses. By 1810, there were 4,000 cafés in Paris. At the beginning of the 20th century, writers Arthur Schnitzler, Stefan Zweig, Peter Hills, and Franz Grillparzer regularly camped in the plush booths of Viennese coffee houses, whose vast salons, overhung with ornate chandeliers and fringed by lavish zinc bars, doubled as reading rooms.

Authors even did a fair amount of writing in these establishments, hunched in corners, nursing their steaming black libations. Henri Murger died thinking he had done himself in by drinking an excess of coffee. From the days the Cavalier Poets swished through Covent Garden's java dens, to those of London's exclusive Scriblerus Club, Kit-Kat, and Hanover, and on to those of the cliques of international avant-gardists who assembled at Montmarte's Lapin Agile, writers have enjoyed the spirit of informal rendezvous and bonhomie fostered by such habitats, and the caffeine-abetted pleasures of sitting and talking all day long or late into the night.

The roster of writers guilty of habitual alcohol use and of penning words of praise or disparagement on its behalf, would stretch from Timbuctu to Zanzibar but, among the literary drinkers of monumental proportions must certainly be numbered Dylan Thomas, Brendan Behan, Ernest Hemingway, Jack Kerouac, Alexander Grin, Leonid Andreyev, and John Berryman. The Mermaid Tavern in Elizabethan London was a crapulous nest where Shakespeare, Marlowe, Donne, Beaumont, Fletcher, and Johnson knocked back countless tankards of ale; Samuel Johnson and Oliver Goldsmith met once a week at the Turk's Head; Verlaine and Rimbaud frequented the humbler cafés of Paris, where they shared more than one glass of opalescent absinthe with poet Charles Cros. Guillaume Apollinaire published a volume entitled *Alcools* while Jean Moréas published a piece called *Absinthe Dream*, which details the hallucinations of a character who has downed a tumbler too many of that "pale fire." F. Scott Fitzgerald authored an account of his alcoholic misfortunes titled *The Crack-Up.* In Malcolm Lowry's *Under the Volcano,* the protagonist, the Consul, stumbles through the entire novel in an alcoholic haze. In "The Orange Distillers," a story by Horacio Quiroga, the Poe of Uruguay, a high-proof liquor distilled from fermented oranges causes a man to go mad and murder his child. The perpetrator, Dr. Else, an alcoholic physician suffering from delerium tremens, guzzles the liquor "unstintingly, just as it dripped from the plates of the still; with all its brain poisons." Before he dies from downing a "liter of carbureted lamp alcohol," the protagonist first sees *fauna alcoholica* in the form of a "centipede crawling around the walls," then mistakes his daughter for a "monstrous rat" and beats her to death. Some take a condemnatory stance towards alcohol. Both Walt Whitman and Upton Sinclair saw fit to pen temperance novels. Whitman's book, *Franklin Evans, or The Inebriate,* appeared in 1842 while Sinclair's offering, *The Wet Parade,* riding the crest of volsteadism, hit the shelves in 1931. During the interim between these dates, Robert Ingersoll wrote: "I believe that alcohol, to a certain degree, demoralizes those who make it, those who sell it, and those who drink it. I believe from the time it issues from the coiled and poisonous worm of the distillery until it empties into the hell of crime, death, and dishonor, it demoralizes everybody who touches it. I do not believe that anybody can contemplate the subject without becoming prejudiced against this liquid crime. All you have to do is to think of the wrecks upon either bank of this stream of death—of the suicides, of the insanity, of the poverty, of the ignorance, of the distress, of the little children tugging at the faded dresses of weeping and despairing wives, asking for bread; of the men of genius it has wrecked; of the millions who have struggled with imaginary serpents produced by this devilish thing. And when you think of the jails, of the almshouses, of the prisons, and of the scaffolds upon either bank—I do not wonder that every thoughtful man is prejudiced against the damned stuff called alcohol." Tolstoy despised it and drug use, as witness the piece included in this anthology, "Why Men Stupefy Themselves."

For the better part of the past two centuries, opiates have figured prominently in world literature, as well as in the lives of literature's practitioners. During the early 1800s, English poet Samuel Taylor Coleridge, who also sampled hashish, chloral hydrate, and henbane, was addicted to opium to the extent that he consumed two pints of laudanum a day. His younger contemporary Thomas De Quincey sometimes neared a pint a day of the "ruby-red elixir." Coleridge and De Quincey had the same physician, one Dr. Beddoes of

Bristol, who liberally prescribed opium as a sort of panacea. Coleridge's favorite brand was Lancashire Genuine Black Drop, which had about three times the potency of other brands on the market. Both poets binged intermittently for the rest of their lives, and Coleridge was never able to fully wean himself away from "Old Blacky," but he ultimately found contentment on the transcendentalist lecture circuit in America, where he was the subject of a major personality cult. De Quincey, who made his drug habit famous with his *Confessions of an English Opium-Eater,* wrote of being "hooted at, grinned at, chattered at by monkeys ... kissed with cancerous kisses by crocodiles and laid, confounded with unutterable slimy things, amongst reeds and nilotic mud." Additional English poppy heads were the novelist Wilkie Collins, and the poets George Crabbe and Francis Thompson. Frequent users were Keats, Shelley, Byron, Elizabeth Barrett Browning, Lord Bulwer-Lytton, Jane Welsh Carlyle, and Dickens. Sir Walter Scott used opium as an anodyne, though he regarded it as a miserable nostrum. Graham Green and Jean Cocteau were also users. Cocteau has written that "everything one does in life, even love, occurs in an express train racing toward death. To smoke opium is to get out of the train while it is still moving. It is to concern oneself with something other than life or death." In the early 1900s, Albert de Pouverville circulated pro-opium tracts, and Louis Lalloy authored the opium-extolling *The Book of Smoking.* As a topic of general fiction, opium has often found favor. There are *Opium* by Paul Bonnetain, *Opium* by Geza Csath, and *Opium* by Guillaume Apollinaire; *The Opium Smokers* by Jules Boissiere; *Out of the Silence* by Claude Farrere; and *Dead End* by Sadegh Hedayat. In *The Opium-Eater* by Iqbal Ahmad, an eccentric Pakistani misanthrope named Sanki is addicted to opium pellets, along with his bald pet parrot which can recite a few lines of Hafiz when sober. Gradually Sanki becomes more and more withdrawn, lives in a world of poetry, doesn't eat or sleep, and dies of his addiction, speaking of worlds "beyond the clouds, even beyond the stars." In the Burmese folk tale "The Opium-Eater and the Four Ogres," an opium-drunkard oblivious to his surroundings, à la Mr. Magoo, inadvertently outwits and confounds four evil spirits who intend to make a meal of him but instead leave him a tribute in the form of a pot of gold so that he wakes from his opium reverie in the haunted house to find himself a rich man though he has no recollection how or why.

Victorian children were often dosed with Mrs. Winslow's Soothing Syrup, Godfrey's Cordial, or Collis Browne's Chlorodyne, which served as all-purpose palliatives; all of them consisted of liquid opium. Many pharmaceutical supply houses owe their early successes to the manufacture of morphine, since, until the end of the 19th century, morphine-based commercial medicines were available cheaply and without prescription. Around the turn of the last century, "free trial bottles" of heroin were handed out on streetcorners. Patent medicines of the time, available through mail-order, often contained high concentrations of morphine. This heyday for hard opiates produced such sensational fiction as Marcel Mallat's *Countess Morphine* and Maurice Talmeyr's *By Morphium Possessed,* lurid accounts of morphine degeneration.

Cannabis or hemp, sometimes known by its epithets "marijuana," "grass," "boo," "pot," "weed," "muggles," or "mary jane," appears in many guises. In India, its sobriquet is "bhang"; in Jamaica, where it is the sacrament of Rastafarianism, it is known as "ghanja"; in Islamic nations, it is called "hashish," "kif," and "dawamesc"; in Dutch Africa, where it is used by the Zulu, Bantu, and Hottentot, its name is "dagga"; to the ancient Hindus, it was "Indracanna," the "heavenly guide." Fitz Hugh Ludlow called hashish the "drug of travel." "Hashish makes a man like God" says a character in a story by Nerval. There is no question but that those who have had encounters with this fabled herb or its sticky, dark brown concentrate, have been profoundly impressed. Around the year 1200 CE, journals of travelers returning from the Orient began to take note of the drug. Actually, it had been in use since antiquity, and Herodotus had touched on it as early as 450 BCE, but written accounts of cannabis use dropped off, along with almost everything else, during the Middle Ages. Marco Polo mentions it around 1300 CE. Arnold of Lubeck, another early explorer, also comments on it. Travel narratives by visitors to India on the eve of the Renaissance remark that hens which nibble on cannabis seeds "return to it again and again, extravagantly." The tradition of traveler's tales continued throughout the Renaissance in the logs of globetrotters Garcia de Orta, Jan Huyghen van Linschoten, Laurent d'Arvieux, Jean Chardin, Gerhard Rohlfs, and Henri-Alexandre Junod. Antoine Sylvestre de Sacy, a member of Napoleon's Egyptian Expedition, discusses it at length. Bayard Taylor's "The Vision of Hashish," a pseudo-travelog description of a hashish experience in Syria, appeared in an 1854 issue of *Putnam's Monthly.* Taylor went on to author *A Slight Experience of Hashish,* and his best-known treatise on the subject, *Land of the Saracens.* Tales about hashish appear in *The Thousand and One Arabian Nights.* Alexandre Dumas and Louisa May Alcott feature it in their writings. Alcott wrote a story titled "Perilous Play," which centers around a box of marijuana bonbons. Gérard de Nerval wrote "Hashish," an atmospheric parable of hemp intoxication. Lord Dunsany wrote a story titled "The Hashish Man." The Arabian comic morality tale "The Three Haschich Eaters" by Hassan Abdallah, recounts the outlandish acts, each exceeding the last in foolishness, of three users of hashish. In mid-19th century Paris, a literary coterie calling itself the Hashish Club met monthly at the Hôtel Lauzun, an elegant old edifice in the Latin Quarter also known as Pimodan House. There, Charles Baudelaire, Théophile Gautier, and Gérard de Nerval regularly luxuriated in the "ivresse divine" of hashish rapture, and Alexandre Dumas and Honoré de Balzac were known to drop in for an occasional romp. François Lallemand wrote *Hashish* during this period. The visionary prose-poems of Adolphe Rette's *Bourne of Mists* are said to have been written under the influence of hashish. Still other works devoted to the subject are Jules Giraud's "How I Came to Hashish"; Henry de Monfried's "The Hashish Crossing"; Thomas Bailey Aldrich's poem "Hashisch"; John Greenleaf Whittier's poem of the same title; "The Girl and the Hashish-Smoker" by Albert Cossery; "The Oblivion Seekers" by Isabelle Eberhardt; and *M'Hashish* by Mohammed Mrabet. Perhaps the most high-flown acolyte of hashish consumption was 19th century American author Fitz Hugh Ludlow, whose drug-inflamed passages have been described as cascades of "grand spectral processions, beautiful houris, and the solemn patriarchs of ancient religions and religions unknown …" in which "… demons, machines, Mandarins, monuments and tabernacles pullulate, in settings that sail from the Great Wall of China across the Hindu Koosh into the labyrinthine bowels of the earth at the indent of a paragraph."

The most notable writings concerning the effects of nitrous oxide or "laughing gas" are those which were composed during the earliest period of systematic scientific investigation of its distinctive properties. Beginning in 1799, as an assistant to Dr. Beddoes, the physician who prescribed opium for Coleridge, De Quincey, and other British literary contemporaries, Humphrey Davy kept records of his investigations of the "physiological effects of æriform fluids" while director of the Medical Pneumatic Institution in Bristol, England. As part of a study of the therapeutic applications of gases, these experiments, reckless in their daring, involved inhaling not only nitrous oxide, but also pure hydrogen and carbonic acid. At one point, Davy had himself sealed inside an air-tight "breathing box," into which twenty quarts of nitrous oxide were introduced. Davy, who referred to nitrous oxide as "dephlogisticated nitrous gas," wrote a 600-page book titled *Researches Concerning Nitrous Oxide and its Respiration.* Davy's are mostly straightforward laboratory log accounts detailing adjustments in dosage, dilution levels, and so on. Peter Mark Roget, of thesaurus fame, was another of Beddoes's assistants, and also subjected himself to the effects of nitrous oxide, as did the Romantic poets Robert Southey and Samuel Taylor Coleridge. Moses Thomas wrote about laughing gas in 1814 after witnessing a public exhibition of its effects in Washington, D.C. According to Thomas, volunteers from the audience took turns interacting with an apparatus fitted with a large bladder inflated with “the newly discovered exhilarating gas.” As at a hypnosis demonstration, each volunteer proceeded to make a fool of himself after inhaling “a potent dose of the delicious poison.” Benjamin Paul Blood, writing on the effects of nitrous oxide in 1874, contemplated, in mystico-religious terms, the revelation residing in the “anesthetic trance,” comparing it to an awareness of the “genius of being.” In articles such as "Subjective Effects of Nitrous Oxide," William James emphasizes what he calls “the tremendously exciting sense of an intense metaphysical illumination”; specifically, James contends that “the centre and the periphery of things seem to come together. The ego and its objects, the meum and the tuum are one.” James goes on to say that he has the sense that there is a Hegelian reconciliation of opposites; that “every opposition … vanishes in a higher unity” and that “difference and no-difference merge in one. The mind sees how each term belongs to its contrast through a knife-edge moment of transition which is effected, and which, perennial and eternal, is the nunc stans of life.” The experience terminates, James says, “either in a laugh at the ultimate nothingness, or in a mood of vertiginous amazement at a meaningless infinity.” In the mid-19th century, “itinerant chemists” conducted laughing gas exhibitions as a form of public entertainment. Theodore Dreiser wrote a one-act play about laughing gas; Allen Ginsberg wrote a poem about it; poet Gregory Corso and novelist Ken Kesey used it. Since breathing the "gas of paradise" causes a numbing sensation and will, in sufficient quantity, knock the user unconscious, descriptions of gas sessions tend to be somewhat repetitious, which suggests that the imagination and skill of the writer is an important factor in producing literature from the experience.

Intoxication by other inhalants presents a similar dilemma, in that anyone inspiring volatile solvent fumes, for example, is so disoriented by the practice, that he has little idea of where he is, let alone how to describe his sensations and perceptions in cogent terms. Consequently, there is little literature on record concerning the subjective experience of solvent vapor inebriation or hydrocarbon misuse. Such substances do not necessarily inhibit creativity, however. Vincent Van Gogh, who was addicted to absinthe, had a fatal weakness for terpenes, including camphor, and had to be prevented, on at least one occasion, from drinking a quart of turpentine. The classic picture of the solvent abuser is that of some pubescent guttersnipe collapsed in an alleyway holding a paper bag soaked with airplane glue. Indeed, those solvents found in adhesives which can intoxicate when present in sufficient concentrations are toluene, hexanes, heptanes, ethyl acetate, isopropyl acetate, acetone, methyl ethyl ketone, methylene chloride, and trichlorethane. But commercially available cleaning fluids usually contain trichlorethylene, perchlorethylene, or both, and butane, gasoline, lighter fluid, acetone, and industrial solvents are just as likely to be inhaled to get high. Other recreational inhalants include nail polish remover, anti-freeze, marking pencils, lacquer thinners, typewriter correction fluid, refrigerants, ærosols and room sanitizers, and propellants in spray cans of whipped cream, engine treatments, furniture polish, and spot remover. A waxed or plastic bag frequently serves as a dispenser. Liquids are usually poured or squeezed onto a rag or handkerchief which, when saturated, is pressed, like a pad, against the nose and mouth. Fumes are just as likely to be inhaled directly from solvent storage vats as from solvents siphoned into lemonade bottles, so as to be made portable. Respiratory intrajection of the toxic fumes of noxious chemicals is known, among street urchins, as a "butane bash." Impairment from exposure to these agents of intoxication is such that those affected are usually incapable of speaking, let alone imparting accurate details of their adventures. An exception to the incommunicability rule attaching to these states of stupefaction is Jordan Jones's spooky essay "René Daumal's Experiments with Carbon Tetrachloride," an extensive elaboration of the French poet's oneiric exploits in the Realm of Twilight Death, while a fine example of fiction treating the subject of inhalant abuse is Greg Boyd's short story "Unglued," a rather malignant peek into the private world of an adolescent model airplane builder.

Sedatives or hypnotics have been featured in numerous trashy novels, particularly since the 1940s and 1950s. Since barbiturates, or "goofballs," in the vernacular, were first synthesized in Germany in 1903, billions of doses have been dispensed. Of the more than 2,500 varieties eventually developed, veronal, or barbital, and luminal, or phenobarbital, are probably most familiar to readers of murder mysteries, where they are the cause of both real and staged suicides by means of an "overdose of sleeping pills." In fact, contemporary fiction abounds with morose toxicomaniacs rendering themselves comatose with handfuls of psychodysleptics, and countless references to tranquilizers such as Valium, Librium, and Miltown can be found. Another ataraxic, quaalude, stars in Benjamin Stein's awful 1982 novel *'Ludes,* which concerns a thoroughly unsympathetic loser named Lenny, who calms and soothes himself to the point of insanity.

Then there are the ego drugs such as cocaine and methedrine, lowest common denominator psychostimulants which make "dumb people feel smart and little people feel big." Cocaine, the "caviar of drugs" has been the subject of William Martindale's *Coca, Cocaine, and Its Salts;* William Alexander Hammond's "Coca: Its Preparations and Their Therapeutic Qualities, with Some Remarks on the So-Called Cocaine Habit"; and Sigmund Freud's "On the General Effects of Cocaine and Contribution to the Knowledge of the Effect of Cocaine." Freud, at first a fanatic booster for cocaine, used it messianically. He even performed surgery on himself, applying it as an anesthetic. But though initially championing the drug as a panacea, he later repented, recanting his first professional paper about the subject, and publishing a second report detailing untowards side effects. Cocaine is derived from the plant Erythroxylon coca. Endemic to South America, coca leaf, in pre-Columbian times, was the special preserve of Inca royalty. Chewing the leaves produces a benign sense of well-being. When added to alcohol, cocaine makes coæthylene, the basis for popular beverages such as Vin Mariani which, in decades past, was drunk and endorsed by kings and popes. It was claimed that "even mummies stand up and walk after taking a drink" of this cocaine- laced tonic. Coca leaves mashed into a paste and reduced to a salt, yields cocaine hydrochloride, the familiar powder snorted by thrill-seekers. Cocainum muriaticum in a 1% water solution is a traditional formula for injection and, at one point in history, people commonly used cocaine to get off morphine and morphine to get off cocaine, intravenous administration being the preferred route. "Crack" is melted, smokable cocaine. The "Brompton cocktail" was a blend of cocaine, alcohol, and heroin once considered, in some medical circles, as a compassionate mode of euthanasia. At one time manufactured by Parke Davis and other major pharmaceutical houses, cocaine was, around 1900, as apt to be used by children and housewives as by actors and sharpshooters, and was a common ingredient in patent medicines. But it has always been as a high-powered pleasure drug that cocaine has enjoyed its greatest celebrity.

Always chic among the fashionable set, conspicuous consumption of "blow" by wealthy and glamorous cocainists has given rise to an entrenched association of the drug with society's upper echelons. Images of aristocratic pilgrims on the "Great White Way" summoning "servants to grate rocks of cocaine into champagne glasses" while idly anticipating wild and wanton orgies have filled the pages of countless potboilers. During the 1920s, Italian writer Dino Segre (under the pseudonym Pitigrilli) wrote a novel entitled *Cocaine* and Pendleton King authored a one-act play by the same name. Proust mentions cocaine use by one of his characters in *Remembrance of Things Past* and, along with many other drugs, it is procured, through "secret channels," by the character Pablo in Hermann Hesse's *Steppenwolf.* To bolster him for the last two weeks of his life, Adolf Hitler received injections of strychnine, which is a powerful central nervous system stimulant in low doses; milder versions of analeptics or "strength' drugs are the amphetamines benzedrine, dexedrine, methedrine, etc. Beat Era American fiction is rife with amphetamine and its analogs, primarily in the work of such authors as Jack Kerouac, whose hipster characters, like long-haul truck drivers, chronically pop "bennies," "speed," "whizz," or "billy," in order to stay awake during cross-country drives. For these charging knights of the highway, escape ramps are moot, and when the real thing can't be found, No-Doz will do.

Among other exhilarants are betel and qat, a shrub the chewing of whose stimulating leaves is the national habit of Yemen, where it was introduced from Ethiopia around 1200 CE. Qat users attempt to reach a state they call "al kayf" or "taradi": one of relaxed euphoria. Yet a higher stage is known as "khedra," which means "drugged"; it refers to a level of qat intoxication in which the user feels numbed to impinging stimuli. This is the condition attained by the protagonist of Lebanese author Haydar Haydar's story "The Ants and the Qat"; in which he is so elated by qat that he can't feel the ants which devour him alive as he languishes in a daze of ecstatic torpor.

The family of major psychedelics has perhaps generated the most fascinating of all drug literature. For millennia, men have been freeing their minds with psychoactive plants, the geographical distribution of which is global. There are 100 species of hallucinogens in the Americas alone. Tlitlitzin, ololiuqui, and coaxihuitl or "snakeplant" were mesoamerican psychedelic substances used by the Aztecs. Teonanacatl, or "flesh of gods" is what the Aztecs called their sacred psilocybin mushrooms. Yaqui Indians smoked Scotch broom flowers, boletus and psilocybin mushrooms are eaten by New Guinea natives, pituri is chewed and smoked by Australian aborigines. Iboga is a favorite of autocthonic Gabonese in coastal French Equatorial Africa, while voaconga is used elsewhere in the dark continent. Amanita muscaria, the toadstool or fly-agaric fungus, is consumed ceremonially by Asian nomads who call it muchamor. Panther caps, another mushroom, although highly toxic, have also been consumed. Cohoba snuff is made from the ground seeds of fermented mimosa pods; Guahibo and Otomac Indians also call it niopo, and it is called parica by the Catauxis and Mura Indians. Some tribes absorb the drug in suppository form. Other psychoactive powders taken via a nose pipe are epena, anadenanthera, and yopo. Natema, oo-koey, and ebene are Amazonian psychedelics, as is virola, which is orally administered. Syrian rue is known to induce visions. Nutmeg, morning glory, calamus, also called sweet flag, and datura, also called jimson weed and thorn apple, are psychedelics used by Incas and other American Indians. Mimosa hastibus is used in Brazil. Jurema wine, harmel flowers, Hawaiian woodrose, the San Pedro cactus, and the Amazonian vine banisteriopsis caapi, which yields yage or ayahuasca, are all powerful hallucinogenics. Traditionally, certain of these plants have been regarded as religious sacraments, able to confer powers of telepathy, divination, and disclosure of occult secrets. The oloiuqui sacred to the Aztecs comes from bindweed seeds they called the divine food. Aztecs believed that when a person slept after swallowing the seeds, "plant children" would come to talk to him to impart hidden knowledge.

During the Middle Ages, witches were thought to employ "flying ointments," or salves made from such substances as mandrake, henbane, and belladonna, also known as deadly nightshade. Anointed with these "sorceror's herbs," witches would lapse into "babbling trances" during the delirium of "waking" coma, in the throes of which they claimed to "fly" through the air in the company of bizarre animal familiars.

Hallucinations tend to conform to certain predictable patterns in peyote and mescaline experiences. Optical phenomena such as brilliant, vivid colors and supernaturally illumined landscapes, repetitive architectonic forms and geometric figures, visions of mythic beasts, surges of endless waves of energy, and the sense that physical laws have been suspended, are typical characteristics of the experience Aldous Huxley described as charged with "being-awareness-bliss" and "grace, transfiguration." French poet Henri Michaux's mescaline experiences are lyrically described in "Turbulent Infinity." The active ingredient of the peyote cactus is mescaline, so named on account of its use by Mescalero Apaches. The effects of mescaline exaltation are markedly Pythagorean: again and again users make reference to a stripping away of veils on the infinite, to reveal skeins of sacred geometry constituting the substructure of matter. Many literary figures have sampled mescaline and documented its properties. Michael McClure wrote "Peyote Poem"; Huxley refers to the "peyotyl trances of Swinburne"; Weir Mitchell, a novelist and physician, turned on psychologists William James and Havelock Ellis; Ellis, in turn, gave some to Irish poet William Butler Yeats; mountebank occultist Aleister Crowley gave it to British author Katherine Mansfield. Jack Green's Beat Era prose-poem "Peyote," typed entirely in lower-case letters, was composed at a time when peyote was legal and cheaply available by mail order. Green defines the cactus scientifically, discusses dosages and methods of preparation, and presents detailed descriptions of the drug's elations and dangers, as well as its ability to suspend habitual ideation and allow higher, truer perceptions to break through. Octavio Paz's book *Alternating Current* discusses the mescaline and psilocybin experiments of Henri Michaux and the manner in which American Indians and Asian and African peoples use drugs ritually and religiously, while reliving his own experiences with bhang during a religious festival in India. In the 1962 memoir *The Prime of Life,* Simone de Beauvoir relates how her friend, French philosopher and writer Jean-Paul Sartre, took mescaline during a psychiatrically supervised session, in order to observe his own hallucinations in connection with a study in perceptions he was conducting. Late nineteenth century and early twentieth century researchers Louis Lewin and Karl Beringer in Germany, and Alexandre Rouhier in France, authored scientific papers concerning mescaline. Swiss physiologist Dr. Beringer, an associate of Carl Gustav Jung and Hermann Hesse, published his book *Mescaline Inebriation* in 1927 and, in 1928, another early author, Heinrich Kluver, brought out a study of mescaline titled *Mescal*.

Important non-fiction works devoted to the "magic mushrooms" psilocybin and stropharia cubensis are Robert Gordon Wasson's *Soma: Divine Mushroom of Immortality*; and *The Road to Eleusis*; which he authored along with Carl Ruck. Wasson, a New York banker and amateur ethnobotanist, wrote exhaustively and compellingly about mycology and brain chemistry and made a compelling case for the origin of many religions in magic mushroom cults. DMT, DET, DPT and other short-acting tryptamines have been thoroughly examined by both neurobiologists and pharmacologic adventurers. Albert Hoffmann, chemist, director of research at Sandoz Laboratories in Switzerland, and discoverer of lysergic acid, participated in LSD sessions with Europe's leading writers and philosophers. In Germany in 1962, at the house of the head forester of Stauffenberg Castle, Hoffmann dropped psilocybin with novelist Ernst Junger and two other friends. Junger and Hoffmann separately wrote about their experiences during this "mushroom symposium." Anaïs Nin took LSD in a private session with a psychiatrist and wrote about her experiences in her celebrated diary. Publishing establishment figures like Henry and Claire Booth Luce used psychedelics; other socialites and celebrities of the 1950s took lysergic acid both for enlightenment and for "kicks." The mid-1960s saw an explosion in the popular use of psychedelics, and drug-fueled antics were widely chronicled in mass-circulation books and journals of the period. The 1970 story "Psychedelic" by Alain Bosquet, is a lyrical interpretation of the LSD experience. Among the pioneers of the consciousness-dilation movement of the 1960s was chemical philosopher Timothy Leary, who produced a plethora of provocative writing on the subject, and whose classic, *The Psychedelic Experience*, co-authored by Richard Alpert, is a roadmap through uncharted regions of inner space. Leary was incarcerated 40 times in prisons in several nations; the hysteria with which he was met was such that he can be fairly likened to a sort of latter-day Socrates, relentlessly hounded corrupter of youth. During the 1960s, "Blue Cheer," "Purple Haze," "Orange Sunshine," and "Windowpane" acid gave endless insights into the "nature of the universe and the purpose of life." What Daumal, during the 1940s, designated as a veil beyond which the ordinary world was still visible but charged with the higher significance of "the unbroken substance of the Immobile," became, during the 1960s, the "ceaseless wonder" and "annihilating illumination" of the "love-pill," lysergic acid. Soon, neuropsychologists the world over were discussing the pharmacodynamics of entheogens, serotonin levels, and brain metabolism. Social philosophers such as Aldous Huxley postulated that the "mind-detergent," LSD, was cleansing doors of perception ordinarily closed off by the brain in order to prevent its circuits from being overloaded by the limitless and ineffable glory of the universe.

Designer drugs, substances synthesized in laboratories, sometimes in private laboratories according to custom-orders from daredevils, subsume the newly emerged group of psychochemicals called phenethylamines, which include MDMA, known as "E," "Adam," "166," "X," and "Ecstasy"; MDE, popularly known as "EVE"; MDA or methylenedioxyamphetamine; and 2CB, known in street parlance as "Bromo"; as well as several other variants. Known as empathogens, these euphorics facilitate emotional communion and validate, in the minds of their advocates, the slogan of the DuPont Corporation, "Better Living Through Chemistry," although one such item, alpha-methyl fentanyl or "China White," has caused profoundly deleterious neurological symptoms in at least one user. Chronicles of the contemporary club scene which speak of youthful adherents of "Acid House" and "Rave" culture eed up on Ecstasy, dancing all night to "trance music," oblivious to everything but one another, clearly delineate them as descendants of the characters populating the "pill party" pulp novels of the 1960s, later supplanted by serious pop novels such as *Almost Transparent Blue.*

Police drugs such as sodium amytal and scopolamine, the so-called "truth serum," figure prominently in spy novels, where they are usually employed as an assist in extracting confessions. They, and other substances, have also played a part in government thought control experiments. Medical misuse of drugs, as in Soviet punitive psychiatry, has been well documented. Nootropics, or "smart drugs," which include hydergine, piracetum, and vasopressin, and the monoamine oxidase inhibitor selegiline hydrochloride or Deprenyl, are of the same family as the fictitious intelligence booster which transforms a mentally retarded man into a genius in Daniel Keyes' *Flowers for Algernon*, the 1966 novel made into the popular movie *Charlie*.

Aphrodisiacs, substances which excite erotic desire, spice the literature of all times and places. Debauchees have always cited wine and hemp as agents of sensual arousal. Cocaine carries a similar reputation. The herb eryngium was believed by the ancients to be an aphrodisiac; yohimbe has been traditionally used in Africa as an adjunct to orgiastic rituals; khala-khiji, damiana, cocoa, and saffron have all been considered, in certain cultures, as aphrodisiacs. In eighteenth century England, aristocratic members of the Hellfire Club, using cantharides or "Spanish fly" at their resort of Medenham Abbey, drugged virgins, and secreted the "nymphs" in the bushes, where they waited to be discovered by roving "fauns." Similar tales of sensuality and the use of chemical tools as an aid to seduction continue into the present day with newspaper reports of innocent girls lured into acts of depravity through the use of such "date rape" drugs as I-4 and gamma-hydroxybutyrate. Also known as GBH or "scoop," gamma-hydroxybutyrate is slipped in a drink as a Mickey Finn, in order to render the victim pliant. Viagra, a male potency promoter, has enjoyed much publicity in recent years, while bromocriptine, manufactured by Sandoz Pharmaceuticals under the name Parlodel, is another chic substance with a street rep as a supposed "sex starter."

"Natural" drug culture has spawned a host of cheap, legal, nutritional supplements with trade names like "Ultimate Xphoria," "Cloud 9," and "Herbal Ecstasy." Constituents of these compounds include herbs like lobelia, comfrey, ephedra, sassafras, senna, yohimbe, pennyroyal, coltsfoot and germander. Most of these "herbal extracts" and "dietary supplements" are intended as natural mood boosters and euphoriants. Related literature has taken the form of personal testimonials or journalistic admonitions about the dangers of overstimulation from the synergistic effects of ephedrine and caffeine which certain of these products contain. Other novelties which have come to light in recent years and provided sensational fodder for supermarket tabloids have been "ice" crack, teen "toad-licking" parties, at which guests ingest bufotonine venom secreted by glands on the undersides of Bufo toads or at which toadskins are brewed into a tea, and the consumption, by jungle tribespeople, of a marine specimen known as the "dream fish," which contains psychedelic chemicals.

The panorama of factual and fictional accounts of drug experiences is far too vast to encompass in a single volume. But it seems to bear out philosopher Edmund Burke's assertion that "under the pressure of the cares and sorrows of our mortal condition, men have at all times, and in all countries, called in some physical aid to their moral consolations—wine, beer, opium, brandy, or tobacco." Echoing Burke, Aldous Huxley contended that "in the course of history many more people have died for their drink and their dope than have died for their religion or their country." Huxley also commented that "everywhere and at all times, men and women have sought, and duly found, the means of taking a holiday from the reality of their generally dull and often acutely unpleasant existence. A holiday out of space, out of time, in the eternity of sleep or ecstasy, in the heaven or the limbo of visionary phanstasy. 'Anywhere, anywhere, out of the world.'" Allowing that most known drugs are treacherous and harmful, Huxley nevertheless noted that prohibition has proven unsuccessful and, since people crave some means of escape and are more than willing to employ pharmaceutical avenues in pursuit of it, there will never be a cure for drug abuse until some feasible substitute is afforded suffering humanity. "Despite all," ethnobotanist William Emboden corroborates, "man has used, and continues to use, narcotics to endure the duress of an otherwise intolerable existence."

In spite of pleas for what poet Allen Ginsberg has termed "the honorific use of drugs," and apart from the fact that the legal drugs alcohol and tobacco, along with prescription drugs, cause one hundred times as many deaths per year as do all illegal drugs combined, the "drug controversy" persists and, regardless of valiant efforts to resist the twin ogres ignorance and hypocrisy, the ongoing battle against the "drug problem" will likely never be won since, if it were, numberless armies of gangsters, police agents, military personnel, and government bureaucrats would find themselves unemployed. Meanwhile, drug use surges unabated and, whether at laboratories such as Sloan-Kettering in New York or Botanic Dimensions in Hawaii, where plants are systematically investigated for potential applications in medicinal therapeutics, or at pharmaceutical firms such as Eli Lilly or Ciba, where scientists continue to synthesize new drugs so fast that the average shelf life is mere months before the Food and Drug Administration bans them and they are replaced by batches of newer synthetics, the lure of chemical inebriants remains stubbornly undiminished.

The human animal has always sought ways to escape pain through intoxication, has always expressed a need to bend the mind and derange the senses. French poet and playwright Antonin Artaud, unabashedly and unapologetically a drug fiend, half-mad but wholly ingenious, composed a famous "Letter to the Legislator (of the Law Governing Stupefacients)" which begins: "Mister Legislator, you are a cunt!" In this same letter, Artaud proclaims opium to be "sovereign against the malady called "Anguish"; against "the anguish which makes madmen; against the anguish which makes suicides; against the anguish which makes men damned; against the anguish which medicine cannot know; against an anguish the doctors cannot understand; against the anguish which injures life; which pinches life at the umbilical." Artaud wrote that "as long as we haven't been able to abolish a single cause of human desperation, we do not have the right to try to suppress the means by which man tries to clean himself of desperation." He observed that "there are people who have built excremental and famous industries out of their pretended indignation against an inoffensive group of the damned of the drug," and he pointed out that "... the fury against toxics ... is without effect against the need for toxics which, satisfied or not, is innate to the soul and would induce it to resolutely antisocial gestures, even if the toxics did not exist; furthermore, it exasperates the social need for toxics and changes it into a secret vice." Finally, Artaud asserts that so long as governments and religions cannot offer man other means of ameliorating his misery, he should not be faulted for resorting to what remedies are available to him.

There is little doubt man will continue to use drugs and write about the experience. What will be written about drugs of the future and the "trips" they produce, however, can scarcely be imagined.

# Get Drunk

*Charles Baudelaire*

One should always be drunk. It's the answer to the sole question. To keep from suffering the burden of Time, which weighs upon your shoulders and presses you down to the earth, you must get drunk constantly.

But drunk on what? Wine, poetry or virtue—whichever you prefer—only get drunk.

And if, from time to time, whether on the stairs of a palace or in the green grass of a ditch, or in the gloomy loneliness of your room, you awaken less inebriated or already sober, then ask the wind and the waves, the stars, the bird, the clock, ask whatever spins or turns or sings or talks, ask them what time it is: then the wind and wave and star and bird and clock will answer you: "it's time to get drunk! So to keep from being the martyred slaves of Time, get drunk without respite, on wine, poetry or virtue, whichever you prefer."

*—Translated from the French*
*by Greg Boyd*

# Alcohol and the Absolute

*William James*

The next step into mystical states carries us into a realm that public opinion and ethical philosophy have long since branded as pathological, though private practice and certain lyric strains of poetry bear witness to its ideality. I refer to the intoxicants and anæsthetics, especially by alcohol. The sway of alcohol over mankind is unquestionably due to its power to stimulate the mystical faculties of human nature, usually crushed to earth by the cold facts and dry criticisms of the sober hour. Sobriety diminishes, discriminates, and says No; drunkenness expands, unites and says Yes. It is in fact the great exiciter of the Yes function in man. It brings its votary from the chill periphery of things to the radiant core. It makes him for the moment one with truth. Not through mere perversity do men run after it. To the poor and unlettered it stands in the place of symphony concerts and of literature; and it is part of the deeper mystery and tragedy of life that whiffs and gleams of something that we immediately recognise as excellent should be vouchsafed to so many of us only in the fleeting earlier phases of what in its totality is so degraded a poisoning. The drunken consciousness is one bit of the mystic consciousness, and our total opinion of it must find its place in our opinion of that larger whole.

Nitrous oxide and ether, especially nitrous oxide, when sufficiently diluted with air, stimulate mystical consciousness in an extraordinary degree. Depth beyond depth of truth seems revealed to the inhaler. This truth fades out, however, or escapes, at the moment of coming to; and if any words remain over in which it seemed to clothe itself, they prove to be the veriest nonsense. Nevertheless, the sense of a profound meaning having been there persists; and I know more than one person who is persuaded that in the nitrous oxide trance we have a genuine metaphysical revelation.

Some years ago I myself made some observations of this aspect of nitrous oxide intoxication, and reported them in print. One conclusion was forced upon my mind at that time, and my impression of its truth has ever since remained unshaken. It is that our normal waking consciousness, rational consciousness as we call it, is but one special type of consciousness, whilst all about it, parted from it by the filmiest of screens, there lie potential forms of consciousness entirely different. We may go through life without suspecting their existence; but apply the requisite stimulus and at a touch they are there in all their completeness, definite types of mentality which probably somewhere have their field of application and adaptation. No account of the universe in its totality can be final which leaves these other forms of consciousness quite disregarded.

# *from* Wormwood

*Marie Corelli*

MEANWHILE I WAS cold and tired and starved; I would go home,—home if I could walk there,—and if my limbs were not too weak and stiff to support me—Oh, for a draught of *Absinthe!*—that would soon put fire into my veins and warm the numbness of my heart! I paused a moment, still gazing at the dull water and the dull mists; then all at once a curious sick fear began to creep through me; an awful premonition that something terrible was about to happen, though what it was I could not imagine. My heart began to beat heavily;—I kept my eyes riveted on the scene immediately opposite, for while the sensation I speak of mastered me, I dared not look behind. Presently I distinctly heard a low panting near me like the breathing of some heavy creature—and my nervous dread grew stronger. For a moment I felt that I would rather fling myself into the Seine than turn my head. It was an absurd sensation,—a cowardly sensation; one that I knew I ought to control and subdue, and after a brief but painful contest with myself I gathered together a slight stock, not of actual courage but physical bravado,—and slowly, irresolutely looked back over my own shoulder, then unspeakably startled and amazed at what I saw, I turned my whole body round involuntarily and confronted the formidable beast that lay crouched there on the Pont Neuf, watching me with its sly green eyes and apparently waiting on my movements. A leopard of the forest at large in the heart of Paris!—could anything be more strange and terrifying? I stared at it,—and it stared at me! I could almost count the brown velvet spots on its tawny hide,—and I saw its lithe body quiver with the pulsations of its quick breath,—and for some minutes I was perfectly paralysed with fear and horror;—afraid to stir an inch! Presently, as I stood inert and terror-stricken, I heard steps approaching, and a labourer appeared carrying some tin cans which clinked together merrily,—he whistled as he came along, and seemed to be in cheerful humour. I watched him anxiously. What would he do,—what would he say when he caught sight of that leopard lying on the bridge, obstructing his progress? Onward he marched indifferently,—and my heart almost ceased to beat for a second as I saw him coming nearer and nearer to the horrible creature.... What! was he blind?—Could he not see the danger before him? I strove to cry out, but my tongue was like stiff leather in my mouth,—I could not utter a syllable;—and lo!—while my fascinated gaze still rested on him he had passed me!—passed apparently over or through the animal I saw and dreaded!

The truth flashed upon me in an instant,—I was the dupe of my own frenzy—and the leopard was nothing but a brain-phantom! I laughed aloud, buttoned my coat close over me and drew myself erect,—as I did this, the leopard rose with slow and stealthy grace, and when I moved prepared to follow me. Again I looked at it—again it looked at me,—again I counted the spots on its sleek skin,—the thing was absolutely real and distinct to my vision,—was it possible that a diseased brain could produce such seemingly tangible shapes? I began to walk rapidly,—and another peculiarity of my hallucination discovered itself,—namely, that *before* me as I looked I saw nothing but the usual surroundings of the streets and the passing people,—but *behind* me, I knew, I felt the horrible monster at my heels,—the monster created by my own poisoned thought,—a creature from whom there was no possible escape. The enemies of the body we can physically attack, and often physically repel,—but the enemies of the mind,—the frightful phantoms of a disordered imagination—these no medicine can cure, no subtle touch disperse!

And yet I could not quite accept the fact of the nervous havoc wrought upon me. I saw a boy carrying a parcel of "*Figaros*" to a neighbouring *kiosque* and stopping him, I purchased one of his papers.

"Tell me," I then said, lightly and with a feigned indifference. "Do you see a—a great dog following me? I chanced upon a stray one on the Pont Neuf just now, but I don't want it at my lodgings. Can you see it?"

The boy looked up and down and smiled.

"Je ne vois rien, monsieur!"

"Merci!" and nodding to him I strolled away, resolved not to look back again till I reached my own abode.

# Absinthia Tetra

*Ernest Dowson*

GREEN CHANGED TO white, emerald to an opal: nothing was changed.

The man let the water trickle gently into his glass, and as the green clouded, a mist fell from his mind.

Then he drank opaline.

Memories and terrors beset him. The past tore after him like a panther and through the blackness of the present he saw the luminous tiger eyes of the things to be.

But he drank opaline.

And that obscure night of the soul, and the valley of humiliation, through which he stumbled were forgotten. He saw blue vistas of undiscovered countries, high prospects and a quiet, caressing sea. The past shed its perfume over him, to-day held his hand as it were a little child, and to-morrow shone like a white star: nothing was changed.

He drank opaline.

The man had known the obscure night of the soul, and lay even now in the valley of humiliation; and the tiger menace of the things to be was red in the skies. But for a little while he had forgotten.

Green changed to white, emerald to an opal: nothing was changed.

# Nightmare Alley

*Jean Richepin*

I HAVE NEVER deluded myself into pretending that my friend Harry Sloughby is a sober man; many is the time I have watched him absorb, at a single sitting, under the pretext of fortifying himself with a tonic refreshment to which he euphemistically refers as "brandy and soda", more eau-de-vie than would be needed to render dead drunk four sappers and their corporal.

Far be it from me to offer the slightest guess as to why he has taken to promulgating cautionary sermons against the perils of drink, insisting with perfervid and unshakable conviction upon his opposition to alcoholic excess, especially when he himself has affirmed, in all apparent sincerity, that he has never in his life been soused to the point of losing his rationality; though many is the time, after one of his monumental ingurgitations of alcohol, when I have seen him reduced to the state of an inert lump barely able to carry himself off and collapse onto his bed, thoroughly bereft of any awareness of what he was doing or any recollection of his actions.

But I must, on the other hand, acknowledge that, until the precise moment when he drops, brusquely overwhelmed by intoxication, my honorable friend Harry Sloughby retains complete mastery of his thoughts, and of his imagination, and that he has never been the type, even when enwreathed by the thickest alcoholic fumes, to grab at phantoms or prop himself up against lampposts. I feel myself compelled also to avow that, following a preliminary period of being stiff as a judge, he exercises powers of observation which are nothing less than remarkable; he is able to warehouse in his memory everything taking place around him, in a fashion detached and almost mechanical; so much so, in fact, that these involuntary observations are recorded with what can only be described as photographic and phonographic fidelity!

Thanks to which, since he has traveled widely, in all parts of the world, and since, everywhere, he has irrigated himself with brandy and soda (though the doses nowadays are formulated at half-strength), his conversation has always been rich with rare imagery yielding vivid and precise pictures of the most diverse civilizations.

Yet I do not believe that any of these pictures has ever so interested me, so intrigued me, I would venture to say, to the point of amazing me, as has that which he presented the other evening, when he conjured up the picture of the extraordinary, the strange, the fantastic and demonic street to which he had assigned the ever-so-appropriate title: Nightmare Alley.

That which he had thus designated seemed to indicate a street situated in some English city. In any case, it was situated somewhere; my honorable friend skirted the issue at first, confessing that he had given the street this name, not knowing what it was called in actuality, and confessing, moreover, something far more serious: that he was ignorant of the name of the city in which he found himself, let alone of how to find in it a specific street.

Without doubt, he had strayed there one day when just at the point of blacking out, and later awakened to begin a new bout of intoxication, during which he observed everything with his usual habit of involuntary memorization, but after which he could recall neither how he had got there, nor how he had got out; that part of the business only cloudily recurring to him, as if it had all been a dream.

But, if the evidence was to be believed, it hadn't been a dream. That is to say, rather, that my honorable friend Harry Sloughby had been, that day, subject to a miracle unique in his life; because never, but never before, in his life, had he dreamed such a dream; of that he was sure, as indisputably sure as anyone can be, of anything in this world.

The only challenge which could be put forward in defiance of the reality of these very tangible memories of Nightmare Alley, was that, extraordinarily this time, his memory hadn't been that photographic, and that the phonographic impressions were blurred and indistinct, as if the negatives had been overexposed and the inscriptions on the recording cylinder mixed up in an acoustic jumble comprised of sounds heard both before and after, as well as those correctly registered during the passage through Nightmare Alley.

These sonic superimpositions, forming confusion and an incomprehensible hubbub, were in the French language; so unmistakably, in fact, were the words of the foreign and unknown tongue spoken in Nightmare Alley marked by a French musicality that, in spite of being cloaked by fallacious inflections, they seemed about to differentiate themselves at any second, and to make themselves understood.

The photographic memories, on the other hand, were of an absolute purity; living proof; vivid as projections in a cinema, and they demonstrated, moreover, that if Nightmare Alley was neither an English street nor a French street, it was incontestably a street of an enormous modern city, by no means exotic and, in all likelihood, European, because the men and women there were dressed in the attire of the Old World.

But what abominable examples of that Old World! The men, save for some very rare exceptions, had the atrocious appearance of bandits; and almost all the women looked like prostitutes of the very lowest class. The children exhibited on their haggard faces, and in their impudent eyes, all the markings of vice and crime. This, at least, was the judgment of my friend Harry Sloughby, who likened the inhabitants of Nightmare Alley to ferocious and epileptic apes, to lunatics breaking out of an asylum, to convicts breaking out of prison and, finally, as he put it, to perfect demons.

These perfect demons swarmed over a tightly confined space, because Nightmare Alley wasn't more than two hundred fifty paces long, by some fifteen paces wide. The throng was incessantly replenished by the spillover from a succession of gaudily dismal dives, where one drinks while standing in front of splendid white metal countertops. These dives were arranged, one after the other, in a line, interrupted only by some food stalls, some butcher shops, and three or four vast department stores filled with hats and shoes and perfumes, which not a soul inhabited and which seemed to have no purpose for being there except to tempt, with their open windows and exposed wares, the itchy hands of thieves.

On one corner stood three music halls, on the other a theater, irresistibly attractive to my friend Harry, who wanted to enter everywhere, and who mixed with the people deliriously; here smiling, there laughing in unrestrained outbursts at the sight of some clowns accompanied by the shrilling, squalling refrains of a combined canine-feline chorale; weeping warm tears at the ups and downs of some dreadfully tenebrous drama; everywhere surrounded by an infernal din, composed of pleas and propositions, loud shouts and quarrelsome vociferations; vicious verbal battles regularly degenerating into knife-fights.

One phenomenon made an unforgettable impression on my friend Harry, always a liquor-hound of the first order: it was a dram shop, above the open door of which a large placard announced some spectacle, and in the penetralia of which my honorable friend had the queer and unexpected pleasure of drinking with a giant eight feet tall, a dwarf two feet tall, a Negress weighing four hundred twelve pounds, and a man sporting a beard which hung to his knees.

But that which topped off my friend's astonishment and not only mystified but decidedly unnerved him, was the precise location of Nightmare Street, since the passersby spoke an unknown language with French inflections, while the giant conversed in Norwegian, the dwarf in Spanish, the negress in Creole English, and the man with the beard in Dutch; details which lent to the pandemonium the air of a cosmopolitan Black Sabbath.

My friend Harry Sloughby had reached this point in the story of his extraordinary vision, and we listened with mouths agape, reconstructing in our imaginations this strange, fantastic, demoniac, and mysterious street, invested by him with the all-too-apt appellation of Nightmare Alley, when suddenly, at the evocation of the bearded Dutchman, a lightning bolt shot through my memory, and I cried out, plunging my honorable friend Harry and all his listeners into a state of stupefaction.

—But, yes, yes, of course, that's it! I've been there! Hear me out! The theater, the three music halls, it all fits! The Gangloff Hall! Bobino! There ... do you see? Beyond a doubt! And the Cabaret of Monsters! But of course! Of course! Your formidable and unrecoverable Nightmare Alley is the rue de la Gaïté, and none other, by God! The rue de la Gaîté, in Montparnasse![1]

*—Translated from the French*
*by Gilbert Alter-Gilbert*

# *from* Wine and Hashish

*Charles Baudelaire*

O PROFOUND JOYS of wine, who has not known you? Anyone who has had a remorse to appease, a memory to evoke, a grief to drown, a castle in Spain to build—that is to say everyone, has invoked you, O mysterious deity hidden in the fibers of the vine. How grand are the spectacles of wine, illuminated by that inner sunlight! How true and passionate, that second youth which man derives therefrom! But also, how dangerous are its overwhelming pleasures and its nerve-racking delights! And yet, you judges, legislators, men of the world, all you persons for whom good fortune makes virtue and health so easy—tell me, who among you will be bold and cruel enough to condemn the man who drinks for his genie?

Moreover, wine is not always a fearsome combatant sure of victory and sworn to have no pity nor mercy. Wine is like man: one never knows to what extent it can be cherished or despised, loved or hated, nor how many sublime deeds or monstrous crimes it is capable of. So let us be no more cruel toward it than toward ourselves, and let us treat it as our equal.

It sometimes seems to me that I can hear wine talking—it speaks with its soul, with a spiritual voice audible only to spirits. "Man, my dear friend, I want to convey to you, despite my glass prisons and my cork stoppers, a song of brotherhood, a song of joy, of sunlight and hope. I am no ingrate; I know full well I owe you my life. I know what it has cost you in hard labor and in hot sun on your shoulders. You have given me life, and I shall reward you therefor. I shall pay my debt in full; for I feel a special joy when I flow down a gullet made thirsty by hard labor. The stomach of a good man is a resting-place much more to my liking than those cold, gloomy cellars. That stomach is a happy tomb where I achieve my destiny with enthusiasm. I cause a great stir and bustle in the working man's stomach, and from there via invisible staircases I rise into his brain, where I perform my matchless dance.

"Can you hear ringing and echoing in me the powerful refrains of olden times, the songs of love and glory? I am the soul of the patrie, half lover, half soldier. I am the saving grace of Sunday. World on week-days is for money; wine makes Sundays happy days. With elbows on the family table and sleeves rolled up, you will sing my praises for making you truly happy.

"I shall light up the eyes of your old wife, the aging partner in all your problems and your oldest dreams; I will make your glance tender and will put the sparkle of youth into her eyes. And your dear little son, pale and wan, that poor little ass's colt harnessed to the same routine as his wheel-horse, I shall restore to him the bright colors of his cradle, and I shall be, for this young athlete of life, the essential oil with which wrestlers of antiquity used, to restore their muscle-tone.

"I shall penetrate deep into your breast like a plant-ambrosia. I shall be the seed that makes fertile the furrow so painfully prepared. Our intimate union will create poetry. The two of us will make a God, and we will flutter off toward the infinite, like birds, butterflies, sons of the Virgin, heady perfumes and all winged things."

That is what wine sings about in its mysterious language. Woe to the man whose selfish heart, closed to the suffering of his brothers, has never heard that song!

* * *

If wine were to disappear from human production, I believe this would create in the physical and intellectual life of our planet a void, an emptiness, a defectiveness much more serious than all the excesses and deviations for which wine is held responsible. Is it not reasonable to think that people who never drink wine, be they naive or narrow-minded, are fools or hypocrites: fools who have no knowledge of humanity or nature; artists who reject all the traditional approaches to art; workmen who curse their tools;—hypocrites, that is, "closet" gluttons, braggarts who proclaim their sobriety, drinking on the sly and having their wine stashed away somewhere? A man who drinks nothing but water has a secret to hide from his fellow men.

* * *

An anonymous author once wrote: Nothing equals the joy of the man who drinks, lest it be the joy of the wine in being drunk. Indeed, wine plays an intimate role in the life of mankind—so intimate, that I am not surprised by the fact that, intrigued by a pantheistic concept, certain reasonable minds attribute to it a kind of personality. Wine and mankind seem to me to be like two friendly wrestlers, always fighting, always reconciled. The loser always embraces the winner.

* * *

When hemp is being harvested, strange phenomena sometimes occur in the personality of both male and female workers. One would say there rises from the harvest a kind of vertiginous spirit which flows around the legs and rises maliciously toward the brain. The head of the harvester fills with swirling eddies, and at other times with mental fantasies. Arms and legs become weak and refuse to serve. Furthermore, when I was a child, I experienced some similar phenomena upon rolling in piles of lucerne.

Attempts have been made to make hashish out of French hemp. All such efforts have failed thus far, and enthusiasts who will at all costs procure for themselves such magical pleasures have continued to use hashish from across the Mediterranean, that is, made from Indian or Egyptian hemp. Hashish is derived from an extract of Indian hemp, butter and a small quantity of opium.

It is a greenish jam with a very strong odor, so strong that it becomes rather sickening, as any fine aroma does when pressed to its maximum strength and "density." Take a walnut-sized lump of it, fill a little spoon with it, and happiness is yours—an absolute euphoria with all its intoxication, all its youthful follies, and also its infinite beatitudes. The essence of happiness is right there, in the form of a little blob of jam; don't be afraid to take some, it won't kill you; the physical organs are not seriously affected thereby. Of course your will may be weakened; that's another matter.

Generally, in order to give hashish its full strength and development, it must be steeped in very hot black coffee, and taken without food; dinner must be postponed until ten o'clock or midnight; only a very light soup is permissible. An infraction of this simple rule would produce either vomiting (dinner clashing with the drug) or inefficacy of the hashish. Many ignorant or stupid fools who ignore these precautions accuse the hashish of impotence.

Once the little drug has been absorbed (an operation which, by the way, demands a certain fortitude, for, as I have said, the mixture is so odoriferous that it causes some people to become nauseous), you find yourself immediately in a state of anxiety. You have heard vaguely of the marvelous effects of hashish, your imagination has created for itself a particular idea, an ideal of intoxication, and you are eager to find out whether the resulting reality will measure up to your preconception of it. The time that elapses between absorption of the beverage and the first symptoms varies with personal temperaments and also with practice. Persons who are regular practitioners of hashish sometimes experience the first symptoms of its onset after about a half-hour.

* * *

Most of the time novices, in their first initiation, complain of the slowness of its effects. They await them anxiously, and when things don't happen quickly enough to suit them, they start yammering in disbelief, which greatly amuses those who know what hashish can do and how it behaves. It's rather amusing to see the first effects appear and multiply, right in the middle of this incredulity. First, you are seized by a kind of preposterous and irresistible hilarity. The most vulgar words, the simplest ideas take on a new and bizarre aspect. You can't stand this change in yourself; but it's useless to balk. The demon has gotten into you; all the efforts you make to resist will serve only to speed the progress of the mal. You laugh at your own silliness and folly; your comrades laugh in your face, and you don't hold it against them; for benevolence is beginning to manifest itself.

This listless gaiety, this malaise within happiness, this insecurity, this indecision about malady usually lasts only a short time. It sometimes happens that individuals completely inept at word games improvise an interminable series of puns, completely improbable associations of ideas and facts calculated to lead astray the strongest masters in this preposterous art. After a few minutes, the connections between your ideas become so vague, the threads which link your conceptions are so tenuous, that only your accomplices, your co-religionists, are able to understand you. Your playfulness, your peals of laughter seem the height of silliness to anyone who is not in the same condition as you are.

The wisdom of the unfortunate "other fellow" delights you beyond measure; his composure pushes you to the very limits of irony; he seems to you the maddest, most ridiculous of men. As for you and your comrades, you all understand each other perfectly. Soon you will understand each other only via your eyes. In truth, this is quite a comic situation—one in which men are enjoying a kind and degree of gaiety incomprehensible to anyone who is not in the same world as they are. They conceive a profound pity for such a person. Thenceforth, the feeling of your own superiority reaches the zenith in your mind. Soon it will grow immeasurably greater.

* * *

The second phase begins with a sensation of coolness in the extremities, a general weakness; you have, as they say, a hand of butter, a heaviness of the head and a general stupefaction throughout your being. Your eyes grow larger, as if they were being pulled in all directions by an implacable ecstasy. Your face fills with pallor, becomes livid and greenish. The lips shrink, becoming shorter and seeming to want to be drawn inward. Deep, raucous sighs escape from your chest, as if your former nature could not bear the weight of your new nature. The senses take on an extraordinary acuity. Your eyes pierce infinity. Your ears perceive the slightest and the most piercing of sounds.

Hallucinations begin. External objects take on monstrous forms, which reveal themselves in forms previously unknown to you. Then they change shapes, transforming themselves, and finally enter into your being, or you enter into them. The most amazing ambiguities, the most unexplainable transposals of ideas take place. Sounds have a color, colors have a sound. Musical notes are numbers, and you resolve with frightful rapidity prodigious arithmetical calculations, as music surges into your ears. You are seated and are smoking; you think you are sitting inside your pipe, and it is you who are being smoked by your pipe; it is yourself that you are exhaling, in the form of the bluish cloud.

You feel fine at this point; only one thing worries you and makes you uneasy. How will you get out of your pipe? This question persists for an eternity. In a moment of lucidity, a tremendous effort enables you to glance at the clock. This eternity has lasted one minute. Another current of ideas carries you away; it will carry you off for one minute in its living whirlwind, and that minute will become another eternity. The proportions of time and consciousness are deranged by the vast number and intensity of sensations and ideas. One lives several lifetimes in the space of an hour. That's really the subject of *Peau de Chagrin.* There is no longer any fixed equation between sense organs and pleasures.

From time to time, one's personality disappears. Objectivity, which characterizes certain pantheistic poets and all great actors, becomes such that you confuse yourself with other beings. Now you are a tree, sighing in the wind, singing plant-like melodies to Nature. Now you are soaring in the vastly expanded blue of the sky. All pain has disappeared. You no longer struggle; you are carried away, no longer master of yourself, and this no longer distresses you. In a little while the concept of time will disappear completely.

From time to time another brief awakening takes place. You seem to be emerging from a marvelous, fantastic world. You retain, however, the faculty of observing yourself, and by tomorrow you will have remembered some of your sensations. But this mental faculty you can no longer apply. I defy you to take up a quill pen or a pencil; that would be a task beyond your capacity.

At other times, music recites to you endless poems, places you in frightening or fairy-like situations. This music is associated with objects which are before your eyes. Paintings on the ceiling, even mediocre or poor ones, take on a striking reality. Clear, enchanted water flows through trembling grass. Beguiling nymphs look at you with great blue eyes more limpid than water and sky. You will assume your place and your role in the naughtiest paintings, the most vulgar painted wallpapers covering the walls of hostelries.

I have noticed that water has an appalling effect on the minds of all somewhat artistic persons who are "lit up" by hashish. Running water, fountains, dramatic waterfalls, the full immensity of the sea go on rolling, soothing, singing lullabies to the very depths of your mind. It would perhaps not be advisable to leave a man in this condition on the shore of a limpid body of water; he might let himself be carried off by Ondine.

Towards the end of the evening, one may eat; but this operation is not accomplished without difficulty. One finds himself so far above material things that he would certainly prefer to remain supine, deep in his intellectual paradise. Sometimes, however, the appetite is stimulated to an extraordinary degree; but it takes great courage to handle a bottle, a fork and a knife.

The third phase, distinguishable from the second by a redoubling of crisis, a dizzying drunkenness followed by a new malaise, is something quite indescribable. This is what the Orientals call the kief; it is happiness in the absolute. No longer is it whirling and tumultuous. It's a state of calm and motionless beatitude. All philosophical problems are resolved. All the difficult questions which theologians struggle with and which are the despair of reasoning mankind are simple and clear. All contradiction has become unity. Man has become god.

There is something within you that says: "Thou art superior to all men; no one can fathom what thou art thinking and feeling at this moment. Other men are incapable even of understanding the tremendous love thou art feeling for them. But thou must not hate them for that; thou must have pity for them. A plethora of happiness and virtue is opening before thee. No one will ever understand the degree of virtue and intelligence thou hast reached. So live thy life in the solitude of thine own thought, and afflict not anyone else."

One of the most grotesque effects of hashish is the fear, carried to the most meticulous extreme, of afflicting someone, anyone. You would even disguise, if you had the strength, the super-natural condition you are in, in order not to cause anyone at all any anxiety.

* * *

The next morning, when you see the light of day filling your room, your first sensation is complete surprise. A period of time has completely disappeared. A little while ago it was nighttime; now it's daytime. "Have I slept, or haven't I? Did my drunkenness last all night, and the concept of time being suppressed, has the whole night, for me, amounted to less than one second? Or, have I been shrouded in the toils of a sleep filled with dreams?" It is impossible to be sure.

It seems to you that you are experiencing a state of well-being and a marvelous lightness of mind and spirit; no fatigue whatever. But scarcely are you on your feet when an old familiar symptom of drunkenness manifests itself. Your weak legs carry you timidly; you are afraid you will break yourself like a fragile object. A great lassitude, not without charm, takes possession of your mind. You are incapable of work and of physical activity.

This is the deserved punishment for the impious prodigality with which you have made such a great expenditure of nervous energy. You have scattered your personality to the four winds of heaven, and now you have the problem of reassembling and concentrating it.

*—Translated from the French*
*by Kendall Lappin*

# Hashish

*Théophile Gautier*

For some time now we'd been hearing, without knowing quite what to believe, about the marvelous effects produced by hashish. While we'd experienced hallucinations from smoking opium, we knew hashish only by name. Some orientalist friends of ours had promised us a taste a number of times, but due to difficulties in procuring the substance or to any number of other reasons, it simply hadn't happened. Yesterday it did, and so finally the analysis of our sensations will replace the imagined plots of those plays in which we hadn't acted.

The peoples of the Near East, whose religion forbids the drinking of wine, have through the ages researched other methods of satisfying the common human need for mental stimulation, which those of us living in the Western nations indulge through strong spirits and fermented drinks. The desire to approach an ideal mental state is so strong in Man that he strives as much as he can to unlock the shackles that confine the soul within the body, and as ecstasy is far beyond the reach of most temperaments, he drinks his mirth, he smokes his forgetfulness and he ingests his folly, in the form of wine, tobacco and hashish.—What an extraordinary situation! A little red liquor, a puff of smoke, a spoonful of greenish paste, and the soul, that impalpable essence, is instantly transformed; serious people act foolish, words gush forth involuntarily from the mouths of the silent, Heraclitus roars with laughter and Democrates weeps.

Hashish is an extract from the hemp flower (Canibus indica), which sautéed in butter, along with pistachios, almonds and honey, forms a kind of paste reminiscent of apricot jam in consistency and tasting not half-bad besides.—It was hashish that the deposed Nizar the Elder fed his murderous partisans in their mountain strongholds, and from there originates the word assassin—in Arabic, hashashin, or "users of hashish."

A single spoonful is a large enough dose for those unused to the delights of the true believer. First we washed the hashish down with cups of strong, unsweetened coffee, prepared in the Arab fashion, and then we sat at the table as usual—for it takes some time for the hemp to produce an effect. One of our companions, Doctor ____, who has traveled extensively in the East, and who is a resolute hashish eater, was taken first, having ingested a larger dose than us; he saw stars in his plate, and the sky at the bottom of the soup-tureen; then he pressed his nose to the wall, talking to himself, roaring with laughter, eyes bright and in a profound state of jubilation. Until the end of dinner, I felt perfectly calm, even though the pupils of my fellow diners had begun to sparkle strangely and to turn a completely unnatural shade of turquoise-blue. The dishes cleared from the table, I went to sit down, still having my wits about me, on the sofa, where

I made myself comfortable between two Moroccan pillows while waiting for ecstasy to arrive. At the end of several minutes, a general numbness overcame me. It seemed as though my body had dissolved and become transparent. I saw quite clearly within my stomach the hashish I'd eaten take the form of an emerald, from which shone millions of tiny sparks; my eyelashes lengthened indefinitely, unwinding like golden threads on ivory spinning wheels that turned themselves with dazzling speed. Around me, gem stones of every color collapsed and fell in liquid Arabesques of never-repeated floral patterns that I would best compare to the view through a kaleidoscope; I saw again my comrades at certain instants, but disfigured—half men, half plants, with the thoughtful air of an Ibis standing on one leg, or an ostrich flapping its bizarre wings—so that I was contorted with laughter in my corner, and to better enter into the nonsense of the spectacle, I began to toss my pillows into the air, catching them and spinning them with the dexterity of an Indian juggler. One of these figures began speaking to me in Italian, which the hashish, through its uncanny powers, transformed into Spanish. The questions and responses were almost reasonable, and concerned routine matters, news of the theater and literary gossip.

Thus ended my first encounter.—After several minutes, I found myself with all my senses once again intact, without a trace of headache, without any of the symptoms that accompany drunkenness from wine, and very much surprised at what had just transpired.—Barely half an hour passed before I fell back into the realm of hashish. This time the vision was more complex and more extraordinary. In a vaguely luminous air, thousands of butterflies fluttered in a perpetual swarm, wing-beats humming like whipping fan-blades. Huge flowers like crystal chalices—giant hollyhocks, gold and silver lilies—rose and opened around me with an explosive crackling like the grand finale of a fireworks display. My hearing was so greatly enhanced that I could perceive the sound of colors. Green, red, blue and yellow sounds came to me in perfectly distinct wave-lengths. An overturned glass, the creaking of a chair, a whispered word, vibrated and resounded in me like thunder claps; my own voice seemed so loud that I dared not speak for fear of tumbling the walls or exploding myself like a bomb; more than five hundred clocks sang me the hour, their fluted voices silver-toned and sonorous. Even the slightest motion produced a note from a harmonica or an æolian harp. I was swimming in an ocean of resonance in which opera motifs floated like islands of light. Never had such beatitude overwhelmed me with its emanations: I was so absorbed by the wave, at once free and lost, so outside my self, that obnoxious witness that accompanies me everywhere, that for the first time I understood how elemental spirits, angels and souls without bodies could exist. I was like a sponge in the middle of the sea: each minute tides of bliss washed over me, entering and exiting through my pores, for I had become permeable, and, down to the smallest capillary vessel, my entire being was injected with the colors of this fantastic realm into which I had fallen. Sounds, smells, light, came to me through a multitude of tubes as thin as hairs, through which I heard the hissing of magnetic currents.—By my estimation, this state lasted about 300 years, for the series of sensations following one upon the next was so numerous and condensed as to render any accurate sense of time impossible.—The trip over, I saw that it had lasted fifteen minutes.

What is most singular about a hashish high is that it is not continual; it grabs hold of you and leaves you, blasts you up into the sky and drops you back on the ground without transition—like moments of lucidity surfacing from the depths of insanity. A third trip, the last and the most bizarre, ended my hash party: during this one my vision doubled—two images were reflected on my retina and produced a complete symmetry. Then the completely-digested magic paste produced an even stronger effect upon my brain and for the next hour I became totally out of my mind. All the Pantagruelian dreams came to me in my imagination: goat-footed mules, flirting cranes, licornes, griffins, bridled oysters and saddled nightmares. A whole menagerie of monstrous dreams trotted, leaped, flew and yelped around the room: there were elephant trunks that ended in foliage, hands with fish fins instead of palms, anomalous beings with chair legs for limbs and dial-plates for eyeballs, huge noses that danced the cha-cha on chicken feet. As for me, I imagined that I was the parrot belonging to the queen of Sheba, mistress of the late Solomon. And I did my best to imitate the cries of that honorable winged creature. My visions became so baroque that the desire to draw them overtook me and I made, in less than five minutes, with incredible velocity and on any scrap at hand—the back of letters, flyleafs and tickets—fifteen or so of the most extravagant sketches ever seen. One of them was a portrait of Doctor ____, as he appeared to me, seated at the piano, dressed in Turkish attire, a sun on the back of his jacket. The musical notes coming from the instrument were represented in the form of sky-rockets and capriciously curling spirals. Another sketch carrying the caption—a creature of habit—showed a living locomotive with the neck of a swan terminating in the head of a snake, and monstrous feet composed of wheels and pulleys, from which engine spouted puffs of smoke; each pair of feet was accompanied by a pair of wings, and at the tail of this animal one saw the ancient god Mercury, admitting his defeat despite his winged heels. Thanks to the hashish I could draw from life the portrait of a goblin. Up until that time I'd only heard them moan and bustle in my old sideboard.

But that's more than enough insanity for now. To describe in full the hallucinations inspired by hashish would require a fat tome, and a simple journalist is not allowed to rewrite the Book of Revelations!

*—Translated from the French*
*by Greg Boyd*

# The Apocalypse of Hasheesh

*Fitz Hugh Ludlow*

In returning from the world of hasheesh, I bring with me many and diverse memories. The echoes of a sublime rapture which thrilled and vibrated on the very edge of pain; of Promethean agonies which wrapt the soul like a mantle of fire; of voluptuous delirium which suffused the body with a blush of exquisite languor—all are mine. But in value far exceeding these, is the remembrance of my spell-bound life as an apocalyptic experience.

Not, indeed, valuable, when all things are considered. Ah no! The slave of the lamp who comes at the summons of the hasheesh Aladdin will not always cringe in the presence of his master. Presently he grows bold and for his service demands a guerdon as tremendous as the treasures he unlocked. Dismiss him, hurl your lamp into the jaws of some fathomless abyss, or take his place while he reigns over you, a tyrant of Gehenna!

The value of this experience to me consists in its having thrown open to my gaze many of those sublime avenues in the spiritual life, at whose gates the soul in its ordinary state is forever blindly groping, mystified, perplexed, yet earnest to the last in its search for that secret spring which, being touched, shall swing back the colossal barrier. In a single instant I have seen the vexed question of a lifetime settled, the mystery of some grand recondite process of mind laid bare, the last grim doubt that hung persistently on the sky of a sublime truth blown away.

How few facts can we trace up to their original reason! In all human speculations how inevitable is the recurrence of the ultimate "Why?" Our discoveries in this latter age but surpass the old-world philosophy in fanning this impenetrable mist but a few steps further up the path of thought, and deferring the distance of a few syllogisms the unanswerable question.

How is it that all the million drops of memory preserve their insulation, and do not run together in the brain into one fluid chaos of impression? How does the great hand of central force stretch on invisibly through ether till it grasps the last sphere that rolls on the boundaries of light-quickened space? How does spirit communicate with matter, and where is their point of tangency? Such are the mysteries which bristle like a harvest far and wide over the grand field of thought.

Problems like these, which had been the perplexity of all my previous life, have I seen unraveled by hasheesh, as in one breathless moment the rationale of inexplicable phenomena has burst upon me in a torrent of light. It may have puzzled me to account for some strange fact of mind; taking hypothesis after hypothesis, I have labored for a demonstration; at last I have given up the attempt in despair. During the progress of the next fantasia of hasheesh, the subject has again unexpectedly presented itself, and in an instant the solution has lain before me as an intuition, compelling my assent to its truth as imperatively as a mathematical axiom. At such a time I have stood trembling with awe at the sublimity of the apocalypse; for though this be not the legitimate way of reaching the explications of riddles which, if of any true utility at all, are intended to strengthen the argumentative faculty, there is still an unutterable sense of majesty in the view one thus discovers of the unimagined scope of the intuitive, which surpasses the loftiest emotions aroused by material grandeur.

I was once walking in the broad daylight of a summer afternoon in the full possession of hasheesh delirium. For an hour the tremendous expansion of all visible things had been growing toward its height; it now reached it, and to the fullest extent I realized the infinity of space. Vistas no longer converged, sight met no barrier; the world was horizonless, for earth and sky stretched endlessly onward in parallel planes. Above me the heavens were terrible with the glory of a fathomless depth. I looked up, but my eyes, unopposed, every moment penetrated further and further into the immensity, and I turned them downward lest they should presently intrude into the fatal splendors of the Great Presence. Joy itself became terrific, for it seemed the ecstasy of a soul stretching its cords and waiting in intense silence to hear them snap and free it from the enthrallment of the body. Unable to bear visible objects, I shut my eyes. In one moment a colossal music filled the whole hemisphere above me, and I thrilled upward through its environment on visionless wings. It was not song, it was not instruments, but the inexpressible spirit of sublime sound—like nothing I had ever heard-impossible to be symbolized; intense, yet not loud; the ideal of harmony, yet distinguishable into a multiplicity of exquisite parts. I opened my eyes, yet it still continued. I sought around me to detect some natural sound which might be exaggerated into such a semblance, but no, it was of unearthly generation, and it thrilled through the universe an inexplicable, a beautiful yet an awful symphony.

Suddenly my mind grew solemn with the consciousness of a quickened perception. I looked abroad on fields, and water, and sky, and read in them all a most startling meaning. I wondered how I had ever regarded them in the light of dead matter, at the furthest only suggesting lessons. They were now grand symbols of the sublimest spiritual truths, truths never before even feebly grasped, utterly unsuspected.

Like a map, the arcana of the universe lay bare before me. I saw how every created thing not only typifies but springs forth from some mighty spiritual law as its offspring, its necessary external development; not the mere clothing of the essence, but the essence incarnate.

Nor did the view stop here. While that music from horizon to horizon was still filling the concave above me, I became conscious of a numerical order which ran through it, and in marking this order I beheld it transferred from the music to every movement of the universe. Every sphere wheeled on in its orbit, every emotion of the soul rose and fell, every smallest moss and fungus germinated and grew, according to some peculiar property of numbers which severally governed them and which was most admirably typified by them in return. An exquisite harmony of proportion reigned through space, and I seemed to realize that the music which I heard was but this numerical harmony making itself objective through the development of a grand harmony of tones.

The vividness with which this conception revealed itself to me made it a thing terrible to bear alone. An unutterable ecstasy was carrying me away, but I dared not abandon myself to it. I was no seer who could look on the unveiling of such glories face to face.

An irrepressible yearning came over me to impart what I beheld, to share with another soul the weight of this colossal revelation. With this purpose I scrutinized the vision; I sought in it for some characteristic which might make it translatable to another mind. There was none! In absolute incommunicableness it stood apart, a thought, a system of thought which as yet had no symbol in spoken language.

For a time, how long, a hasheesh-eater alone can know, I was in an agony. I searched every pocket for my pencil and note-book, that I might at least set down some representative mark which would afterwards recall to me the lineaments of my apocalypse. They were not with me. Jutting into the water of the brook along which I wandered lay a broad flat stone. "Glory in the Highest!" I shouted exultingly, "I will at least grave on this tablet some hieroglyph of what I feel!" Tremblingly I sought for my knife. That, too, was gone! It was then that in a frensy I threw myself prostrate on the stone, and with my nails sought to make some memorial scratch upon it. Hard, hard as flint! In despair I stood up.

Suddenly there came a sense as of some invisible presence walking the dread paths of the vision with me, yet at a distance as if separated from my side by a long flow of time. Taking courage, I cried, "Who has ever been here before me, who in years past has shared with me this unutterable view?" In tones which linger in my soul to this day, a grand, audible voice responded, "Pythagoras!" In an instant I was calm. I heard the footsteps of that sublime sage echoing upward through the ages, and in celestial light I read my vision unterrified, since it had burst upon his sight before me. For years previous I had been perplexed with his mysterious philosophy. I saw in him an isolation from universal contemporary mind for which I could not account. When the Ionic school was at the height of its dominance, he stood forth alone, the originator of a system as distinct from it as the antipodes of mind. The doctrine of Thales was built up by the uncertain processes of an obscure logic, that of Pythagoras seemed informed by intuition. In his assertions there had always appeared to me a grave conviction of truth, a consciousness of sincerity, which gave them a great weight with me, though seeing them through the dim refracting medium of tradition and grasping their meaning imperfectly. I now saw the truths which he set forth, in their own light. I also saw, as to this day I firmly believe, the source whence their revelation flowed. Tell me not that from Phoenicia he received the wand at whose signal the cohorts of the spheres came trooping up before him in review, unveiling the eternal law and itineracy of their evolutions, and pouring on his spiritual ear that tremendous music to which they marched through space. No!

During half a lifetime spent in Egypt and in India, both motherlands of this nepenths, doubt not that he quaffed its apocalyptic draught, and awoke, through its terrific quickening, into the consciousness of that ever-present and all-pervading harmony "which we hear not always, because the coarseness of the daily life hath dulled our ear." The dim penetralia of the Theban Memnonium, or the silent spice groves of the upper Indua may have been the gymnasium of his wrestling with the mighty revealer; a priest or a gymnospohist may have been the first to anoint him with the palæstric oil, but he conquered alone. On the strange intuitive characteristics of his system, on the spheral music, on the government of all created things and their development according to the laws of number, yes, on the very use of symbols which could alone have force to the esoteric disciple, (and a terrible significancy, indeed, has the simplest form, to a mind hasheesh-quickened to read its meaning)—on all these is the legible stamp of the hasheesh inspiration.

It would be no hard task to prove, to a strong probability, at least, that the initiation into the Pythagorean mysteries and the progressive instruction that succeeded it, to a considerable extent, consisted in the employment, judiciously, if we may use the word, of hasheesh, as giving a critical and analytic power to the mind which enabled the neophyte to roll up the murk and mist from beclouded truths, till they stood distinctly seen in the splendor of their own harmonious beauty as an intuition.

One thing related of Pythagoras and his friends has seemed very striking to me. There is a legend that, as he was passing over a river, its waters called up to him, in the presence of his followers, "Hail, Pythagoras!" Frequently, while in the power of the hasheesh delirium, have I heard inanimate things sonorous with such voices. On every side they have saluted me; from rocks, and trees, and waters, and sky; in my happiness, filling me with intense exultation, as I heard them welcoming their master; in my agony, heaping nameless curses on my head, as I went away into an eternal exile from all sympathy. Of this tradition on Iamblichus, I feel an appreciation which almost convinces me that the voice of the river was, indeed, heard, though only in the quickened mind of some hasheesh-glorified esoteric. Again, it may be that the doctrine of the Metempsychosis was first communicated to Pythagoras by Theban priests; but the astonishing illustration, which hasheesh would contribute to this tenet, should not be overlooked in our attempt to assign its first suggestion and succeeding spread to their proper causes.

A modern critic, in defending the hypothesis, that Pythagoras was an impostor, has triumphantly asked, "Why did he assume the character of Apollo at the Olympic games? Why did he boast that his soul had lived in former bodies, and that he had been first Acthalides, the son of Mercury, then Euphorbus, then Pyrrhus of Delos, and at last Pythagoras, but that he might more easily impose upon the credulity of an ignorant and superstitious people!" To us these facts seem rather an evidence of his sincerity. Had he made these assertions without proof, it is difficult to see how they would not have had a precisely contrary effect from that of paving the way to a more complete imposition upon the credulity of the people. Upon our hypothesis, it may be easily shown, not only how he could fully have believed these assertions himself, but, also, have given them a deep significance to the minds of his disciples.

Let us see. We will consider, for example, his assumption of the character of Phoebus at the Olympic games. Let us suppose that Pythagoras, animated with a desire of alluring to the study of his philosophy a choice and enthusiastic number out of that host who, along all the radii of the civilized world, had come up to the solemn festival at Elis, had, by the talisman of hasheesh, called to his aid the magic of a preternatural eloquence; that, while he addressed the throng whoin he had charmed into breathless attention by the weird brilliancy of his eyes, the unearthly imagery of his style, and the oracular insight of his thought, the grand impression flashed upon him from the very honor he was receiving, that he was the incarnation of some sublime deity. What wonder that he burst into the acknowledgment of his godship as a secret too majestic to be hoarded up; what wonder that this sudden revelation of himself, darting forth in burning words and amid such colossal surroundings, wended down with the accessories of time and place along the stream of perpetual tradition?

If I may illustrate great things by small, I well remember many hallucinations of my own which would be exactly parallel to such a fancy in the mind of Pythagoras. There is no impression more deeply stamped upon my past life than one of a walk along the brook which had frequently witnessed my wrestlings with the hasheesh-afreet, and which now beheld me, the immortal Zeus, descended among men to grant them the sublime benediction of renovated life. For this cause I had abandoned the serene seats of Olympus, the convocation of the gods, and the glory of an immortal kingship, while, by my side, Hermes trod the earth with radiant feet, the companion and dispenser of the beneficence of deity. Across lakes and seas, from continent to continent, we strode; the snows of Hæimus and the Himmalehs crunched beneath our sandals; our foreheads were bathed with the upper light, our breasts glowed with the exultant inspiration of the golden ether. Now resting on Chimborazo, I poured forth a majestic blessing upon all my creatures, and in an instant, with one omniscient glance, I beheld every human dwelling-place on the whole sphere irradiated with an unspeakable joy.

I saw the king rule more wisely, the laborer return from his toil to a happier home, the park grow green with an intenser culture, the harvest-field groan under the sheaves of a more prudent and prosperous husbandry; adown blue slopes came new and more populous flocks, led by unvexed and gladsome shepherds, a thousand healthy vineyards sprang up above their new-raised sunny terraces, every smallest heart glowed with an added thrill of exaltation, and the universal rebound of joy came pouring up into my own spirit with an intensity that lit my deity with rapture.

And this was only a poor hasheesh-eater, who, with his friend, walked out into the fields to enjoy his delirium among the beauties of a clear summer afternoon! What, then, of Pythagoras?

The tendency of the hasheesh-hallucination is almost always toward the supernatural or the sublimest forms of the natural. As the millennial Christ, I have put an end to all the jars of the world; by a word I have bound all humanity in etern alignments of brotherhood; from the depths of the grand untrodden forest I have called the tiger, and with bloodless jaws he came mildly forth to fawn upon his king, a partaker in the universal amnesty. As Rienzi hurling fiery invective against the usurpations of Colonna, I have seen the broad space below the tribune grow populous with a multitude of intense faces, and within myself felt a sense of towering into sublimity, with the consciousness that it was my eloquence which swayed that great host with a storm of indignation, like the sirocco passing over reeds. Or, uplifted mightily by an irresistible impulse, I have risen through the ethereal infinitudes till I stood on the very cope of heaven, with the spheres below me. Suddenly, by an instantaneous revealing, I became aware of a mighty harp, which lay athwart the celestial hemisphere, and filled the whole sweep of vision before me. The lambent flame of myriad stars was burning in the azure spaces between its strings, and glorious suns gemmed with unimaginable lustre all its colossal frame-work. While I stood overwhelmed by the visions, a voice spoke clearly from the depths of the surrounding ether, "Behold the harp of the universe!" Again I realized the typefaction of the same grand harmony of creation, which glorified the former vision to which I have referred; for every influence, from that which nerves the wing of Ithuriel down to the humblest force of growth, had there its beautiful and peculiar representative string. As yet the music slept, when the voice spake to me again—"Stretch forth thine hand and wake the harmonies!" Trembling yet daring, I swept the harp, and in an instant all heaven thrilled with an unutterable music. My arm strangely lengthened, I grew bolder, and my hand took a wider range. The symphony grew more intense; overpowered, I ceased, and heard tremendous echoes coming back from the infinitudes. Again I smote the chords; but, unable to endure the sublimity of the sound, I sank into an ecstatic trance, and was thus borne off unconsciously to the portals of some new vision.

But, if I found the supernatural an element of happiness, I also found it many times an agent of most bitter pain. If I once exulted in the thought that I was the millennial Christ, so, also, through a long agony, have I felt myself the crucified. In dim horror, I perceived the nails piercing my hands and feet; but it was not that which seemed the burden of my suffering. Upon my head, in a tremendous and ever-thickening cloud, came slowly down the guilt of all the ages past, and all the world to come; by a dreadful quickening, I beheld every atrocity and nameless crime coming up from all time on lines that centred in myself. The thorns clung to my brow, and bloody drops stood like dew upon my hair, yet, these were not the instruments of my agony. I was withered like a leaf in the breath of a righteous vengeance. The curtain of a lurid blackness hung between me and heaven, mercy was dumb forever, and I bore the anger of Omnipotence alone. Out of a fiery distance, demon chants of triumphant blasphemy came surging on my ear, and whispers of ferocious wickedness ruffled the leaden air about my cross. How long I bore this vicarious agony, I have never known; hours are no measure of time in hasheesh. I only know that, during the whole period, I sat perfectly awake among objects which I recognized as familiar; friends were passing and repassing before me, yet. I sat in speechless horror, convinced that to supplicate their pity, to ask their help in the tortures of my dual existence, would be a demand that men in time should reach out and grasp one in eternity, that mortality should succor immortality.

In my experience of hasheesh there has been one pervading characteristic—the conviction that, encumbered with a mortal body, I was suffering that which the untrammeled immortal soul could alone endure. The spirit seemed to be learning its franchise and, whether in joy or pain, shook the bars of flesh mightily, as if determined to escape from its cage. Many a time, in my sublimest ecstasy, have I asked myself, "Is this experience happiness or torture?" for soul and body gave different verdicts.

Hasheesh is nothing to be played with as a bauble. At its revealing, too-dread paths of spiritual life are flung open, too tremendous views disclosed of what the soul is capable of doing, and being, and suffering, for that soul to contemplate, till, relieved of the body, it can behold them alone.

Up to the time that I read in the September number of this Magazine the paper entitled "The Hasheesh-eater." I had long walked among the visions of "the weed of insanity." The recital given there seemed written out of my own soul. In outline and detail it was the counterpart of my own suffering. From that day, I shut the book of hasheesh experience, warned with a warning for which I cannot express myself sufficiently grateful. And now, as utterly escaped, I look back upon the world of visionary yet awful realities, and see the fountains of its Elysium and the flames of its Tartarus growing dimmer and still dimmer in the mists of distance, I hold the remembrance of its apocalypse as something which I shall behold again, when the spirit, looking no longer through windows of sense, shall realize its majesty unterrified, and face to face gaze on its infinite though now unseen surroundings..

# Cannabis Indica Poisoning

*J. C. O'Day, M.D.*

Believing an experience I once had with cannabis indica to be of interest to some of the readers of the Plexus, will be my apology for contributing this article.

It has never been the inclination of the writer to indulge the feeling of egotism; and as the pronoun "I" may appear frequently, you will please bear in mind my desire of accurately and truthfully recounting the event as it actually occurred.

Some few years prior to my taking up the study of medicine, I was employed in northwestern Pennsylvania as locomotive engineer on the Bradford, Bordell & Kinzua Railway. My run was to double the road with the way freight.

One day I pulled into Bradford suffering with an attack of acute bronchitis, and, having a few minutes to spare, ran over to a corner drugstore to consult the clerk about my cough. He recommended Piso's Cure for Consumption, and I bought a bottle and returned to my engine.

Taking a mouthful of the cure I completed the shifting of the freight cars in the yard and made up my train for the trip out. This consumed about one-half hour. Before leaving the yard the conductor (George Caswell) came to the engine telling me we had two car loads of cinders in our train and instructed me to stop at "Hard Scrable" that the Italian section hands might unload the cinders.

My cough was very distressing, and so, as we sped along, I made frequent requisition on the bottle. The more I partook the more I had need to partake.

We had covered about seven miles of the road when I suddenly became aware that I had been dreaming, and that I had forgotten that the responsibility for the safety of the engine and the train rested on my shoulders. The realization of this responsibility shocked me, but did not dispel an illusion that one of my legs was larger than the top of the smoke-stack, my arms like ponderous levers and my hands capable of encircling a flour barrel.

Just then my fireman yelled, "O'Day, what is the matter with you!" and the conductor came clambering over the tender, calling to me to know why I had not stopped at Hard Scrable to allow the unloading of the cinders. About this time I began to realize that I had been imbibing too freely of Piso's Cure, and made a desperate effort to concentrate my mind on my work. I reversed my engine and backed away toward the dumping spot. Looking back I was astonished to find that my train appeared to be more than a mile long, and that the Italian shovelers on the loads of cinders were expanding into enormous misty phantoms.

The sight unnerved me, and I again forgot to stop at Hard Scrable. So wrapped up in the novelty of my new surroundings was I that I forgot my place at the lever until the conductor came forward the second time and told the fireman I must be going crazy. This sobered me somewhat and the ashes were at last dumped at the desired place.

Before starting again I began to wander away into a land of giants and monsters, and fearing that some erratic impulse might seize me I told the fireman to watch me closely and to take charge of the engine if he saw anything wrong with me.

As I responded to the signal to go ahead, I noticed the great length of my engine. The telegraph poles shot upward until their cross arms pierced the blue vault above. Dogs as large as Durham bulls ran out and barked at us as we passed. Flocks of English sparrows with spread of wing greater than the condor rose from the road-bed and flew away. I had run over the road day and night for some years, until I knew every whistling post, but things did not have the old familiar look, and I could not tell whether I was running up grade or down, and was curious to see what the next curve would reveal. The cab grew to enormous proportions, and the fireman stood at his post more than one hundred feet away.

After what seemed to be days of running, and when we had covered what seemed hundreds of miles of track, I began to realize that we were nearing Kinzua Junction, and I slowed up.

The effects of the drug were wearing away and were soon gone, so that I knew how to handle my engine, and persons and objects shrank down to their old proportions.

The intoxication did not last more than three-quarters of an hour.

When a student of medicine in Baltimore, I ran across Prof. H. C. Wood's classic description of cannabis indica intoxication, as experienced by himself, and immediately attributed my peculiar sensations and illusions to hemp in the Cure for Consumption.

A medical journal published in India has recently made very free use of Dr. Wood's article in describing the effects of the drug on its habitués who, it claims, are becoming very numerous in that country.

# The Dance of the Ouled-Na'ils

*Hendrik DeLeeuw*

My English friend of the Egyptian Narcotics Division, urbane and ruddy-faced, who had so kindly offered to initiate me in the idiosyncrasies of the traffic in drugs, had called for me at the appointed hour.

Like long lost brothers we engaged in earnest conversation, so that soon much that had been unknown to me about Egypt's traffic in drugs was imparted to me. I was particularly keen on learning something about hashees, since in America its ally, the Marihuana weed, had taken such a hold as to become a serious menace.

"It was not until the year 1929," said the Major, "that Egypt realized that the country was confronted with a drug visitation that was more severe than any other plague it has had since pre-Biblical times, although true enough, the country has had the problem of hashees for centuries. The fact that it was possible to derive pleasant sensations from the use of hashees seems to have been discovered at a very early date too.

"Paleographists discovered on some clay tablets in a Mesopotamian tongue, a reference to a herb that could make one see visions and what is more, make one indulge in prophetic dreams. Now the exact nature of that herb seems to have been veiled in obscurity, although it may have been the Cannabis Indica, the plant from which the drug known as hashees is extracted and which is probably a sister, a brother or an aunt of the plant grown on American soil which, under the name of Marihuana, has made its ugly presence felt. Now so old is the habit of hashees smoking in the Near East that some philologists assure us that the word Assassin, derived from the word hashis, denotes a person performing some murderous work while under the influence of the drug. Syria has been the largest grower of Cannabis Indica or hashees and numerous mystical societies have flourished in the Syrian hill lands, that were not only devoted to Allah, but also consecrated to strangling dissenters with a gut bow string. This noble service was performed by these self-same assassins whose name, curiously enough, so we are told, derives from the Arabic words hdbit-hashashin, meaning eaters of hashees. These societies, or their adherents, rather, were a sect of the Ismail faction of Islam who believed that their Ismail line, descendants of Ali, carried also with it the highest authority of the Moslemites. It was their paramount duty to attend to the strangulation acts, for which they expected to reap rich rewards in the Moslem hereafter."

At this point I asked the Major to tell me something about the preparation of hashees and whether its process was as simple as that of preparing Marihuana.

"While in America the process of preparing Marihuana is a very simple one," he replied, "and, if my information is correct, is also widely used in the making of many brands of cigarettes so as to enhance their sale, the method adopted in the Near East and in Egypt is not so simple. I perhaps ought to acquaint you with some of the idiosyncrasies and peculiarities of the Cannabis or hashees plant itself.

"It matures toward the end of September and, assuming an amber-colored tint, it becomes very sticky. Of this plant the seeds only are used for the preparation of hashees. These seeds are carefully inspected to determine whether they are ripe and if so are taken to the drying sheds. After ten or twelve days of extensive sun-drying they are placed on linen sheets, special care being taken that they lose none of the fine, amber-colored powder which is so abundant in the seed pods.

"Then follows the shed-drying process, during which the seeds are given a thorough flailing by workers who, with long sticks, separate the powder from the seeds. The powder is then graded, run through sieves and put into bags. The bags are carefully sewed up, flattened out and placed in a cooking apparatus. During this process, which takes about fifteen minutes, the hashees softens until it becomes a paste. The hashees is subsequently left in the sun again, when it hardens and is then ready for commercial use.

"The cakes strangely resemble slippers and curiously enough it is by the name of pantoufles (or slippers) that hashees has become known, just as the word bootlegger originated in America. The word pantoufle originated in the days when the smugglers used to place the cakes of hashees inside their shoes. Most of the smuggling, by the way, took place at Port Said and half of that port's population derived its income from the illicit trade in hashees."

When I asked the Major how hashees principally was used, he told me that it was extensively used in religious rituals, despite the otherwise so rigid tenets of the church. First it was mixed with tobacco and extensively used in cigarettes which, like the weeds in America, were always in great demand. The most common use of hashees was in the Goza or water pipe. This Goza, by the way consists of a bowl in which the tobacco, mixed with hashees, is placed on a vertical tube. This tube in turn rests in a bowl of water, which permits the hashees and tobacco to cool off before the smoker begins to inhale the fumes.

We were soon wending our way towards the native section of Cairo, through narrow streets and lanes, past minaretted mosques and innumerable little shops, that were protected from the sun merely by ragged awnings and that would have become a heap of dust were it not for that most important of street tradesmen, the water carriers. Of these water carriers, by the way, there were some six or seven varieties. There were, for instance, those who were concerned only with the sprinkling of the streets. Then there were the Sakha, who, lumbering under the weight of a goatskin bag, dispensed unfiltered water, and the Sussi, who from their terra cotta pots dispensed copious draughts of drinking water. There were the Sherbutli, vendors of sherbets and lemonade, who carried a variety of huge water bottles holding the lemonade and sherbet of rainbow hues and which presented a rather colorful sight as they shone through the transparent glass of the bottles.

One tradesman who held me rather fascinated, as he must have thousands of other travellers, was the incense burner who, for a mere pittance, made it his specialty to fumigate one's raiment or one's place of business. And I could not help thinking how customs are established out of sheer necessity. For woe be to those who are endowed with too good a proboscis and consequently keen at detecting things. Unless the incense be generously sprayed about, he with the proverbial dog's nose, upon entering a merchant's shop, would do a fast about-face. In fact life in Cairo might become a terrible nightmare for him.

Major Dunwoodie proposed that he take me to one of the wine bars, where the followers of Mahomet so cunningly connive in violating the tenets of the Prophet, more especially that which prohibits them from imbibing strong drinks, and where, with that insatiable desire for novelties, they also indulge in other dissipations in which hashees has become a necessary accessory.

We came to a district where women with brightly-painted lips, shapely formed bodies and naked breasts were peeping from open doorways. Here the traffic was thick and evil seemed to float from everywhere. I looked back for a moment through the tortuous lanes and in the dull glow of a lantern behind a door I could see figures pass. I also heard the booming of a drum. Beggars shouted out to us and held out dirty hands. Nondescript natives, like Biblical figures, sat on the curb.

In a little square we came to a halt. At the entrance to the wine shop sat a ragged beggar woman with a soiled and protesting baby clasped to her naked breast. Her veil, a final bulwark of outraged modesty, was none too closely drawn and actually revealed a face that still might be useful in attracting sots, although no longer the delight of a harem. From her mouth filtered the omnipresent whining, echoing plaint of the Near and Far East, "Bakshees for the love of Allah, Allah be Merciful!" We slipped her a couple of coins and entered the wine shop, where Major Dunwoodie was well known. A café-au-lait–colored servant who, so I heard afterwards, was also a secret service man, bowed us through the heterogeneous throng.

Fragrant fumes of coffee, absinthe and cognacs blew into our faces. Oil lamps in the apparently badly lighted place were swinging from the rafters and cast a ruddy glow on a heavily-carpeted dais. As my eyes became more accustomed to the dim light of the place, I was able to distinguish rugs, shawls and scrolls emblazoned with strange golden devices, and broad carpeted divans covered with strips of crimson cloth and heavily embroidered, imparting a warm and colorful effect to what at first had looked like deep gloom. Cushions were littered about and were used by the natives, who squatted cross-legged beside little tables.

The crowd seemed a variegated one: To begin with we noticed the lower-class Egyptians, whose ill-fitting and sagging trousers and discolored jackets were much the worse for wear. There were also a few fleshy-lipped and lusty-eyed Tunisians, a Berber or two, some Moors, Jews, and Maltese, while to my great surprise I spotted also a Tonkinese, who surely was a long way from home. And then of course there were the women, whose nationalities were as undefinable as their morals.

The atmosphere was somewhat heavy. Clouds of spiral smoke blended and leaped apart. The odors that I was able to detect now were those of garlic, onions and a pungent smell of overhot humanity, which made a blend totally unlike that of an attar of roses.

On all sides were the sucking, gobbling noises, not so much of the nargilehs this time, as those of soup and other concoctions which the patrons seemed to imbibe by the countless platefuls.

In a small alcove, a rather benevolent-faced and aged Mussulman was making coffee over a charcoal-filled brazier. I have never quite forgotten the attire of this extraordinary creature, though I have seen his counterpart at times in comic opera. He wore a maroon-colored jacket and yellow waistcoat, with sleeves richly covered with golden braid. His breeches also were of an indescribable color and with red stockings, curly-toed slippers and green broad belt he made a very impressionistic picture. His multi-colored kaftan, however, was what intrigued me most of all. I do not believe that one color in this fanciful raiment had been overlooked.

The particular duty of this fellow, whom we had named Omar the Coffee Maker, was to make coffee for the visitors and he did it with the deftness for which Arabs and many others of the Near East are so well known.

When we entered the shop and he had seen us, his face lighted up. When we had given our order for his brew, the mannerisms of Omar, as he made our coffee, became such as are hard to describe. He took one teaspoonful of the powder, added to it a similar amount of sugar, put both into one of the little brass pots and repeated the performance three times. He then placed the pots before him in a semi-circle upon his bench. Then he poured the boiling water and thrust the brass pots into the heart of the fire.

This part of the ceremony over, Omar just sat, with arms folded before him, and he kept looking at us, then at his pots, and vice versa until at last the coffee started to froth. This was the supreme moment for which Omar, the Grand Potentate, had been waiting. He jerked the brass vessels off the coals and with a ceremonial gesture handed these to the attendant, who rushed the brew over to us and, as he poured it into rather dainty cups, apologized profusely and expressed the fervent hope that the Effendis would find the broth nothing short of a drink of the gods.

The fumes of tobacco mingled with the fumes of something indefinable at that particular moment, but decidedly sweeter than coffee, began to permeate our nostrils. The patrons appeared to be bringing their long and short noses together in conversation and in fierce flurries of laughter. The fezzed and turbanned occupants of the cushions on the floor puffed and gurgled their nargilehs and drew in their hashees and other concoctions, while sleek flunkeys cantered to and fro to replenish the pipe and cup.

My mind at this moment brimmed with flashes of color, of a movement of bodies, half naked and otherwise, of chatter of all kinds in mysterious vernaculars, of ejaculations of joy and of women screaming like magpies, when their companions became too daring.

My attention was drawn towards a party of three men and a woman. The men were better-class Egyptians and the woman was of that Near-Eastern type of womanhood renowned for its great beauty. The antics of these people fascinated me greatly, since they were smoking hashees. One of the men placed a piece of hashees on the smoldering tobacco. He then took a long whiff and passed the pipe first to the woman, who also took a long whiff, and then to the others in the party, who did likewise. They seemed to enjoy the thing immensely, and that would have ended the matter as far as my interest was concerned, if after a short while the hashees had not begun to take effect. The laughter and conversation which at first had been subdued, now became almost hilarious. The woman seemed to lose her composure and she became extremely agitated. A spasm that wrenched her blazing mind was getting fiercer. Her eyes grew darker. She flung her arms about wildly, until finally they hung limply at her sides, and she fell back upon the cushions, showing the fullness of her body and the sharp rise of her exquisitely-formed breasts.

Gradually all the men in her party went through identical experiences, dropping by the wayside. I watched this exhibition for some time. These people seemed to have been stripped of all vitality. Their eyes remained open and not a sound issued from their lips. They were like corpses.

As Major Dunwoodie pointed out, the effect of the drug in this particular case seemed to be identical in all four persons, although, as he added, the effect varies, depending on the temperament of the individual. It may have no disastrous repercussions at all on certain people, whereas in the cases of others it may render the devotees somnolent or numb. And in still others it produces such a disastrous effect as to end in a mad frenzy, which often makes the users run amok. When thus affected they may be seized with sudden bursts of madness or frenzy and they become a real danger to the community. "Strange as it may sound," concluded the Major, "such madness usually occurs at the time of the full moon."

As the Major stopped talking I became aware of a lull which seemed almost uncanny. Fumes of tobacco and hashees swirled over the crowd of men and women. Behind us I could hear some one's quickened breathing. I turned around and beheld a native madly clasping a light-colored Nubian girl in his arms.

Then as the effects of the hashees in many of the devotees seemed to be wearing off, a plump-ish woman, wearing a semi-transparent gown, bedecked with tawdry jewelry and bedaubed with much powder and paint, precipitated herself from one of the alcoves and was joined by a negro in a savage dance. They pressed their bodies together and swayed their hips in lascivious oscillations. The strumming and fiddling of the Derbouka, Gimbri and Viola, handled by a small band hidden in an alcove, accelerated the tempo and pace.

When after a while the music stopped and the couple panting for breath had sunk to the floor, their act was followed by that of three Ouled-Naïls, the dancing girls from the hills.

These girls were lithe and slender and the crowd admired their most attractive figures that revealed, beneath clinging satin tunics, supple breasts supported by coral-studded girdles. Heavy coils of night-black hair, entwined with golden and silver coins, almost hid their huge earrings of gold and coral. Anklets dangled and tinkled with their every movement as they made ready for their performance. Their small, arched feet and long and rounded arms were bare save for some bizarre jewelled bracelets. Their hands glittered with rings and their finger tips were stained with henna.

They broke into a gesture dance, the sort of stuff usually staged for foreign consumption. Each girl, on her own little square of carpet, began to undulate her body to the tempo of the thumping, strumming, sobbing and droning of uncanny music, and to twist her pointed fingers. They coiled and serpentined themselves into every conceivable pose and contortion. Their black, arched eyebrows, made blacker with kohl, their faces peach-complexioned and scarlet-lipped, made them appear even more mask-like and expressionless.

The heat of the place, unquestionably due to the very low ceiling, became at times insufferable. The fumes of food, drink, tobacco and hashees, together with the sweet, though overpowering, odors of the dancing women, produced a strange combination jarring to one's olfactory nerves. The white glow of a few specially constructed lamps, spraying an often eerie light upon the dancing women, contrasted weirdly with the cherry red of the nargilehs of the smokers.

The tempo of the music increased. The girls leaped like cats into the air and dropped down again with a soft thud as their bodies began to contort. Their masks of indifference were thrown aside and in the gleam of the reddish-tinted lamps overhead, their onyx-black eyes seemed ablaze with mocking laughter. Through red, pouting lips came again and again a glint of dazzling teeth. Now furiously, then passionately, then again coquettishly, they sprang and gyrated, bent and rose, advanced and retreated and moved so fast that it was difficult to follow them. They coiled their straight, slim limbs about them, while their flexible hips continued to shake. Their arms circled nearly white against the dark background. Their breasts swelled, as they panted. The single piece of silk that covered each of their bodies dropped to the floor, in some mysterious and dexterous movement, reminiscent of the best of strip-tease acts, and they danced stark naked before the drugged and sex-intoxicated audience.

One of the girls, the most attractive in the lot—very supple and gracefully formed, detached herself from the others for a moment. Permitting a faint smile to pass over her pretty face, this one did a bit of business of her own. She wriggled her pelvis while jogging her well- shaped breasts up and down like water bags on a mule.

The audience, due to the cataleptic state brought about by the use of hashees, was led to a transport of enthusiasm.

The solo dancer was joined again by the others and their warm, impassioned bodies, brimful of the sap of life, exuded a most irresistible magnetism that attracted and drew all eyes. What had first been ecstasy now became violence and obscenity. The music grew more uproarious. What had been close to endearment now became sheer lust, as the girls continued to whirl and writhe like snakes. For a brief moment they stood rigid like young poplars; then they bent backward and, splitting their legs wide, their dance assumed sensual motions full of erotic meaning. They delighted and repelled, irritated and fascinated. Sometimes their ardor seemed cold and refined, then again it was hot, fierce and cruel. The smokers in the audience gazed spellbound, having found at last something that matched their hubble-bubble paradise.

The last figure of the dance presented a pattern of an exotic flower as the girls began to move with mincing steps. This made a most beautiful decoration, daring and yet not obscene. Out of each movement sprang color intended to vanquish the heart, and each gesture, each nod joyously appealed to the audience until, as if by magic, the barbaric music stopped on an ear-piercing, long-drawn note. With flame in their eyes and with odd-sounding, gurgling moans, the three graceful nymphs collapsed into motionless heaps and the dance was over.

From the audience guttural voices burst into shouts. Some stamped their feet. Others beat a tattoo on the tables. Coins fell onto the carpets.

The night was young and the Levantine waiter, bald as a coot, whined through an oily smile that the best was yet to come. Still we decided not to remain for the next act. It had been enough for one evening's entertainment.

Soon we filed into the gloomy street. A large and round, silvery moon sailed overhead in a sapphire-gemmed sky which ran like a twisted, spangled and luminous ribbon between the high-bracketed, inky-black roofs and daintily-laced minarets of the mosques. Not a sound was heard save the occasional howl of a dog, possibly barking at the moon.

We passed a native watchman.

"Aleikum es Salaam," said my friend, who spoke Arabic as well as he did his native tongue.

The watchman mumbled a reply.

The trembling lights of lanterns faded, then climbed again into brightness. A patriarchally-draped Arab, with turban and cane, emerged from the shadows of a doorway. From another, sparsely lighted, a Berber or Tunisian prostitute importuned. On and on, through a world of smells, creeps and shudders, we walked, until all noise dwindled to silence, except for the thud of our footsteps.

Spooks, occult and malign, began to rise, and shapes and shadows danced on ahead of us. We continued in this manner until, half an hour later, we emerged again into the lights of mysterious Cairo.

# The Pleasures of Opium

*Thomas de Quincey*

It is so long since I first took opium, that if it had been a trifling incident in my life, I might have forgotten its date: but cardinal events are not to be forgotten; and from circumstances connected with it, I remember that it must be referred to the autumn of 1804. During that season I was in London, having come thither for the first time since my entrance at college. And my introduction to opium arose in the following way. From an early age I had been accustomed to wash my head in cold water at least once a day: being suddenly seized with toothache, I attributed it to some relaxation caused by an accidental intermission of that practice; jumped out of bed: plunged my head into a basin of cold water; and with hair thus wetted went to sleep. The next morning, as I need hardly say, I awoke with excruciating rheumatic pains of the head and face, from which I had hardly any respite for about twenty days. On the twenty-first day, I think it was, and on a Sunday, that I went out into the streets; rather to run away, if possible, from my torments, than with any distinct purpose. By accident I met a college acquaintance who recommended opium. Opium! dread agent of unimaginable pleasure and pain! I had heard of it as I had of manna or of ambrosia, but no further: how unmeaning a sound was it at that time! what solemn chords does it now strike upon my heart! what heart-quaking vibrations of sad and happy remembrances! Reverting for a moment to these, I feel a mystic importance attached to the minutest circumstances connected with the place and the time, and the man (if man he was) that first laid open to me the Paradise of Opium-eaters. It was a Sunday afternoon, wet and cheerless: and a duller spectacle this earth of ours has not to show than a rainy Sunday in London. My road homewards lay through Oxford-street; and near 'the stately Pantheon' (as Mr Wordsworth has obligingly called it) I saw a druggist's shop. The druggist, unconscious minister of celestial pleasures!—as if in sympathy with the rainy Sunday, looked dull and stupid, just as any mortal druggist might be expected to look on a Sunday: and, when I asked for the tincture of opium, he gave it to me as any other man might do: and furthermore, out of my shilling, returned to me what seemed to be real copper halfpence, taken out of a real wooden drawer. Nevertheless, in spite of such indications of humanity, he has ever since existed in my mind as the beatific vision of an immortal druggist, sent down to earth on a special mission to myself. And it confirms me in this way of considering him, that, when I next came up to London, I sought him near the stately Pantheon, and found him not: and thus to me, who knew not his name (if indeed he had one) he seemed rather to have vanished from Oxford-street than to have removed in any bodily fashion. The reader may choose to think of him as, possibly, no more than a sublunary druggist: it may be so: but my faith is better: I believe him to have evanesced, or evaporated. So unwillingly would I connect any mortal remembrances with that hour, and place, and creature, that first brought me acquainted with the celestial drug.

Arrived at my lodgings, it may be supposed that I lost not a moment in taking the quantity prescribed. I was necessarily ignorant of the whole art and mystery of opium-taking: and, what I took, I took under every disadvantage. But I took it:—and in an hour, oh! heavens! what a revulsion! what an upheaving, from its lowest depths, of the inner spirit! what an apocalypse of the world within me! That my pains had vanished, was now a trifle in my eyes:—this negative effect was swallowed up in the immensity of those positive effects which had opened before me—in the abyss of divine enjoyment thus suddenly revealed. Here was a panacea—a remedy for all human woes: here was the secret of happiness, about which philosophers had disputed for so many ages, at once discovered: happiness might now be bought for a penny, and carried in the waistcoat pocket: portable ecstasies might be had corked up in a pint bottle: and peace of mind could be sent down in gallons by the mail coach. But, if I talk in this way, the reader will think I am laughing: and I can assure him, that nobody will laugh long who deals much with opium: its pleasures even are of a grave and solemn complexion; and in his happiest state, the opium-eater cannot present himself in the character of l'Allegro: even then, he speaks and thinks as becomes Il Penseroso. Nevertheless, I have a very reprehensible way of jesting at times in the midst of my own misery: and, unless when I am checked by some more powerful feelings, I am afraid I shall be guilty of this indecent practice even in these annals of suffering or enjoyment. The reader must allow a little to my infirm nature in this respect: and with a few indulgences of that sort, I shall endeavour to be as grave, if not drowsy, as fits a theme like opium, so antimercurial as it really is, and so drowsy as it is falsely reputed.

And, first, one word with respect to its bodily effects: for upon all that has been hitherto written on the subject of opium, whether by travellers in Turkey (who may plead their privilege of lying as an old immemorial right), or by professors of medicine, writing ex cathedrá,—I have but one emphatic criticism to pronounce—Lies! lies! lies! I remember once, in passing a bookstall, to have caught these words from a page of some satiric author:—"By this time I became convinced that the London newspapers spoke truth at least twice a week, viz., on Tuesday and Saturday, and might safely be depended upon for—the list of bankrupts." In like manner, I do by no means deny that some truths have been delivered to the world in regard to opium: thus it has been repeatedly affirmed by the learned, that opium is a dusky brown in colour; and this, take notice, I grant: secondly, that it is rather dear; which also I grant: for in my time, East-India opium has been three guineas a pound, and Turkey eight: and, thirdly, that if you eat a good deal of it, most probably you must do—what is particularly disagreeable to any man of regular habits, viz. die. These weighty propositions are, all and singular, true: I cannot gainsay them: and truth ever was, and will be, commendable. But in these three theorems, I believe we have exhausted the stock of knowledge as yet accumulated by man on the subject of opium. And therefore, worthy doctors, as there seems to be room for further discoveries, stand aside, and allow me to come forward and lecture on this matter.

First, then, it is not so much affirmed as taken for granted, by all who ever mention opium, formally or incidentally, that it does, or can produce intoxication. Now, reader, assure yourself, meo periculo, that no quantity of opium ever did, or could intoxicate. As to the tincture of opium (commonly called laudanum) that might certainly intoxicate if a man could bear to take enough of it; but why? because it contains so much proof spirit, and not because it contains so much opium. But crude opium, I affirm peremptorily, is incapable of producing any state of body at all resembling that which is produced by alcohol: and not in degree only incapable, but even in kind: it is not in the quantity of its effects merely, but in the quality, that it differs altogether. The pleasure given by wine is always mounting, and tending to a crisis, after which it declines: that from opium, when once generated, is stationary for eight or ten hours: the first, to borrow a technical distinction from medicine, is a case of acute—the second, of chronic pleasure: the one is a flame, the other a steady and equable glow. But the main distinction lies in this, that whereas wine disorders the mental faculties, opium, on the contrary (if taken in a proper manner), introduces amongst them the most exquisite order, legislation, and harmony. Wine robs a man of his self-possession: opium greatly invigorates it. Wine unsettles and clouds the judgment, and gives a preternatural brightness, and a vivid exaltation to the contempts and the admirations, the loves and the hatreds, of the drinker: opium, on the contrary, communicates serenity and equipoise to all the faculties, active or passive: and with respect to the temper and moral feelings in general, it gives simply that sort of vital warmth which is approved by the judgment, and which would probably always accompany a bodily constitution of primeval or antediluvian health. Thus, for instance, opium, like wine, gives an expansion to the heart and the benevolent affections: but then, with this remarkable difference, that in the sudden development of kind-heartedness which accompanies inebriation, there is always more or less of a maudlin character, which exposes it to the contempt of the bystander. Men shake hands, swear eternal friendship, and shed tears—no mortal knows why: and the sensual creature is clearly uppermost. But the expansion of the benigner feelings, incident to opium, is no febrile access, but a healthy restoration to that state which the mind would naturally recover upon the removal of any deep-seated irritation of pain that had disturbed and quarrelled with the impulses of a heart originally just and good. True it is, that even wine, up to a certain point, and with certain men, rather tends to exalt and to steady the intellect: I myself, who have never been a great wine-drinker, used to find that half a dozen glasses of wine advantageously affected the faculties—brightened and intensified the consciousness—and gave to the mind a feeling of being 'ponderibus librata suis': and certainly it is most absurdly said, in popular language, of any man, that he is disguised in liquor: for, on the contrary, most men are disguised by sobriety; and it is when they are drinking (as some old gentleman says in Athenæus), that men—display themselves in their true complexion of character; which surely is not disguising themselves. But still, wine constantly leads a man to the brink of absurdity and extravagance; and, beyond a certain point, it is sure to volatilize and to disperse the intellectual energies: whereas opium always seems to compose what had been agitated, and to concentrate what had been distracted. In short, to sum up all in one word, a man who is inebriated, or tending to inebriation, is, and feels that he is, in a condition which calls up into supremacy the merely human, too often the brutal, part of his nature: but the opium-eater (I speak of him who is not suffering from any disease, or other remote effects of opium,) feels that the diviner part of his nature is paramount; that is, the moral affections are in a state of cloudless serenity; and over all is the great light of the majestic intellect.

This is the doctrine of the true church on the subject of opium: of which church I acknowledge myself to be the only member—the alpha and the omega—but then it is to be recollected, that I speak from the ground of a large and profound personal experience: whereas most of the unscientific authors who have at all treated of opium, and even of those who have written expressly on the materia medica, make it evident, from the horror they express of it, that their experimental knowledge of its action is none at all. I will, however, candidly acknowledge that I have met with one person who bore evidence to its intoxicating power, such as staggered my own incredulity: for he was a surgeon, and had himself taken opium largely. I happened to say to him, that his enemies (as I had heard) charged him with talking nonsense on politics, and that his friends apologized for him, by suggesting that he was constantly in a state of intoxication from opium. Now the accusation, said I, is not prima facie, and of necessity, an absurd one: but the defence is. To my surprise, however, he insisted that both his enemies and his friends were in the right: 'I will maintain,' said he, 'that I do talk nonsense; and secondly, I will maintain that I do not talk nonsense upon principle, or with any view to profit, but solely and simply, said he, solely and simply,—solely and simply, (repeating it three times over), because I am drunk with opium; and that daily.' I replied that, as to the allegation of his enemies, as it seemed to be established upon such respectable testimony, seeing that the three parties concerned all agreed in it, it did not become me to question it; but the defence set up I must demur to. He proceeded to discuss the matter, and to lay down his reasons; but it seemed to me so impolite to pursue an argument which must have presumed a man mistaken in a point belonging to his own profession, that I did not press him even when his course of argument seemed open to objection: not to mention that a man who talks nonsense, even though 'with no view to profit,' is not altogether the most agreeable partner in a dispute, whether as opponent or respondent. I confess, however, that the authority of a surgeon, and one who was reputed a good one, may seem a weighty one to my prejudice: but still I must plead my experience, which was greater than his greatest by 7000 drops a day; and, though it was not possible to suppose a medical man unacquainted with characteristic symptoms of vinous intoxication, it yet struck me that he might proceed on a logical error of using the word intoxication with too great latitude, and extending it generically to all modes of nervous excitement, instead of restricting it as the expression for a specific sort of excitement, connected with certain diagnostics. Some people have maintained, in my hearing, that they had been drunk upon green tea: and a medical student in London, for whose knowledge in his profession I have reason to feel great respect, assured me, the other day, that a patient, in recovering from an illness, had got drunk on a beef-steak.

Having dwelt so much on this first and leading error, in respect to opium, I shall notice very briefly a second and a third; which are, that the elevation of spirits produced by opium is necessarily followed by a proportionate depression, and that the natural and even immediate consequence of opium is torpor and stagnation, animal and mental. The first of these errors I shall content myself with simply denying; assuring my reader, that for ten years, during which I took opium at intervals, the day succeeding to that on which I allowed myself this luxury was always a day of unusually good spirits.

With respect to the torpor supposed to follow, or rather (if we were to credit the numerous pictures of Turkish opium-eaters) to accompany the practice of opium-eating, I deny that also. Certainly, opium is classed under the head of narcotics; and some such effect it may produce in the end: but the primary effects of opium are always, and in the highest degree, to excite and stimulate the system: this first stage of its action always lasted with me, during my noviciate, for upwards of eight hours; so that it must be the fault of the opium-eater himself if he does not so time his exhibition of the dose (to speak medically) as that the whole weight of its narcotic influence may descend upon his sleep. Turkish opium-eaters, it seems, are absurd enough to sit, like so many equestrian statues, on logs of wood as stupid as themselves. But that the reader may judge of the degree in which opium is likely to stupify the faculties of an Englishman, I shall (by way of treating the question illustratively, rather than argumentatively) describe the way in which I myself often passed an opium evening in London, during the period between 1804 and 1812. It will be seen, that at least opium did not move me to seek solitude, and much less to seek inactivity, or the torpid state of self-involution ascribed to the Turks. I give this account at the risk of being pronounced a crazy enthusiast or visionary: but I regard that little: I must desire my reader to bear in mind, that I was a hard student, and at severe studies for all the rest of my time: and certainly I had a right occasionally to relaxations as well as other people: these, however, I allowed myself but seldom.

The late Duke of _____ used to say, 'Next Friday, by the blessing of heaven, I purpose to be drunk': and, in like manner, I used to fix beforehand how often, within a given time, and when, I would commit a debauch of opium. This was seldom more than once in three weeks: for at that time I could not have ventured to call every day (as I did afterwards) for "a glass of laudanum negus, warm, and without sugar" No: as I have said, I seldom drank laudanum, at that time, more than once in three weeks: this was usually on a Tuesday or a Saturday night; my reason for which was this. In those days Grassini sang at the Opera: and her voice was delightful to me beyond all that I had ever heard. I know not what may be the state of the Opera-house now, having never been within its walls for seven or eight years, but at that time it was by much the most pleasant place of public resort in London for passing an evening. Five shillings admitted one to the gallery, which was subject to far less annoyance than the pit of the theatres: the orchestra was distinguished by its sweet and melodious grandeur from all English orchestras, the composition of which, I confess, is not acceptable to my ear, from the predominance of the clangorous instruments, and the absolute tyranny of the violin. The choruses were divine to hear: and when Grassini appeared in some interlude, as she often did, and poured forth her passionate soul as Andromache, at the tomb of Hector, &c. I question whether any Turk, of all that ever entered the paradise of opium-eaters, can have had half the pleasure I had. But, indeed, I honour the Barbarians too much by supposing them capable of any pleasures approaching to the intellectual ones of an Englishman. For music is an intellectual or a sensual pleasure, according to the temperament of him who hears it. And, by the by, with the exception of the fine extravaganza on that subject in Twelfth Night, I do not recollect more than one thing said adequately on the subject of music in all literature: it is a passage in the Religio Medici of Sir T. Brown; and, though chiefly remarkable for its sublimity, has also a philosophic value, inasmuch as it points to the true theory of musical effects. The mistake of most people is to suppose that it is by the ear, they communicate with music, and, therefore, that they are purely passive to its effects. But this is not so: it is by the reaction of the mind upon the notices of the ear, (the matter coming by the senses, the form from the mind) that the pleasure is constructed: and therefore it is that people of equally good ear differ so much in this point from one another. Now opium, by greatly increasing the activity of the mind generally, increases, of necessity, that particular mode of its activity by which we are able to construct out of the raw material of organic sound an elaborate intellectual pleasure. But, says a friend, a succession of musical sounds is to me like a collection of Arabic characters: I can attach no ideas to them! Ideas! my good sir? there is no occasion for them: all that class of ideas, which can be available in such a case, has a language of representative feelings. But this is a subject foreign to my present purposes: it is sufficient to say, that a chorus, &c. of elaborate harmony, displayed before me, as in a piece of arras work, the whole of my past life—not as if recalled by an act of memory, but as if present and incarnated in the music: no longer painful to dwell upon: but the detail of its incidents removed, or blended in some hazy abstraction; and its passions exalted, spiritualized, and sublimed. All this was to be had for five shillings. And over and above the music of the stage and the orchestra, I had all around me, in the intervals of the performance, the music of the Italian language talked by Italian women: for the gallery was usually crowded with Italians: and I listened with a pleasure such as that with which Weld the traveller lay and listened, in Canada, to the sweet laughter of Indian women; for the less you understand of a language, the more sensible you are to the melody or harshness of its sounds:

for such a purpose, therefore, it was an advantage to me that I was a poor Italian scholar, reading it but little, and not speaking it at all, nor understanding a tenth part of what I heard spoken.

These were my Opera pleasures: but another pleasure I had which, as it could be had only on a Saturday night, occasionally struggled with my love of the Opera; for, at that time, Tuesday and Saturday were the regular Opera nights. On this subject I am afraid I shall be rather obscure, but, I can assure the reader, not at all more so than Marinus in his life of Proclus, or many other biographers and auto-biographers of fair reputation. This pleasure, I have said, was to be had only on a Saturday night. What then was Saturday night to me more than any other night? I had no labours that I rested from; no wages to receive: what needed I to care for Saturday night, more than as it was a summons to hear Grassini? True, most logical reader: what you say is unanswerable. And yet so it was and is, that, whereas different men throw their feelings into different channels, and most are apt to show their interest in the concerns of the poor, chiefly by sympathy, expressed in some shape or other, with their distresses and sorrows, I, at that time, was disposed to express my interest by sympathising with their pleasures. The pains of poverty I had lately seen too much of; more than I wished to remember: but the pleasures of the poor, their consolations of spirit, and their reposes from bodily toil, can never become oppressive to contemplate. Now Saturday night is the season for the chief, regular, and periodic return of rest to the poor: in this point the most hostile sects unite, and acknowledge a common link of brotherhood: almost all Christendom rests from its labours. It is a rest introductory to another rest: and divided by a whole day and two nights from the renewal of toil. On this account I feel always, on a Saturday night, as though I also were released from some yoke of labour, had some wages to receive, and some luxury of repose to enjoy. For the sake, therefore, of witnessing, upon as large a scale as possible, a spectacle with which my sympathy was so entire, I used often, on Saturday nights, after I had taken opium, to wander forth, without much regarding the direction or the distance, to all the markets, and other parts of London, to which the poor resort on a Saturday night, for laying out their wages. Many a family party, consisting of a man, his wife, and sometimes one or two of his children, have I listened to, as they stood consulting on their ways and means or the strength of their exchequer, or the price of household articles. Gradually I became familiar with their wishes, their difficulties, and their opinions. Sometimes there might be heard murmurs of discontent: but far oftener expressions on the countenance, or uttered in words, of patience, hope, and tranquility. And, taken generally, I must say, that, in this point at least, the poor are far more philosophic than the rich—that they show a more ready and cheerful submission to what they consider as irremediable evils, or irreparable losses. Whenever I saw occasion, or could do it without appearing to be intrusive, I joined their parties; and gave my opinion upon the matter in discussion, which, if not always judicious, was always received indulgently. If wages were a little higher, or expected to be so, or the quarter loaf a little lower, or it was reported that onions and butter were expected to fall, I was glad: yet, if the contrary were true, I drew from opium some means of consoling myself. For opium (like the bee, that extracts its materials indiscriminately from roses and from the soot of chimneys) can overrule all feelings into a compliance with the master key. Some of these rambles led me to great distances: for an opium-eater is too happy to observe the motion of time. And sometimes in my attempts to steer homewards, upon nautical principles, by fixing my eye on the pole-star, and seeking ambitiously for a north-west passage, instead of circumnavigating all the capes and headlands I had doubled in my outward voyage, I came suddenly upon such knotty problems of alleys, such enigmatical entries, and such sphinx's riddles of streets without thoroughfares, as must, I conceive, baffle the audacity of porters, and confound the intellects of hackney-coachmen. I could almost have believed, at times, that I must be the first discoverer of some of these terræ incognitæ, and doubted, whether they had yet been laid down in the modern charts of London. For all this, however, I paid a heavy price in distant years, when the human face tyrannized over my dreams, and the perplexities of my steps in London came back and haunted my sleep, with the feeling of perplexities moral or intellectual, that brought confusion to the reason, or anguish and remorse to the conscience.

Thus I have shown that opium does not, of necessity, produce inactivity or torpor; but that, on the contrary, it often led me into markets and theatres. Yet, in candour, I will admit that markets and theatres are not the appropriate haunts of the opium-eater, when in the divinest state incident to his enjoyment. In that state, crowds become an oppression to him; music even, too sensual and gross. He naturally seeks solitude and silence, as indispensable conditions of those trances, or profoundest reveries, which are the crown and consummation of what opium can do for human nature. I, whose disease it was to meditate too much, and to observe too little, and who, upon my first entrance at college, was nearly falling into a deep melancholy, from brooding too much on the sufferings which I had witnessed in London, was sufficiently aware of the tendencies of my own thoughts to do all I could to counteract them.—I was, indeed, like a person who, according to the old legend, had entered the cave of Trophonius; and the remedies I sought were to force myself into society, and to keep my understanding in continual activity upon matters of science. But for these remedies, I should certainly have become hypochondriacally melancholy. In after years, however, when my cheerfulness was more fully re-established, I yielded to my natural inclination for a solitary life. And, at that time, I often fell into these reveries upon taking opium; and more than once it has happened to me, on a summer night, when I have been at an open window, in a room from which I could overlook the sea at a mile below me, and could command a view of the great town of L____, at about the same distance, that I have sat, from sun-set to sun-rise, motionless, and without wishing to move.

I shall be charged with mysticism, Behemenism, quietism, &c. but that shall not alarm me. Sir H. Vane, the younger, was one of our wisest men; and let my readers see if he, in his philosophical works, be half as unmystical as I am.—I say, then, that it has often struck me that the scene itself was somewhat typical of what took place in such a reverie. The town of L____ represented the earth, with its sorrows and its graves left behind, yet not out of sight, nor wholly forgotten. The ocean, in everlasting but gentle agitation, and brooded over by a dove-like calm, might not unfitly typify the mind and the mood which then swayed it. For it seemed to me as if then first I stood at a distance, and aloof from the uproar of life; as if the tumult, the fever, and the strife, were suspended; a respite granted from the secret burthens of the heart; a sabbath of repose; a resting from human labours. Here were the hopes which blossom in the paths of life, reconciled with the peace which is in the grave; motions of the intellect as unwearied as the heavens, yet for all anxieties a halcyon calm: a tranquillity that seemed no product of inertia, but as if resulting from mighty and equal antagonisms; infinite activities, infinite repose.

Oh! just, subtle, and mighty opium! that to the hearts of poor and rich alike, for the wounds that will never heal, and for "the pangs that tempt the spirit to rebel," bringest an assuaging balm; eloquent opium! that with thy potent rhetoric stealest away the purposes of wrath; and to the guilty man, for one night givest back the hopes of his youth, and hands washed pure from blood; and to the proud man, a brief oblivion for

Wrongs unredress'd, and insults unavenged;

that summonest to the chancery of dreams, for the triumphs of suffering innocence, false witnesses; and confoundest perjury; and dost reverse the sentences of unrighteous judges:—thou buildest upon the bosom of darkness, out of the fantastic imagery of the brain, cities and temples, beyond the art of Phidias and Praxiteles—beyond the splendour of Babylon and Hekatómpylos: and 'from the anarchy of dreaming sleep,' callest into sunny light the faces of long-buried beauties, and the blessed household countenances, cleansed from the 'dishonours of the grave.' Thou only givest these gifts to man; and thou hast the keys of Paradise, oh, just, subtle, and mighty opium!

I now pass to what is the main subject of these latter confessions, to the history and journal of what took place in my dreams; for these were the immediate and proximate cause of my acutest suffering.

The first notice I had of any important change going on in this part of my physical economy, was from the re-awakening of a state of eye generally incident to childhood, or exalted states of irritability. I know not whether my reader is aware that many children, perhaps most, have a power of painting, as it were, upon the darkness, all sorts of phantoms: in some, that power is simply a mechanic affection of the eye; others have a voluntary, or a semi-voluntary power to dismiss or to summon them; or, as a child once said to me when I questioned him on this matter, 'I can tell them to go, and they go; but sometimes they come, when I don't tell them to come.' Whereupon I told him that he had almost as unlimited a command over apparitions, as a Roman centurion over his soldiers.—In the middle of 1817, I think it was, that this faculty became positively distressing to me: at night, when I lay awake in bed, vast processions passed along in mournful pomp; friezes of never-ending stories, that to my feelings were as sad and solemn as if they were stories drawn from times before Œdipus or Priam—before Tyre—before Memphis. And, at the same time, a corresponding change took place in my dreams; a theatre seemed suddenly opened and lighted up within my brain, which presented nightly spectacles of more than earthly splendour. And the four following facts may be mentioned, as noticeable at this time:

1. That, as the creative state of the eye increased, a sympathy seemed to arise between the waking and the dreaming states of the brain in one point—that whatsoever I happened to call up and to trace by a voluntary act upon the darkness was very apt to transfer itself to my dreams; so that I feared to exercise this faculty; for, as Midas turned all things to gold, that yet baffled his hopes and defrauded his human desires, so whatsoever things capable of being visually represented I did but think of in the darkness, immediately shaped themselves into phantoms of the eye; and, by a process apparently no less inevitable, when thus once traced in faint and visionary colours, like writings in sympathetic ink, they were drawn out by the fierce chemistry of my dreams, into insufferable splendour that fretted my heart.

2. For this, and all other changes in my dreams, were accompanied by deep-seated anxiety and gloomy melancholy, such as are wholly incommunicable by words. I seemed every night to descend, not metaphorically, but literally to descend, into chasms and sunless abysses, depths below depths, from which it seemed hopeless that I could ever reascend. Nor did I, by waking, feel that I had reascended. This I do not dwell upon; because the state of gloom which

attended these gorgeous spectacles, amounting at least to utter darkness, as of some suicidal despondency, cannot be approached by words.

3. The sense of space, and in the end, the sense of time, were both powerfully affected. Buildings, landscapes, &c. were exhibited in proportions so vast as the bodily eye is not fitted to receive. Space swelled, and was amplified to an extent of unutterable infinity. This, however, did not disturb me so much as the vast expansion of time; I sometimes seemed to have lived for 70 or 100 years in one night; nay, sometimes had feelings representative of a millennium passed in that time, or, however, of a duration far beyond the limits of any human experience.

4. The minutest incidents of childhood, or forgotten scenes of later years, were often revived: I could not be said to recollect them; for if I had been told of them when waking, I should not have been able to acknowledge them as parts of my past experience. But placed as they were before me, in dreams like intuitions, and clothed in all their evanescent circumstances and accompanying feelings, I recognized them instantaneously. I was once told by a near relative of mine, that having in her childhood fallen into a river, and being on the very verge of death but for the critical assistance which reached her, she saw in a moment her whole life, in its minutest incidents, arrayed before her simultaneously as in a mirror; and she had a faculty developed as suddenly for comprehending the whole and every part. This, from some opium experiences of mine, I can believe; I have, indeed, seen the same thing asserted twice in modern books, and accompanied by a remark which I

am convinced is true; viz. that the dread book of account, which the Scriptures speak of, is, in fact, the mind itself of each individual. Of this, at least, I feel assured, that there is no such thing as forgetting possible to the mind; a thousand accidents may, and will interpose a veil between our present consciousness and the secret inscriptions on the mind; accidents of the same sort will also rend away this veil; but alike, whether veiled or unveiled, the inscription remains for ever; just as the stars seem to withdraw before the common light of day, whereas, in fact, we all know that it is the light which is drawn over them as a veil—and that they are waiting to be revealed, when the obscuring daylight shall have withdrawn.

* * *

May 1818.

The Malay has been a fearful enemy for months. I have been every night, through his means, transported into Asiatic scenes. I know not whether others share in my feelings on this point; but I have often thought that if I were compelled to forego England, and to live in China, and among Chinese manners and modes of life and scenery, I should go mad. The causes of my horror lie deep; and some of them must be common to others. Southern Asia, in general, is the seat of awful images and associations. As the cradle of the human race, it would alone have a dim and reverential feeling connected with it. But there are other reasons. No man can pretend that the wild, barbarous, and capricious superstitions of Africa, or of savage tribes elsewhere, affect him in the way that he is affected by the ancient, monumental, cruel, and elaborate religions of Indostan, &c. The mere antiquity of Asiatic things, of their institutions, histories, modes of faith, &c. is so impressive, that to me the vast age of the race and name overpowers the sense of youth in the individual. A young Chinese seems to me an antediluvian man renewed. Even Englishmen, though not bred in any knowledge of such institutions, cannot but shudder at the mystic sublimity of castes that have flowed apart, and refused to mix, through such immemorial tracts of time; nor can any man fail to be awed by the names of the Ganges, or the Euphrates. It contributes much to these feelings, that Southern Asia is, and has been for thousands of years, the part of the earth most swarming with human life; the great oficina gentium. Man is a weed in those regions. The vast empires also, into which the enormous population of Asia has always been cast, give a further sublimity to the feelings associated with all Oriental names or images. In China, over and above what it has in common with the rest of Southern Asia, I am terrified by the modes of life, by the manners, and the barrier of utter abhorrence, and want of sympathy, placed between us by feelings deeper than I can analyze. I could sooner live with lunatics, or brute animals. All this, and much more than I can say, or have time to say, the reader must enter into before he can comprehend the unimaginable horror which these dreams of Oriental imagery, and mythological tortures, impressed upon me. Under the connecting feeling of tropical heat and vertical sun-lights, I brought together all creatures, birds, beasts, reptiles, all trees and plants, usages and appearances, that are found in all tropical regions, and assembled them together in China or Indostan. From kindred feelings, I soon brought Egypt and all her gods under the same law. I was stared at, hooted at, grinned at, chattered at, by monkeys, by paroquets, by cockatoos. I ran into pagodas: and was fixed, for centuries, at the summit, or in secret rooms; I was the idol; I was the priest; I was worshipped; I was sacrificed. I fled from the wrath of Brama through all the forests of Asia: Vishnu hated me: Seeva laid wait for me. I came suddenly upon Isis and Osiris: I had done a deed, they said, which the ibis and the crocodile trembled at. I was buried, for a thousand years, in stone coffins, with mummies and sphinxes, in narrow chambers at the heart of eternal pyramids. I was kissed, with cancerous kisses, by crocodiles; and laid, confounded with all unutterable slimy things, amongst reeds and Nilotic mud.

I thus give the reader some slight abstraction of my Oriental dreams, which always filled me with such amazement at the monstrous scenery, that horror seemed absorbed, for a while, in sheer astonishment. Sooner or later, came a reflux of feeling that swallowed up the astonishment, and left me, not so much in terror, as in hatred and abomination of what I saw. Over every form, and threat, and punishment, and dim sightless incarceration, brooded a sense of eternity and infinity that drove me into an oppression as of madness. Into these dreams only, it was, with one or two slight exceptions, that any circumstances of physical horror entered. All before had been moral and spiritual terrors.

But here the main agents were ugly birds, or snakes, or crocodiles; especially the last. The cursed crocodile became to me the object of more horror than almost all the rest. I was compelled to live with him; and (as was always the case almost in my dreams) for centuries. I escaped sometimes, and found myself in Chinese houses, with cane tables, &c. All the feet of the tables, sofas, &c. soon became instinct with life: the abominable head of the crocodile, and his leering eyes, looked out at me, multiplied into a thousand repetitions: and I stood loathing and fascinated. And so often did this hideous reptile haunt my dreams, that many times the very same dream was broken up in the very same way: I heard gentle voices speaking to me (I hear everything when I am sleeping); and instantly I awoke: it was broad noon; and my children were standing, hand in hand, at my bed-side; come to show me their coloured shoes, or new frocks, or to let me see them dressed for going out. I protest that so awful was the transition from the damned crocodile, and the other unutterable monsters and abortions of my dreams, to the sight of innocent human natures and of infancy, that, in the mighty and sudden revulsion of mind, I wept, and could not forbear it, as I kissed their faces.

# Opium Smoking in America and China

*Henry Hubbell Kane*

A SMOKER ENTERING one of the dens or "joints" in this city, removes his shoes, coat, and collar, hangs them upon a peg and, stretching himself transversely across the platform beside a tray containing the apparatus, calls for a pipe and some opium. The usual call is for "two bits'" or twenty-five cents' worth. For this money the Chinaman gives from 6 to 10 "fãn" (35 to 60 gr.) of No. 1 or first-class, and from 12 to 20 "fãn" (70 to 120 gr.) of No. 2 or second-class opium.

Having the necessary article and materials, the smoker settles himself comfortably upon his side, takes up a little of the treacle-like mass of opium upon the steel needle, or yen hauck, and holding it above the flame of the lamp, watches it bubble and swell to six or seven times its original size. In doing so it loses its inky hue, and becomes of a bright golden-brown color, and gives off a pleasant creamy odor much admired by old smokers. Poor opium does not yield so pleasant an odor, is liable to drop from the needle into the lamp, and rarely gives so handsome a color, the yellow being, here and there, streaked with black. This process is known as "cooking" the opium. Having brought it to a proper consistence, the operator, with a rapid twirling motion of the fingers, rolls the mass upon the smooth surface of the bowl, submitting it occasionally to the flame, now and then catching it upon the edge and drawing it out into strings in order to cook it through more thoroughly. This is called chying the mass. Rolling it again upon the surface of the bowl until the opium is formed into a small pea-sized mass, with the needle as a centre, the needle is forced down into the small hole in the bowl, thus leveling off the bottom of the pea. Then grasping the stem of the pipe, near the bowl, in the left hand, the bowl is held across the flame of the lamp to warm it a little, the bottom of the opium mass is warmed, and by again thrusting the needle into the small aperture in the centre of the bowl and quickly withdrawing it, the mass, with a hole in its centre, is left upon the surface of the bowl, it surrounding the hole that communicates with that of the stem. Inclining the body slightly forward, the smoker tips the pipe-bowl across the lamp until the flame strikes the opium. Inhaling strongly and steadily, the smoke of the burning drug passes into the lungs of the operator and is returned through the nose. This smoke is heavy, white, and has a not unpleasant fruity odor. It is hardly necessary to say that the smoke never passes out through the ears and eyes. Having finished this bolus which requires but one long or a few short inspirations, the smoker cools the bowl of the pipe with a sponge and repeats the operation as often as is necessary to obtain the desired effect. Smokers are classed as "long-draw" and "short-draw" men, according as they consume the pill in one or several inhalations. The long draw is undoubtedly the most injurious.

The wealthier smokers, here and in the East, do not visit these joints, but have rooms fitted up in Oriental style, where a few friends meet to enjoy the pleasures of the pipe. Unlike other forms of the opium-habit, that by smoking finds a special inducement in companionship, especially if the companions are congenial. Men and women often meet to smoke, talk, and enjoy that state that comes as near as it is possible for an American to come to the dolce far niente of the Italian. In the joints, two persons, sometimes three, are usually found about the one tray, one cooking while the other smokes, and vice versa. A package of cigarettes will usually be found upon the tray, they being smoked " between pipes."

To be able to "cook" well is quite an art, and one of which an old smoker is very proud. A novice or a poor cook will bedaub himself and the pipe, and either overdo or underdo the opium, so that it is too sticky or too crisp to smoke well.

A man who smokes large amounts of opium daily is, in this country, called a "fiend." Some Americans have a curious nomenclature for smokers, based upon the number of times in the day and the hour at which a person smokes. Thus, a man who smokes three times is said to have a "triple habit," one who smokes but once, the "single habit," one who smokes early, "the early habit," etc., etc. This is manifestly incorrect.

As to a mixture of habits, I find that it is a rare thing for a smoker to be at the same time an opium-or morphine-taker, save in this way: when on long journeys, or in places where a pipe cannot be had, he will usually cook up a number of pellets of smoking-opium, and take enough of these by the mouth to carry him without discomfort beyond his time for smoking. Occasionally we meet with smokers who are at the same time using opium or morphine by the mouth. This is, however, very rare. I have had one such patient under treatment. Some smokers are of the firm belief that should they swallow a little of the smoking-opium in its raw state certain death would result. This is of course nonsensical. I have taken as high as six grains myself without any ill effect whatever. Many have the idea, evidently taken from the Chinese, that should the yen hauck be thrust through a roach or bed-bug just before taking up the opium upon it, a most horrible and agonizing death will certainly visit the one who smokes that pellet.

Women are never allowed to smoke a good pipe, the Chinese entertaining the belief that it would result in splitting of the stem and a failure to color. There is some truth in this, for moisture will often split the bamboo stems, and it is a notable fact that when women smoke, saliva will, as a rule, get into the aperture against which the lips are placed.

The following is the experience of one of my male nurses, who kindly tried smoking to permit of my experimenting on him. I give it in his own words. He is a man who is perfectly honest and trustworthy, and one not given to exaggeration or an unbridled imagination. Furthermore, he was entirely ignorant of the effect of smoking to excess. The effect upon the pulse is the more conclusive from the fact that in his case, in health, the tension is very low, and the first down-stroke almost reaches the base line.

Fred'k K., æt. 35, M., weight 185 lbs., had taken opium before, by the mouth, without any ill effects.

"July 12, 1881, 2 P.M., I commenced smoking with an habitué who 'cooked' the opium, he and I consuming alternate pipes. On smoking seven pipes I felt a little exhilarated, and continued to feel so until an hour after smoking the ninth pipe. At this time the feeling of exhilaration increased. I felt very talkative, and wished to smoke more, but by Dr. Kane's advice stopped after the tenth pipe. At 6.30 P.M. there was itching of different parts of the body and some nausea. I became very pale. This feeling lasted about twenty minutes. Drank two cups of tea and ate a little supper. Felt natural until about 10 P.M., when nausea rapidly came on, and I suddenly vomited. There was no straining in the act. Read until about 12 midnight. Retired, and was on the point of sleeping when I was possessed with a sudden dread of doing so. Although very sleepy I felt, that if I allowed myself to doze I should jump out of the window, and as I occupied a room on the third floor I was in great terror. I tried several times to reason myself out of the belief, but though I knew that I was extremely foolish to fear such a thing, I could not do so. Finally I was forced to get up and shut the blinds, fastening them securely, close the windows at the top and bottom, light the gas, and place chairs between the bed and the windows, so that if I attempted to reach the windows I would stumble, make a noise and wake myself. Again I tried to sleep, but when just dropping off I would start and look around the room, thinking there was something or somebody there. I would then try to calm myself, saying to myself how foolish and nervous I was. I thought that if I had a rope I could secure myself so as to prevent accidents. I went down on to the first floor, but could not find one. I then listened to see if any of the patients or their nurses were awake, so that I might pass the night with them. But I could not hear a sound. I returned to my room and again tried to sleep, but could in no way overcome my fear of jumping through the window. I lit the gas again, and read and pottered about until 4.30 A.M. On attempting to look out of the window I was obliged to pull my head in, as it seemed as if I must jump out. I then went out into the yard and walked about until people were stirring. At 8 A.M. I ate a hearty breakfast, and at 9 A.M. tried again to sleep. On the fourth attempt I succeeded. Slept till 12 M.; rose and ate a hearty lunch. During the night of the 12th and the succeeding day I seemed to smell the opium cooking and could taste it. My arms felt like lead. All that day I felt as I should imagine a person would feel after a week's drunk."

| | |
|---|---|
| Normal pulse | 68 |
| After smoking three pipes | 84 |
| After ten pipes | 84 |
| The next day | 108 |

During the smoking and for 24 hours afterward, the pupils were firmly contracted. I regret that I did not take the pulse during the night. This is of course not a fair example of the effects of moderate smoking on a novice, for Mr. K. certainly smoked to excess. The gentleman who was smoking with him was a "fiend," and made very "large pipes," that is to say, used about double the ordinary amount of opium each time. As each smoked the same amount, Mr. K. must have used 74 grains in the course of three hours. This is nearly equal to 150 grains of crude opium. One third of the 74 grains became ash. Smoking several times subsequently in smaller quantities produced no such effect. Another of my nurses, illustrating the variable susceptibilities of different persons to this drug, smoked nine large and three small pipes in the course of two hours without any effect save a slowing of the pulse. Subsequently, however, after trying the "long draw," the effect was very decided.

F.R.S., Am., 23, nurse, single, wt. 115 lbs. smoked eight pipes on afternoon of 25th inst. Had smoked nine pipes on afternoon of 23d, with no effect, on account of not inhaling smoke properly.

At the end of fourth pipe began to feel a drowsiness similar to a person partly under the influence of an anæsthetic. Slight dizziness upon attempting to stand, itching, etc. After smoking eighth pipe limbs felt heavy, head felt twice its natural size, increased drowsiness, itching, etc. Went to bed but couldn't sleep on account of itching in all parts of the body, which counterbalanced pleasant effects that old smokers speak of. Four hours after smoking entire left side felt as though under a heavy weight. Severe palpitation of heart (which only lasted ten minutes,) violent twitching of muscles of left eyelid, etc. Nine hours after smoking attempted to urinate but found it impossible. Succeeded two hours later, however. Pulse 40, which arose to 60, after taking $1/48$ gr. atropia.

Pupils greatly contracted.

Now, twenty hours after smoking, feels very languid; no appetite; headache, etc.

The symptoms which he has described are not the result of imagination, as they are the exact reverse of what he expected.

Smoking to excess, especially after hard drinking, is very dangerous. A young man, Mr. D., a very hard smoker now, was taken to a "joint" where he would pawn his wife's clothing for opium. He was in the De Quincey Home just four days and under treatment but ten. He was broken of his habit thus speedily and effectually with almost no suffering,—nothing as compared to what an ordinary smoker would suffer in breaking himself. After leaving me he gained very rapidly in flesh, and is to-day free from the vice and has absolutely no craving for the drug. He had been a hard smoker for from eight to ten years. Others that I have since treated have gone through in the same easy and rapid manner. I hope in a few days to be able to persuade a Chinaman who has been smoking for the past twenty-eight years, and who is said to be the hardest smoker in the city, to let me cure him.

The first patient—the American "fiend"—had once experienced the horrors of sudden deprivation on ship-board, and did not believe, until it was proved to him, that a comparatively painless and rapid cure was possible.

This treatment consists in the use of capsicum, digitalis, and cannabis Indica tincture in large doses, often repeated. The bromides of potassium and sodium, if there is much reflex nervous trouble, may be given. The bromides should be administered in 100 gr. doses twice daily, in plenty of water, as their absorption is more full and rapid. Their use, however, should be continued for only a few days at the most.

In addition to this, bismuth and catechu in large doses for the diarrhoea and vomiting; chloride of gold and soda, ½ gr. every two hours in the form of pill or Fuller's tablets, with fl. ext. gelseminum, to relieve the pains in the limbs; massage and electro-massage, hot baths and cold spray for the same purpose; oxide of zinc and atropia for the profuse perspiration; and hyoscyamus and chloral to produce sleep; stimulants, of which iced champagne is the best, should be freely used for 48 hours only.

Later, to relieve dryness of the throat, fl. extract of jaborandi; muriate of ammonia, and benzoic acid for the bronchitis, and nitrate of silver for the pharyngitis, prove of service. Tonics, short warm baths with cold douche or spray, phosphorus and cod-liver oil, and outdoor exercise, are all called for. Some occupation should be engaged in that does not leave too much leisure time, and a course of reading pursued and associations cultivated that tend to elevate the mental and moral tone of the individual.

Opium-smokers, like opium and morphine takers, can only be reliably and satisfactorily treated in an institution where they can be watched and restrained day and night for at least two weeks.[2]

# Opium's Varied Dreams

*Stephen Crane*

OPIUM SMOKING IN this country is believed to be more particularly a pastime of the Chinese, but in truth the greater number of the smokers are white men and white women. Chinatown furnishes the pipe, lamp, and yen-nock, but let a man once possess a layout, and a common American drug store furnishes him with the opium, and China is discernible only in the traditions that cling to the habit. There are 25,000 opium smokers in the city of New York alone. At one time there were two great colonies, one in the Tenderloin, one, of course, in Chinatown. This was before the hammer of reform struck them. Now the two colonies are splintered into some-thing less than 25,000 fragments. The smokers are disorganized, but they still exist.

The Tenderloin district of New York fell an early victim to opium. That part of the population which is known as the "sporting" class adopted the habit quickly. Cheap actors, race track touts, gamblers, and the different kinds of confidence men took to it generally. Opium raised its yellow banner over the Tenderloin, attaining the dignity of a common vice.

Splendid joints were not uncommon then in New York. There was one on Forty-second street which would have been palatial if it were not for the bad taste of the decorations. An occasional man from Fifth avenue or Madison avenue would have there his private layout, an elegant equipment of silver, ivory, and gold. The bunks which lined all sides of the two rooms were nightly crowded, and some of the people owned names which are not altogether unknown to the public. This place was raided because of sensational stories in the newspapers, and the little wicket no longer opens to allow the fiend to enter.

Upon the appearance of reform, opium retired to private flats. Here it now reigns, and it will be undoubtedly an extremely long century before the police can root it from these little strongholds. Once Billie Hostetter got drunk on whiskey and emptied three scuttles of coal down the dumb-waiter shaft. This made a noise, and, Billie, naturally, was arrested. But opium is silent. The smokers do not rave. They dream, or talk in low tones.

People who declare themselves able to pick out opium smokers on the street usually are deluded. An opium smoker may look like a deacon or a deacon may look like an opium smoker. The fiends easily conceal their vice. They get up from the layout, adjust their cravats, straighten their coat tails, and march off like ordinary people, and the best kind of an expert would not be willing to bet that they were or were not addicted to the habit.

It would be very hard to say just exactly what constitutes a habit. With the fiends it is an elastic word. Ask a smoker if he has a habit and he will deny it. Ask him if someone who smokes the same amount has a habit and he will admit it. Perhaps the ordinary smoker consumes 25 cents worth of opium each day. There are others who smoke $1 worth. This is rather extraordinary, and in this case at least it is safe to say that it is a habit. The $1 smokers usually indulge in high hats, which is the term for a large pill. The ordinary smoker is satisfied with pinheads. Pinheads are of about the size of a French pea.

Habit smokers have a contempt for the sensation smoker, who has been won by the false glamour which surrounds the vice, and goes about really pretending that he has a ravenous hunger for the pipe. There are more sensation smokers than one would imagine. It is said to take one year of devotion to the pipe before one can contract a habit; but probably it does not take any such long time. Sometimes an individual who has smoked only a few months will speak of nothing but pipe, and when a man talks pipe persistently it is a pretty sure sign that the drug has fastened its grip so that he is not able to stop its use easily. When a man arises from his first trial of the pipe, the nausea that clutches him is something that can give cards and spades and big casino to seasickness. If he had swallowed a live chimney sweep he could not feel more like dying. The room and everything in it whirls like the inside of an electric light plant. There comes a thirst, a great thirst, and this thirst is so sinister and so misleading that if the novice drank spirits to satisfy it he would presently be much worse. The one thing that will make him feel again that life may be a joy is a cup of strong black coffee.

If there is a sentiment in the pipe for him, he returns to it after this first unpleasant trial. Gradually the power of the drug sinks into his heart. It absorbs his thought. He begins to lie with more and more grace to cover the shortcomings and little failures of his life. And then, finally, he may become a full-fledged pipe fiend, a man with a yen-yen.

A yen-yen, be it known, is the hunger, the craving. It comes to a fiend when he separates himself from his pipe and it takes him by the heart strings. If, indeed, he will not buck through a brick wall to get to the pipe, he at least will become the most disagreeable, sour-tempered person on earth until he finds a way to satisfy his craving.

When the victim arrives at the point where his soul calls for the drug, he usually learns to cook. The operation of rolling the pill and cooking it over the little lamp is a delicate task, and it takes time to learn it. When a man can cook for himself and buys his own layout, he is gone, probably. He has placed upon his shoulders an elephant which he may carry to the edge of forever. The Chinese have a preparation which they call a cure, but the first difficulty is to get the fiend to take the preparation, and the second difficulty is to cure anything with this cure.

The fiend will defend opium with eloquence and energy. He very seldom drinks spirits, and so he gains an opportunity to make the most ferocious parallels between the effects of rum and the effects of opium. Ask him to free his mind and he will probably say:

"Opium does not deprive you of your senses. It does not make a madman of you. But drink does. See? Who ever heard of a man committing murder when full of hop.

Get him full of whiskey and he might kill his father. I don't see why people kick so about opium smoking. If they knew anything about it, they wouldn't talk that way. Let anybody drink rum who cares to, but as for me, I would rather be what I am."

As before mentioned, there were at one time gorgeous opium dens in New York, but now there is probably not a den with any pretence to splendid decoration. The Chinamen will smoke in a cellar, bare, squalid, occupied by an odor that will float wooden chips. The police took the adornments from the vice and left nothing but the pipe itself. Yet the pipe is sufficient for its slant-eyed lover.

When prepared for smoking purposes, opium is a heavy liquid much like molasses. Ordinarily it is sold in hollow li-shi nuts or in little round tins resembling the old percussion cap boxes. The pipe is a curious affair, particularly notable for the way in which it does not resemble the drawings of it that appear in print. The stem is of thick bamboo, the mouthpiece usually of ivory. The bowl crops out suddenly about four inches from the end of the stem. It is a heavy affair of clay or stone. The cavity is a mere hole, of the diameter of a lead pencil, drilled through the centre. The yen-nock is a sort of sharpened darning needle. With it the cook takes the opium from the box. He twirls it dexterously with his thumb and forefinger until enough of the gummy substance adheres to the sharp point. Then he holds it over the tiny flame of the lamp which burns only peanut oil or sweet oil. The pill now exactly resembles boiling molasses. The clever fingers of the cook twirl it above the flame. Lying on his side comfortably, he takes the pipe in his left hand and transfers the cooked pill from the yen-nock to the bowl of the pipe, where he again moulds it with the yen-nock until it is a little button-like thing with a hole in the centre fitting squarely over the hole in the bowl. Dropping the yen-nock, the cook now uses two hands for the pipe. He extends the mouthpiece toward the one whose turn it is to smoke, and as the smoker leans forward in readiness, the cook draws the bowl toward the flame until the heat sets the pill to boiling. Whereupon the smoker takes a long, deep draw at the pipe, the pill sputters and fries, and a moment later the smoker sinks back tranquilly. An odor, heavy, aromatic, agreeable, and yet disagreeable, hangs in the air and makes its way with peculiar powers of penetration. The group about the layout talk in low voices, and watch the cook deftly moulding another pill. The little flame casts a strong yellow light on their faces as they huddle about the layout. As the pipe passes and passes around the circle, the voices drop to a mere indolent cooing, and the eyes that so lazily watch the cook at his work, glisten and glisten from the influence of the drug until they resemble flashing bits of silver.

There is a similarity in coloring and composition in a group of men about a midnight camp fire in a forest and a group of smokers about the layout tray with its tiny light. Everything, of course, is on a smaller scale with the smoking. The flame is only an inch and a half, perhaps, in height, and the smokers huddle closely in order that every person may smoke undisturbed. But there is something in the abandon of the poses, the wealth of light on the faces, and the strong mystery of shadow at the backs of the people that bring the two scenes into some kind of artistic resemblance. And just as the lazy eyes about a camp fire fasten themselves dreamfully upon the blaze of logs, so do the lazy eyes about an opium layout fasten themselves upon the little flame.

There is but one pipe, one lamp, and one cook to each smoking layout. Pictures of nine or ten persons sitting in armchairs and smoking various kinds of curiously carved tobacco pipes probably serve well enough, but when they are named "Interior of an Opium Den" and that sort of thing, it is absurd. Opium could not be smoked like tobacco. A pill is good for one long draw. After that the cook moulds another. A smoker would just as soon choose a gallows as an armchair for smoking purposes. He likes to curl down on a mattress placed on the floor in the quietest corner of a Tenderloin flat, and smoke there with no light but the tiny yellow spear from the layout lamp.

It is a curious fact that it is rather the custom to purchase for a layout tray one of those innocent black tin affairs which are supposed to be placed before a baby as he takes his high chair for dinner.

If a beginner expects to have dreams of an earth dotted with white porcelain towers and a sky of green silk, he will be much mistaken. "The Opium Smoker's Dream" seems to be mostly a mistake. The influence of dope is evidently a fine languor, a complete mental rest. The problems of life no longer appear. Existence is peace. The virtues of a man's friends, for instance, loom beautifully against his own sudden perfection. The universe is readjusted. Wrong departs, injustice vanishes: there is nothing but a quiet harmony of all things—until the next morning.

And who should invade this momentary land of rest, this dream country, if not the people of the Tenderloin; they who are at once supersensitive and hopeless, the people who think more upon death and the mysteries of life, the chances of the hereafter than any other class, educated or uneducated? Opium holds out to them its lie, and they embrace it eagerly, expecting to find a consummation of peace, but they awake to find the formidable labors of life grown more formidable. And if the pipe should happen to ruin their lives they cling the more closely to it because then it stands between them and thought.

# An "Opium Joint" Raided: Lee Young's Place on Park Street Cleaned Out by the Police

*Anonymous*

All the Chinese resorts in the Sixth Precinct are closely watched to note visits of girls of tender age, who are, in a certain sense, wards of the Society for the Prevention of Cruelty to Children. So last evening, when a girl of twelve years halted in front of Lee Young's opium joint, 104 Park Street, looked up and down the street in a half-scared way, and went swiftly into the place, which is one step down, Detective Joseph Schirmer was alert, and when, ten minutes later, she came out she was followed until out of sight of those who were lounging about the den, and then accosted and taken to the Elizabeth Street Station House.

She began to tell a number of stories and endeavored to make Capt. Brooks believe that she was enticed into the place. No harm befell her, she said, but a Chinaman chatted with her while she watched a number of his countrymen who were smoking opium. This was evidence enough to warrant a raid, and the reserve force of the precinct was called out and a descent was made on the den.

Lee Young and fourteen other Celestials were arrested and locked up. Eleven pipes, 15 bowls, 8 pots, and 5 boxes of opium, 6 "lay outs," 4 trays, scales, 2 revolvers, and $82 in money were seized. Then the girl, who is Catherine Schuyler of 123 Monroe Street, was again questioned and she admitted that she was sent to the den to buy 10 cents worth of opium for Annie Golden of Jefferson and Monroe Streets. No such person was found and after Catherine's parents had been visited the police were of the opinion that a woman in their house sent the child for the drug.

Catherine was sent to the headquarters of Mr. Gerry's society, and will be at the Tombs today, when the prisoners are arraigned.

Young's "joint" was raided a short time ago, when it was kept by Hung Lung. Nineteen persons were arrested, and six of them who were found smoking opium were fined $25 each. No one was smoking when the police burst into the place, which is about 8 by 14 feet.

*New York Times*
September 28, 1891, p. 2.

# *from* The Mystery of Edwin Drood

*Charles Dickens*

An ancient English Cathedral Tower? How can the ancient English Cathedral tower be here! The well-known massive gray square tower of its old Cathedral? How can that be here! There is no spike of rusty iron in the air, between the eye and it, from any point of the real prospect. What is the spike that intervenes, and who has set it up? Maybe it is set up by the Sultan's orders for the impaling of a horde of Turkish robbers, one by one. It is so, for cymbals clash, and the Sultan goes by to his palace in long procession. Ten thousand scimitars flash in the sunlight, and thrice ten thousand dancing-girls strew flowers. Then, follow white elephants caparisoned in countless gorgeous colours, and infinite in number and attendants. Still the Cathedral Tower rises in the background, where it cannot be, and still no writhing figure is on the grim spike. Stay! Is the spike so low a thing as the rusty spike on the top of a post of an old bedstead that has tumbled all awry? Some vague period of drowsy laughter must be devoted to the consideration of this possibility.

Shaking from head to foot, the man whose scattered consciousness has thus fantastically pieced itself together, at length rises, supports his trembling frame upon his arms, and looks around. He is in the meanest and closest of small rooms. Through the ragged window-curtain, the light of early day steals in from a miserable court. He lies, dressed, across a large unseemly bed, upon a bedstead that has indeed given way under the weight upon it. Lying, also dressed and also across the bed, not longwise, are a Chinaman, a Lascar, and a haggard woman. The two first are in a sleep or stupor; the last is blowing at a kind of pipe, to kindle it. And as she blows, and shading it with her lean hand, concentrates its red spark of light, it serves in the dim morning as a lamp to show him what he sees of her.

'Another?' says this woman, in a querulous, rattling whisper. 'Have another?'

He looks about him, with his hand to his forehead.

'Ye've smoked as many as five since ye come in at midnight,' the woman goes on, as she chronically complains. 'Poor me, poor me, my head is so bad. Them two come in after ye. Ah, poor me, the business is slack, is slack! Few Chinamen about the Docks, and fewer Lascars, and no ships coming in, these say! Here's another ready for ye, deary. Ye'll remember like a good soul, won't ye, that the market price is dreffle high just now? More nor three shillings and sixpence for a thimbleful! And ye'll remember that nobody but me (and Jack Chinaman t'other side the court; but he can't do it as well as me) has the true secret of mixing it? Ye'll pay up accordingly, deary, won't ye?'

She blows at the pipe as she speaks, and, occasionally bubbling at it, inhales much of its contents.

'O me, O me, my lungs is weak, my lungs is bad! It's nearly ready for ye, deary. Ah, poor me, poor me, my poor hand shakes like to drop off! I see ye coming-to, and I ses to my poor self, "I'll have another ready for him, and he'll bear in mind the market price of opium, and pay according." O my poor head! I makes my pipes of old penny ink-bottles, ye see, deary—this is one—and I fits-in a mouthpiece, this way, and I takes my mixter out of this thimble with this little horn spoon; and so I fills, deary. Ah, my poor nerves! I got Heavens-hard drunk for sixteen year afore I took to this; but this don't hurt me, not to speak of. And it takes away the hunger as well as wittles, deary.'

She hands him the nearly-emptied pipe, and sinks back, turning over on her face.

He rises unsteadily from the bed, lays the pipe upon the hearth-stone, draws back the ragged curtain, and looks with repugnance at his three companions. He notices that the woman has opium-smoked herself into a strange likeness of the Chinaman. His form of cheek, eye, and temple, and his colour, are repeated in her. Said Chinaman convulsively wrestles with one of his many Gods or Devils, perhaps, and snarls horribly. The Lascar laughs and dribbles at the mouth. The hostess is still.

'What visions can she have?' the waking man muses, as he turns her face towards him, and stands looking down at it. 'Visions of many butchers' shops, and public-houses, and much credit? Of an increase of hideous customers, and this horrible bedstead set upright again, and this horrible court swept clean? What can she rise to, under any quantity of opium, higher than that!—Eh?'

He bends down his ear, to listen to her mutterings.

'Unintelligible!'

As he watches the spasmodic shoots and darts that break out of her face and limbs, like fitful lightning out of a dark sky, some contagion in them seizes upon him: insomuch that he has to withdraw himself to a lean arm-chair by the hearth—placed there, perhaps, for such emergencies—and to sit in it, holding tight, until he has got the better of this unclean spirit of imitation.

Then he comes back, pounces on the Chinaman, and seizing him with both hands by the throat, turns him violently on the bed. The Chinaman clutches the aggressive hands, resists, gasps, and protests.

'What do you say?'

A watchful pause.

'Unintelligible!'

Slowly loosening his grasp as he listens to the incoherent jargon with an attentive frown, he turns to the Lascar and fairly drags him forth upon the floor. As he falls, the Lascar starts into a half-risen attitude, glares with his eyes, lashes about him fiercely with his arms, and draws a phantom knife. It then becomes apparent that the woman has taken possession of this knife, for safety's sake; for, she too starting up, and restraining and expostulating with him, the knife is visible in her dress, not in his, when they drowsily drop back, side by side.

There has been chattering and clattering enough between them, but to no purpose. When any distinct word has been flung into the air, it has had no sense or sequence. Wherefore 'unintelligible!' is again the comment of the watcher, made with some reassured nodding of his head, and a gloomy smile. He then lays certain silver money on the table, finds his hat, gropes his way down the broken stairs, gives a good morning to some rat-ridden doorkeeper, in bed in a black hutch beneath the stairs, and passes out.

# Out of the Silence

*Claude Farrère*

It is the end, the end of everything….

It has been eight, nine, how many? forty days? that I have had nothing to eat,—or drink: my throat no longer knows the taste of tea; there is something on the threshold that stops it, something like dross, like opium, something—I do not know what. It has been forty days, or forty months, that I have had no tea to drink,—and nothing else whatsoever, naturally,—and how many years since I last slept?

I do not know. I know nothing any more. Nothing any more.

Good heavens! in order to know, to reckon, to attain some sort of certitude concerning anything, it would be necessary,—would it not?—to see, to hear, to feel,—to make use, in short, of what men call their senses, their five senses. Five? Are there five? It makes little difference, after all.—Yes, it would be necessary to do all that. But I have no more senses. It has been a long time, indeed, since I had any. I cannot see. I have looked too long at the lamp, and at the yellow opium, budding and crackling above the lamp.—I have looked too long into the night, opening wide my horrified eyes in an effort to compel them to see what men do not see,—the beyond, the pale and terrifying world of phantoms;—my eyes have seen them, and that is why, now, they no longer see anything,—except the lamp, the opium-lamp.—Yes, the phantoms.... As a matter of fact, that is not true; there are no phantoms since I have ceased to see them. An hallucination, an hallucination which has disappeared, that is all. I am well enough aware that there are no phantoms. Alas! There is nothing. There is Nothingness....

I can no longer hear, either. I have listened too intently to the sounds out of the silence, sounds which no one ever heard except myself, who am about to die;—sounds made by the motionless air, and by the earth in repose, and by the infinite little beings who live and die upon the earth. And the buzzing that comes from it all has embedded itself so formidably into my ears that I no longer have any ear-drums left. And now, no sound from without reaches my solitude. My solitary brain clamors and howls in the middle of my cranium,—so loudly that all within me is shattered, as my bones crumble to dust,—that dust which I so soon shall be.

Tell me, do you think that dust will smell of opium? No? And yet, I have smoked much. Three, four, a hundred pipes a day,—or more, even, who knows?

I no longer see, and I no longer hear. And so it is with everything. There is not one human sensation left me, not one human action of which I am capable. Not one, not one. Nothing. Ah! yes, one thing, a verb: to suffer.

Oh, the suffering that I endure! Oh, the fire which rends and devastates my entrails, reddening them to a white heat! Inside me, there is a flaming wound, a wound that begins at my throat and ends lower down than my ankles; a wound that spares nothing, neither vein nor bowel, a wound that is perpetually spouting flames. The rivers, lakes, the sea and all the oceans might roll over those flames without extinguishing them. And it is forever, forever, with no pause, no respite, no sleep. All the way to nothingness, a more terrifying nothingness.

Upon my skin, the opium's itch has bitten in so deeply that I no longer have any epidermis left: I have torn it all away, with my fingernails.

And if that were all! If there were nothing more!

There is the hunger and thirst after opium. Days and days passed without eating or drinking,—all that is nothing, less than nothing:—a pleasure. But an hour without opium, that, that is the terrible, the unutterable thing, the one disease for which there is no cure. It cannot be cured, for the reason that satiety itself does not extinguish such a thirst. Before smoking, I am dying from need of opium, and I die again afterwards, and while I am smoking, and always. My body is in agony from the moment I abandon the pipe. I am that damned one who, in seeking comfort from burning coals, finds only molten lead.

The damned one. That is it; that is exactly it. The Gehenna in which I abide has two penalties, adds insult to injury: to disease of body disease of soul; to the fire, the nightmare.

At first,—how long a time ago it was!—I had only brief sleeping spells, prostrations lasting a few hours, a few minutes, between two intoxications;—a deadening slumber, utterly prostrating, from which I arose more fatigued than by the most violent of love-embraces;—but real sleep, none the less, free of phantasmagoric images, closed to the terrors of the world without. Then, day would come, with its feverish lethargies and its deliriums, filled with bewilderments, atrocities and apocalypses. And it was then that a sort of dismaying proportion was set up: to the degree in which opium abbreviated, cut short my moments of repose,—for it was still repose, almost,—in a corresponding degree, that same opium began filling, heaping and cramming those moments with more bewilderments, with more atrocities and with more apocalypses. Until the superhuman limit of this series, which no mathematician ever will be able to add up, was reached at last: that limit where sleep is reduced to zero and nightmare is raised to a corresponding and inverse power,—one divided by zero equals: infinity!

$$\frac{1}{0} = \infty$$

I do not sleep any more. And nightmare, overstepping the too restricted confines of my slumber, now has spread over all my day. I dream all the time, and that is vastly more atrocious.

Nightmare. No one except opium-smokers ever will know what a nightmare is.

I have heard people say: Last night, I had a frightful dream: the walls came together and crushed me. Or, it may be: I fell down a precipice. Or, perhaps: I saw my wife and children being tortured, without being able to rescue them.

And those persons will raise their hands to their eyes and remark with horror: What a nightmare!

In my own nightmare, there is neither precipice, nor wall, nor wife, nor children. There is the void, nothingness and the night. There is the awful reality of death,—so near, so near, that the condemned man waiting for the guillotine never glimpses eternity so close up as I.

Death, round about me, roves and stagnates. It blocks door and window; it crawls across the mat; it flowers into atmospheric molecules; it enters my lungs, along with the black smoke; and when I emit the smoke, it does not come forth.

Here is a chap who is already dead, like myself. They have tossed him into a well. But wait, where is that well, in reality?

That makes no difference. They have tossed him into a well. There is an eel at the bottom of the well. An eel or a water snake?—Or a water snake!—Do you hear?

The snake has bitten the corpse.—It, in turn, is dead—naturally. They fished it up because it was an eel. And the cat has bitten the eel. The cat! Do you hear?

It is here, the cat. Big as a tiger,—naturally. But with the head of a very small kitten. It is dying. It whirls about the lamp. I whirl, too,—in an opposite direction. We are going to meet ... we are going to meet ...

Ha! ha! ha! Help....

# To Be Dust

*Santiago Dabove*

INEXORABLE SEVERITY OF circumstance! The attending doctors, relenting in the face of my insistent entreaties, of my desperate pleas, had given me a number of injections of morphine and other substances, in order to cover with a velvet glove the claw of the implacable infirmity by which I was incessantly tortured: an atrocious neuralgia of the trigeminal.

I had taken more poisons than Mithradates. It was as if the live current of some sort of voltaic pile or electric coil tormented my trigeminal with throbbing surges of pure, living, pulsing pain. One never tells oneself "surely this martyrdom has reached its limit, nothing could surpass this indomitable pain," since there will always be more suffering, more pain, more tears to endure. For, as I see it, all complaints and expressions of bitterness, whatever the cause, are nothing but variations on the simple and terribly invariable theme: There is no hope for the heart of man! I dismissed the doctors, who left behind some syringes for hypodermic injections, some opium pills, and all the rest of my habitual pharmacologic arsenal.

I mounted my horse, as always, to traverse the twenty miles which separated the villages between which I frequently traveled.

When I reached the edge of the deserted and crumbling cemetery, it occurred to me that here was a double death—that which it housed and its own—since it had disintegrated, stone by stone and brick by brick, into a forlorn, dilapidated ruin and, it seemed to me, disgrace. Looking at these ruins filled me with a sense of fatality, like that felt by Jacob when the angel in the shadows wounded his thigh in order to subdue him, though it couldn't defeat him. Suddenly, an attack of the hemiplegia, the paralysis which had so long menaced me, now struck and threw me from my horse. After I fell, my horse grazed awhile, then gradually wandered off. I had been abandoned on this lonesome route where sometimes not a single person passed for days. There was no point in cursing or bemoaning my fate, because curses had long since clotted on my lips, and no longer had any meaning. For me, cursing had been the same as gratitude to life expressed by a person whose existence had been showered with gifts.

As the soil onto which I had fallen, by the side of the road, was firm, and as I might have to stay there for quite awhile, barely able to move, I patiently devoted myself to digging away, with my pen-knife, the dirt surrounding my body. The task was easy because, below the surface, the earth turned out to be spongy. Little by little I became interred in a sort of pit which made a tolerably comfortable bed warmed by the damp heat of the soil. I dedicated my time to swallowing, regularly and enthusiastically, handfuls of "samples"—opium pills, one after another—and this must have been what determined the "dream" which preceded "my death".

It was a strange waking-dream and a death-in-life. My body felt heavier than lead at times; other times I felt nothing at all, except for my head, which had retained its sensitivity.

Many days, it seemed to me, elapsed while I was in this condition, and the black pills kept popping into my mouth, sliding, descending, settling down below, transforming everything into blackness and into earth.

My head felt and knew that it belonged to an earthen body, inhabited by worms and beetles and riddled with galleries frequented by ants. But I experienced a certain warmth and a certain pleasure in being made of mud and in becoming hollower and hollower. That's how it was—a truly extraordinary situation—only my head had been left undamaged and was nourished by the mud like a plant.

Soon it had to gnash its teeth at the predatory birds which wanted to peck out its eyes and strip the flesh from its face ...

... Judging from the ticklish sensations I feel inside of me, there must be an ant colony somewhere near my heart. I'm happy, but I want to walk, and a man made of mud cannot walk. Everything has to come to me; I cannot go in search of dawn or dusk, or of any living sensation.

... A curious thing: the body is attacked by the gnawing forces of life and becomes a hodgepodge in which no anatomist could distinguish anything but mud, prolix passageways, and the supermeticulous constructions of insects building homes for themselves, yet the brain's intelligence has been preserved ...

I realized that my head was directly receiving the earth's potent nourishment, just as plants do. The sap slowly circulated round and round, the way that blood nervously feeds the heart. What was going to happen next? Things were changing. My head was delighted to become like a bulb, a potato, a tuber, and now it was full of fear. The fear that one of those paleontologists who spend their lives sniffing out death would discover it. Or that those anthropologists who are the other morticians who show up after inhumation would happen past and notice my head's vegetalization. But luckily, they didn't.

... What sadness! To have almost turned to earth and still have hopes of walking, of loving ...

If I try to move it's as if I'm pinned, solidified with the earth. I am dissipating, and soon will be defunct. What a strange plant my head is! Its uniqueness cannot stay secret for long. Men discover everything, even a two-cent coin buried in the mud.

Mechanically I tilted my head towards the pocket watch I had dropped alongside myself when I fell. The lid which closed over the internals was open and a platoon of ants marched in and out. I would have liked to clean it and put it away, but in what remnant of my clothing, since almost all of me had become one with the earth? I felt that my transition to plant was no longer progressing much, since I had a consuming urge to smoke. The most absurd ideas crossed my mind. I wanted to be a tobacco plant, so I wouldn't need to smoke!

The imperious desire to move was giving way to the need to remain entrenched and be nourished by rich, protective earth.

From time to time I distracted myself by watching the clouds sail past. How many forms they assume before lapsing into inexistence, mere masks of steam and vapor! Can they exhaust all variation? Clouds are diverting to those who cannot do anything except look at the sky but, when they repeated to the point of collapse their attempts to take on the shapes of animals, without noticeable result, I felt so dejected that I could have stared with indifference as the blade of a scythe swept straight at my throat.

... I'm becoming a plant though I don't feel it, because plants sense the privileged state of their ecstatic and egotistical life. Their method of amorous complaisance and fulfilment, by means of telegrams of pollen, is probably not as satisfying as our close and carnal love. But it's a question of putting matters into practice, and seeing what their voluptuousness is like ...

... But it isn't easy to resign ourselves, and we would erase what has been written in the Book of Fate if it hadn't already befallen us ...

... How I've come to detest the expression "family tree"; it reminds me too much of my tragic state of vegetable regression. It's not an issue of dignity or prerogatives; planthood is as honorable as animalhood; but, to be logical, why aren't human genealogies symbolized by a deer's antlers? That would more accurately reflect the reality and the animality of things ...

Alone in that desert, the days trickled over my sorrow and my boredom. I calculated the length of time I'd been buried by the growth of my beard. I noticed it was somewhat puffed up, and its horny nature, like that of skin and nails, was now given over to a spongy fluffiness similar in texture to certain plant fibers. I consoled myself with the thought that there are trees as capable of expression as animals or humans. I remember having seen an aspen, a rope dangling from the sky to the earth. It was a leafy tree with stubby branches, quite tall, as stately as a ship's mast with its sails. As the wind played through its foliage, its expressions changed. There was a murmur, so low it was almost soundless, as when the bow of a violin vibrates the strings in varying gradations of speed and intensity.

I heard a man's footsteps—planted by a hiker perhaps or, because he couldn't afford the long distance fare, someone who had converted his legs into driving pistons and his huffing chest into a sort of steam engine. He suddenly stopped as if he had slammed on his brakes in front of my bearded face. At first he was frightened and started to flee, then, overcome by curiosity, he turned and, contemplating crime, bent down to dig me up with a pocket knife. I didn't know whether or not I could talk because my voice had already been semi-silenced by the almost total absence of lungs. As if in secret I said to him, "Leave me alone! Leave me alone! If you pull me out of the ground, as a man I will no longer be functional, and as a plant you will kill me. If you want to preserve my life and not merely behave like a policeman, don't murder me and destroy this mode of existence in which there is something actually innocent, agreeable, and desirable."

The man went on poking and scratching at my head, so I spat in his face. He was offended and struck me with the back of his hand. A surge of blood rose to my head, and my choleric eyes glared at him defiantly, like those of a swordsman who has been buried, along with his blade and its wounding edge and point.

The man's expression was that of a distressed and well-intentioned person, and from this I could tell he wasn't of the race of duellists and cavaliers. Nevertheless something made me shudder; something having to do with myself.

As often happens when someone gets angry, my face was flushed. Everyone has observed that, without a mirror, it's impossible to see any more of your face than the side of your nose and a very small portion of cheek and contiguous lip, all blurry, and visible only with one eye closed. I had shut my left eye as if taking aim with a pistol, and could see, blurred by such close focus, along the fleshy surface of my right cheek, that cheek so recently ravaged by intolerable pain, a glimpse of a deep "green blush." Was it sap, and the chlorophyll of peripheral cells which lent it a greenish cast? I cannot say, but it seems to me each day I'm becoming less and less of a man.

Opposite that ancient cemetery I had been transformed into a solitary cactus in which idle boys would carve their initials. I, with those meaty gloved hands cacti have, would pat their sweaty backs and inhale with relish their "human smell." Their smell? By then, what with? Already my senses had become alarmingly blunted.

Just as the shrill and varied sounds of squeaking hinges will never be considered music, I pondered how my frenzied animality could never be reconciled with the silent and serene life of plants, so made for repose. However highly human activity, change, and freedom of movement are valued, man, in the majority of cases, moves, walks, comes and goes inside a narrow, outstretched cage. He whose horizon consists of four over-familiar walls differs little from he who travels the same, unvarying route every day in order to carry out the same, unvarying tasks under the same, unvarying circumstances. All this wearing oneself out is worthless compared with the mutual kiss and the pact that it seals, between a plant and the sun.

... But this is nothing but a sophism. More and more I am dying as a man, and this death covers me with needles and layers of chlorophyll. And now, across from this crumbling cemetery, across from these anonymous ruins, the cactus "to which I belong" topples on its side, its trunk chopped through by hatchet-blows. Dust to dust! Nihility? Who knows? All I can say is that it will take more than a little fermentation to stir to life again matter like "mine," so punctured by deception and disappointment ...

*—Translated from the Spanish*
*by Gilbert Alter-Gilbert*

# Junkie Monkey

*Ahmad Mahmood*

ALMOST EVERYONE WHO found out just said *the poor thing* with a transient smile, and soon forgot all about it. The clowns, on the other hand, were quite happy.

It was last week that Firooz died. But up until an hour ago, no one knew about his death. All they knew was that he wasn't around for a week and then, when they realized he had died, they didn't want to know how or when.

For a few days a strong stench was coming from the dump behind the latrine of the local tea house. A stench that became stronger and more intolerable every day.

Everybody assumed it was coming from the latrine and cursed Agha Reza, the keeper, for not emptying and cleaning the cesspool.

But as soon as they found Firooz's decomposed body in the dump an hour later, everyone knew that this stench of rancid oil and rotten flesh was coming from Firooz's disintegrating corpse which was found in a squatting position slumped behind the latrine. No one felt sorry, and even those who had cursed Agha Reza didn't feel ashamed. Only the clowns felt joy in their hearts; after all, their toughest rival, the one who had robbed them of their business, had just dropped dead.

It was the first day of the week before that Firooz, as usual, entered the tea house at six sharp. Firooz was strung out and his round, blurry eyes were teary. His small skull, short and hairy forehead, lumpy eyebrows, protruding jaw, and chin were all too heavy on his weak and exhausted neck.

He looked around. Looked at the men who were sitting on rows of chairs smoking long pipes and cigarettes and drinking tea and thought: No! I have never really liked them. They have always laughed at me. Always hurt me, always bothered me. They are pretentious animals. After thinking this thought, which he could never verbalize, he went inside.

A small, limp old man stared at Firooz with his watery eyes, and smiled, showing his yellow, boarish teeth. He mockingly ran his hands over his cheeks and this made Firooz furious. This gesture held a bad meaning for him. But Firooz was old now and couldn't attack like he used to. Firooz gave the old man a tired and scornful look and just grinned and bore it. He who had an imperfect mind sneered at this man who had a perfect mind and walked on two legs and talked, and then he proceeded past him.

When he reached Agha Reza, he stood on his hind legs, and put his long, skinny fingers, with their long, sharp fingernails, on the lacquered cash register and, with the palm of his hand, gently slapped his own cheeks.

Agha Reza, as usual, held a plate in front of his mouth and Firooz spat out the money he had stored inside his cheeks. Agha Reza counted the money with a stick, gave it to the footboy to rinse in the basin, then gave Firooz a few grams of opium.

Firooz took the opium, went into the main room of the tea house, and looked carefully at everyone sitting on the cushions smoking the drug. He ignored the laughter, heckling, and mocking faces. Firooz spotted his friend in a corner smoking. Firooz went over to him, bowed, handed him the opium and squatted down on his callused, dark bottom.

As was his daily practice, Firooz's pal unwrapped the opium pipe, prepared the paste, smoked it, and then blew the smoke into Firooz's mouth.

Firooz inhaled the smoke and then slowly released it through the nostrils of his small, round, upturned nose.

... Firooz was still inhaling. He was high. He felt light-headed. He switched his tail a couple of times and rubbed his eyes with the backs of his shaggy hands.

He forgot everything. The suffering caused by people, the humiliations he had endured, the beatings, the kindnesses, the hecklers, sneers, and kickings ... he forgot it all. He became young again. He felt numb and sick. His round eyes became rounder. He felt that his dirty, dusty, filthy fur was soft, clean, and smooth again, like when he was young. Time and place rolled up like a scroll. He felt the familiar taste of coconut and ripe banana in his mouth. He could sense the damp and intoxicating scent of the forest. He would jump from one tree to another, he would grab one branch and release the other, he would roll in the moist, cool meadow which was covered with leaves, and would play hide and seek with his friends and brothers and sisters who had never harmed him. He would dip his round chin into the limpid, refreshing water of the spring, and drink …

His friend blew another puff into his mouth and Firooz inhaled it, without anyone noticing. He was at the peak of his high. It was at this point that some of the memories of his youth would sprout and begin to grow. He was not at all willing to think about humans. People he had made laugh, and clowns he had made cry … no! No! Did he have any good memories of these two-legged animals? Had they repaid him for all his trouble? Didn't he do enough chores for them in the tea house? Hadn't he shown his respect for "real men" by generously belittling himself? Where are all of those men for whom he would incessantly bring himself down to nothing? No…. All of this is just cunning. Everything that his damned master had taught him was a hoax to make money and feed himself and his offspring. Had any of these talking animals done anything to soothe his pain? … No! … No! … It was useless …

After a few more puffs he turned into nothingness. He dissolved in the opium smoke, he became a spirit, he went beyond matter…. Then he remembered his lover.

He followed her in his delusion and glanced at her shiny brown fur with excited, inflamed eyes. He eagerly watched her red, fresh bottom (which wasn't callused like his). How plump and beautiful she was, what a soft and pretty tail she had … No! … His lover was completely different from the two-legged females he saw in town every now and then.

He himself was so different from the male city dwellers. The urban two-legged animals are spoiled and snobbish; they humiliated him and made snide remarks in return for his troubles. No! He was different from these not-worth-a-dime municipals. He was something else ... His lover was something else. Whenever he desired, he would flirt with her, jump on her back, or carry her on his back, and none of his friends would make fun of him. He had never gone after another one. Hadn't even thought about another.... He remembered that day.... No, he didn't remember, he visualized. His vision was so powerful that he could touch it, that he could see his lover, as if she were right in front of him, dexterously skin a banana and wolf it down. He could see a big snake creeping among the leaves and moving towards her and he would scream in order to save her.... He became pale. He thought that the snake would kill his lover. He squealed, screamed, hopped about and hit his chest.... Suddenly he realized he was in the tea house, and he felt baffled and embarrassed.

Everyone jeered at him. They threw a piece of charcoal at him and said things to him that he didn't understand. All he could tell was that he had disturbed their high and that they were pissed off; his frustration grew. His high was gone. He beggingly looked into his friend's eyes. As if he were saying "please," he stuck out his furry little hand. It was as if he wanted to say, "As I've run out of opium, be nice and give me some of yours." His friend knew exactly what he wanted. He knew he wanted more puffs. He thought to himself what the heck, today I'll give him a little extra and tomorrow I'll pinch half of his dope. He thought this and never wanted to admit that every day he was stealing opium from a monkey, and that every day he would smoke what belonged to Firooz and just blow second-hand smoke into the monkey's mouth.

"Well, what's wrong with that," he mumbled to himself, as he sucked on the pipe and blew a puff to Firooz. Firooz inhaled eagerly. A few moments later he felt that this was to be a painful and bitter high. Involuntarily, he touched his neck with his skinny, lifeless fingers. He thought he was still wearing the chain that "Reza-the-Card" had fastened on him. But nothing was there. Only the trace where the chain had worn away his fur. He was relieved. Even if he was an opium addict, and had to go through hell just to make a few bucks to buy opium, at least he was free. At least he no longer wore the collar and leash of "Reza-the-Card."

The consciousness of freedom made him feel better. He skillfully caught the persistent fly which was tickling his nose, stared at it, then squished it between his fingers. Without asking, he took a sugar cube from his friend's plate and started to chew and ...

He remembered the days when "Reza-the-Card" would set up his opium-smoking kit and there was always tea and sugar cubes. Sometimes he would snatch some sugar. These thefts weren't always trouble-free. If "Reza-the-Card" caught him, he would get mad, hit him, hang a rock around his balls.... But the sweetness of the sugar was worth these rebukes.

Again he touched his neck and again found nothing. Only the missing fur where the collar used to be. The image of his master's bald, shiny, skinny skull, his impudent eyes and his big, strong body came to his mind and shocked him, because this man had caused him more pain than anyone. He had wasted his youth with this loser, without any payoff. He had danced, done somersaults, and entertained at both odd and predictable hours on the streets and at whore-houses. Years performing tricks so that slime Reza could feed himself and his filthy offspring. And now … now what? Now that he had gotten old? Now that he wasn't worth a dime? "Reza-the-Card" had unlatched his leash and tossed him out.

Firooz took another cube of sugar, looked helplessly at his friend and the others, got up, and slowly scampered out of the tea house.

Once on the street, he stopped at the grocery store, clowned a bit, stared miserably at the grocer, and hung around until he got a nickel.

The next day, Firooz arrived at the tea house at six o'clock with his mouth full of coins. He got his opium from Reza, went into the main room and looked everywhere, but couldn't find his friend. So he went outside and sat down.

He waited for more than half-an-hour but still his friend hadn't shown up. Being strung out was killing him. Tears formed in his glassy eyes. His nose was runny. The slightest noise drove him up the wall. It felt like someone was banging on his head with a hammer. There were noises inside his skull. He thought of the days he had seen "Reza-the-Card" swallow the opium instead of smoking it, with a sip of tea to help it down. He had always wondered, in his small brain, why the man did this. With this in mind, he headed towards the basin. With his dingy fingernails he took a pea-sized portion of the opium, popped it in his mouth, and drank some water from the basin. Soon, he no longer felt strung out. He got high. His face opened up and he was content. It was as if he wanted to say now I know why the master eats the opium. Then he looked at the lump of gummy black paste. Perhaps, he assumed, if he took the whole lump he would reach the maximum high, he would feel relieved, he would be free for awhile from ungrateful and unjust humans and could forget them all.

He went to the basin again. But this time he was agile. He was on a spree. He had solved a big puzzle, and was full of himself. He didn't need his friend anymore. To hell with him, he thought. Who cares whether he's around or not? From now on, he could do this on his own. Instead of squatting for two hours next to his friend, he would just help himself.

He took the opium little by little, each time sipping some water from the basin, and wetting his red, round chin. When all the opium was gone, he went out and sat in the yard. He put his feet on the damp soil and had a good time. He played in the grass a bit and enjoyed it. The grass was soft and delicate like his lover's fur. He got goose bumps.... He was in ecstasy. But this ecstasy was impossible to stop. It got stronger by the minute until he imagined that the trees were getting bigger and bigger and then disappeared. He felt as if the walls of the tea house were spinning around his ears, that the water basin had huge waves like the ocean, that the swirls of diffuse, ambiguous noises were swarms of buzzing hornets...

He got up unsteadily and stumbled towards the latrine. Holding onto the wall, he slowly dragged himself to the dump in back. He was quite numb by now. He sat down and held his hairy knees in his shivering arms, blacked out, started snoring, and ...

An hour ago, they found Firooz's worm-eaten corpse behind the latrine. Now everybody knew that the smell of rancid oil and rotten flesh was coming from his disintegrating hulk.

No one felt sorry. They flashed short, sarcastic smiles and said *the poor thing!* And soon they forgot him.

—*Translated from the Persian*
*by Gita Tabatabai*

# Notes on Soma

*Sampurnanand*

WESTERN SCHOLARS ARE of the opinion that Soma was some kind of intoxicating liquor extracted from the leaves of a plant like Bhang (Indian hemp). In the absence of any other worthwhile information on the subject, many educated Indians have also come to believe this. It is certain that Soma was extracted from the leaves of a particular plant and it did have some intoxicating effect. But it was not used normally as an intoxicative drug. The Aryans of those days were familiar with wine and they knew how to prepare fermented intoxicants. They could easily have used some kind of wine, prepared, for instance, from barley or rice. But Soma was something of an entirely different nature and a thing used for an altogether different purpose. There were special rules regarding its transit and sale. There were religious injunctions that, even if two states were at war, there should be no obstruction to the passage of Soma from one to the other. Soma was not sold in the shops like other intoxicants, nor could it be extracted by anyone whenever he chose to do so. It was prepared only in the course of yajna or a Vedic sacrifice. Brahmanas, members of the priestly class, used to say, and they repeat these words today: "Somasmakam Brahmananam Raja":—"Soma is the king of us—Brahmanas." One can easily see that learned priests would not utter such words shamelessly in connection with an ordinary intoxicating drug.

Soma was widely praised in Vedic literature. On the one hand, it is not only a plant by itself but a symbol for plants in general; on the other, the word is also used for that strength and sustenance to all living things which depend on plants for their life and health, directly or indirectly. Soma is also a symbol of Prana, that mysterious energy which functions in the universe at all levels, psychic as well as bodily, and is as such a manifestation of that substance which is at the same time Shiva and Shakti, consciousness and will, God and God's Power. There is this significant passage in the *Veda* about Soma. This is the third mantra of the 85th hymn of the $10^{th}$ book of the *Rig Veda:* "People press the plant with the desire of drinking Soma but the Soma which is known to Brahmanas is not tasted by the ordinary worldly man." This, in brief, is the real mystery of Soma. By drinking it, a special psychic experience is undergone which is similar to that of some of the lower stages of Samadhi, the highest stage of Yoga. Soma helped people to withdraw their minds from the outside world.

A few years ago it might not have been possible to advance such an explanation of the action of Soma. The person coming forward with it would have been laughed out of court forthwith. But recently experiments have been carried out in the West, particularly in the United States, with the juice of certain plants which have been found to possess remarkable psychedelic properties. Mescaline is one such substance. Certain varieties of mushroom are credited with similar properties. It is said that as soon as such a juice is taken, strange psychic experiences begin to occur. The experimenter seems to undergo a remarkable expansion of his self. It seems to him that he is transcending the bonds of space and time. The whole universe seems to reveal its reality and meaning in an instantaneous flash of intuition as it were and the point of time associated with such experience is a moment of truth, as it is called. Infinite peace seems to pervade the mind, and what is particularly remarkable, there is no addiction.

I have no doubt that Soma possesses psychedelic properties more or less of this kind. The condition produced by it was called Baja. This experience was not normally available to the ordinary human being. It was accessible only to the seeker after Brahman, the substratum of reality which pervades all that exists. Not only was Baja a psychic experience itself, it also led directly to certain siddhis, so-called occult powers. It is these siddhis which are being so laboriously investigated and studied in parapsychological laboratories and categorized as ESP and the like. It should not be difficult for anyone acquainted with psychic phenomena and the effects of psychedelic drugs to understand how ESP is made possible by the hyperæsthetic state of mind induced by taking such drugs.

### *Soma and the Interpretation of the Vedas*

I do not accept the view that the Vedic gods represent the great phenomena of nature—sky, sun, moon, thunder-cloud, dawn, anthropomorphized to some extent; I do not believe that the *Rig Veda* bears witness to vagueness about the soul or that there was a cult of Soma, raising this drink to the status of a high god. I am starting from the Vedic period, the period mainly of the hymns of the *Rig Veda* and some of the hymns of the *Atharva Veda*, and it is my firm conviction that, in that age, the religion of the Aryans had already transcended those concepts of which alone Western scholars take cognizance.

The fact of the matter is that having outgrown the outlook of a pastoral people, the Aryan priests, who were the elite among the ruling classes, were reaching out to new horizons, both spiritually and intellectually. They were putting new questions to themselves, questions about the Reality behind phenomena, about what happens after death, about the gods whom their fathers and ancestors had worshipped. Here is an example of such questions: "I ask you what is the end of the earth, I ask you where is the center of the universe, I ask you what is the cause of the sun, I ask you what is the highest region of speech."

Or take this: "Who knows and who can tell us definitely which is the path that leads to the gods? One can see the lower regions of the gods but which is the path that leads to their higher, secret planes?" They had also discovered methods which for a time freed them from the trammels of the body and the waking consciousness and put them in rapport with the Reality, with an infinite expansion of consciousness. The levels of consciousness revealed in the course of this spiritual pilgrimage of the soul, the replies to its questions which the mind formulated in this condition of exaltation—all this experience was startling. The whole universe came to be suffused with a new light. The message had to be brought down. As the *Rig Veda* itself says: "this message ensuring the ultimate good has to be conveyed to all men." But the Vedic seers were not thoughtless iconoclasts, out to disrupt society which they and their fathers had led for generations. The message was, therefore, conveyed in symbolic language mostly. In any case, ordinary language would have been inadequate for the purpose. Some statements, laying down philosophical propositions, were there as beacon lights to draw attention prominently to the new horizon. But very often, the imagery of the old sacrificial rites and the traditions of the race, the old stories of gods and men and the powers of evil, were utilized for the purpose of conveying the new lessons. In this way, the old theology, whatever it might have been, was slowly re-orientated. The old words came very often to clothe new meanings. The popular mind was brought up to a new spiritual level while the key to the passages dealing with the more esoteric facts of experience, the mysteries, was handed down from master to disciple. Unfortunately, this key has been lost.

Anyone who goes through the Vedic texts will see that many of them seem to be puerile and convey fantastic meanings, if any. There is for instance a very famous hymn: "It has four horns, three legs, two heads and seven arms; thrice bound, this bull is roaring. Its power has entered into men." Obviously, such an animal never existed anywhere outside a maniac's dream. If it is a symbol, one should know what it symbolizes. No satisfactory answer is normally forthcoming. People have tried to find grammatical interpretations for such passages but the interpretations fall flat. One wonders how a book containing passages of this kind could have become the scripture of a race endowed with spiritual sensitivities as are apparent in the *Upanishads.* It is considerations such as these which force one to the conclusion that we have lost the key to Vedic interpretation. As Yaska, one of the great commentators, says: "No un-rishi can understand the *Vedas,*" which means that if you want to understand such passages you have to become a rishi (saint). I firmly believe that anyone who tries to understand the *Vedas* with the help of grammar and lexicon alone will fail miserably in the attempt. The key is to be found in yogic experience and there alone. I do not believe that Soma by itself holds the key. My firm conviction is that it has psychedelic virtues and helped those who wanted to go in for the kind of experience that depends on the one-pointedness of the mind.

Not that it was a "must." Everybody need not have used it. Some certainly did. It had some kind of intoxicating effect also. It was necessary, therefore, to hedge it round with all kinds of restrictions so that it should be used only by a special class of people in the course of certain special ceremonies. Apparently, it grew somewhere in Afghanistan or Central Asia. As the Aryans penetrated further into the interior of India, it became more and more difficult to secure fresh supplies. As Vedic sacrifices became more and more rare after the rise of Buddhism, the use of Soma was finally given up till no one today can identify this particular herb.

# Mescal: A New Artificial Paradise

*Havelock Ellis*

It has been known for some years that the Kiowa Indians of New Mexico are accustomed to eat, in their religious ceremonies, a certain cactus called Anhalonium Lewinii, or mescal button. Mescal—which must not be confounded with the intoxicating drink of the same name made from an agave—is found in the Mexican Valley of the Rio Grande, the ancestral home of the Kiowa Indians, as well as in Texas, and is a brown and brittle substance, nauseous and bitter to the taste, composed mainly of the blunt dried leaves of the plant. Yet, as we shall see, it has every claim to rank with hasheesh and the other famous drugs which have procured for men the joys of an artificial paradise. Upon the Kiowa Indians, who first discovered its rare and potent virtues, it has had so strong a fascination that the missionaries among these Indians, finding here a rival to Christianity not yielding to moral suasion, have appealed to the secular arm, and the buying and selling of the drug has been prohibited by Government under severe penalties. Yet the use of mescal prevails among the Kiowas to this day.

It has indeed spread, and the mescal rite may be said to be to-day the chief religion of all the tribes of the southern plains of the United States. The rite usually takes place on Saturday night; the men then sit in a circle within the tent round a large camp fire, which is kept burning brightly all the time. After prayer the leader hands each man four buttons, which are slowly chewed and swallowed, and altogether about ten or twelve buttons are consumed by each man between sun-down and daybreak. Throughout the night the men sit quietly round the fire in a state of reverie—amid continual singing and the beating of drums by attendants—absorbed in the color visions and other manifestations of mescal intoxication, and about noon on the following day, when the effects have passed off, they get up and go about their business, without any depression or other unpleasant aftereffect.

There are five or six allied species of cacti which the Indians also use and treat with great reverence. Thus Mr. Carl Lumholtz has found that the Tarahumari, a tribe of Mexican Indians, worship various cacti as gods, only to be approached with uncovered heads. When they wish to obtain these cacti, the Tarahumari dense themselves with copal incense, and with profound respect dig up the god, careful lest they should hurt him, while women and children are warned from the spot. Even Christian Indians regard Hikori, the cactus god, as coequal with their own divinity, and make the sign of the cross in its presence. At all great festivals Hikori is made into a drink and consumed by the medicine man, or certain selected Indians, who sing as they partake of it, invoking Hikori to grant a "beautiful intoxication"; at the same time a rasping noise is made with sticks, and men and women dance a fantastic and picturesque dance—the women by themselves in white petticoats and tunics—before those who are under the influence of the god.

In 1891 Mr. James Mooney, of the United States Bureau of Ethnology, having frequently observed the mescal rites of the Kiowa Indians and assisted at them, called the attention of the Anthropological Society at Washington to the subject, and three years later he brought to Washington a supply of mescal, which was handed over for examination to Drs. Prentiss and Morgan. These investigators experimented on several young men, and demonstrated, for the first time, the precise character of mescal intoxication and the remarkable visions to which it gives rise. A little later Dr. Weir Mitchell, who, in addition to his eminence as a physician, is a man of marked æsthetic temperament, experimented on himself, and published a very interesting record of the brilliant visions by which he was visited under the influence of the plant. In the spring of the past year I was able to obtain a small sample of mescal in London, and as my first experiment with mescal was also, apparently, the first attempt to investigate its vision-producing properties outside America, I will describe it in some detail, in preference to drawing on the previously published descriptions of the American observers.

On Good Friday I found myself entirely alone in the quiet rooms in the Temple which I occupy when in London, and judged the occasion a fitting one for a personal experiment. I made a decoction (a different method from that adopted in America) of three buttons, the full physiological dose, and drank this at intervals between 2.30 and 4.30 P.M. The first symptom observed during the afternoon was a certain consciousness of energy and intellectual power. This passed off, and about an hour after the final dose I felt faint and unsteady; the pulse was low, and I found it pleasanter to lie down. I was still able to read, and I noticed that a pale violet shadow floated over the page around the point at which my eyes were fixed. I had already noticed that objects not in the direct line of vision, such as my hands holding the book, showed a tendency to look obtrusive, heightened in color, almost monstrous, while, on closing my eyes, afterimages were vivid and prolonged. The appearance of vision with closed eyes was very gradual. At first there was merely a vague play of light and shade which suggested pictures, but never made them. Then the pictures became more definite, but too confused and crowded to be described, beyond saying that they were of the same character as the images of the kaleidoscope, symmetrical groupings of spiked objects. Then, in the course of the evening, they became distinct, but still indescribable-mostly a vast field of golden jewels, studded with red and green stones, ever changing. This moment was, perhaps, the most delightful of the experience, for at the same time the air around me seemed to be flushed with vague perfume—producing with the visions a delicious effect—and all discomfort had vanished, except a slight faintness and tremor of the hands, which, later on, made it almost impossible to guide a pen as I made notes of the experiment; it was, however, with an effort, always possible to write with a pencil. The visions never resembled familiar objects; they were extremely definite, but yet always novel; they were constantly approaching, and yet constantly eluding, the semblance of known things. I would see thick, glorious fields of jewels, solitary or clustered, sometimes brilliant and sparkling, sometimes with a dull rich glow. Then they would spring up into flower-like shapes beneath my gaze, and then seem to turn into gorgeous butterfly forms or endless folds of glistening, iridescent, fibrous wings of wonderful insects; while sometimes I seemed to be gazing into a vast hollow revolving vessel, of whose polished concave mother-of-pearl surface the hues were swiftly changing. I was surprised, not only by the enormous profusion of the imagery presented to my gaze, but still more by its variety. Perpetually some totally new kind of effect would appear in the field of vision; sometimes there was swift movement, sometimes dull, somber richness of color, sometimes glitter and sparkle, once a startling rain of gold, which seemed to approach me. Most usually there was a combination of rich, sober color, with jewel-like points of brilliant hue. Every color and tone conceivable to me appeared at some time or another. Sometimes all the different varieties of one color, as of red, with scarlets, crimsons, pinks, would spring up together, or in quick succession. But in spite of this immense profusion, there was always a certain parsimony and aesthetic value in the colors presented. They were usually associated with form, and never appeared in large masses, or if so, the tone was very delicate. I was further impressed, not only by the brilliance, delicacy, and variety of the colors, but even more by their lovely and various textures—fibrous, woven, polished, glowing, dull, veined, semi-transparent —the glowing effects, as of jewels, and the fibrous, as of insects' wings, being perhaps the most prevalent. Although the effects were novel, it frequently happened, as I have already mentioned, that they vaguely recalled known objects. Thus, once the objects presented to me seemed to be made of exquisite porcelain, again they were like elaborate sweetmeats, again of a somewhat Maori style of architecture; and the background of the pictures frequently recalled, both in form and tone, the delicate architectural effects as of lace carved in wood, which we associated with the mouchrabieh work of Cairo. But always the visions grew and changed without any reference to the characteristics of those real objects of which they vaguely reminded me, and when I tried to influence their course it was with very little success. On the whole, I should say that the images were most usually what might be called living arabesques. There was often a certain incomplete tendency to symmetry, as though the underlying mechanism was associated with a large number of polished facets. The same image was in this way frequently repeated over a large part of the field; but this refers more to form than to color, in respect to which there would still be all sorts of delightful varieties, so that if, with a certain uniformity, jewel-like flowers were springing up and expanding all over the field of vision, they would still show every variety of delicate tone and tint.

Weir Mitchell found that he could only see the visions with closed eyes and in a perfectly dark room. I could see them in the dark with almost equal facility, though they were not of equal brilliancy, when my eyes were wide open. I saw them best, however, when my eyes were closed, in a room lighted only by flickering firelight. This evidently accords with the experience of the Indians, who keep a fire burning brightly throughout their mescal rites. The visions continued with undiminished brilliance for many hours, and as I felt somewhat faint and muscularly weak, I went to bed, as I undressed being greatly impressed by the red, scaly, bronzed, and pigmented appearance of my limbs whenever I was not directly gazing at them. I had not the faintest desire for sleep; there was a general hyperesthesia of all the senses as well as muscular irritability, and every slightest sound seemed magnified to startling dimensions. I may also have been kept awake by a vague alarm at the novelty of my condition, and the possibility of further developments.

After watching the visions in the dark for some hours I became a little tired of them and turned on the gas. Then I found that I was able to study a new series of visual phenomena, to which previous observers had made no reference. The gas jet (an ordinary flickering burner) seemed to burn with great brilliance, sending out waves of light, which expanded and contracted in an enormously exaggerated manner. I was even more impressed by the shadows, which were in all directions heightened by flushes of red, green, and especially violet. The whole room, with its white-washed but not very white ceiling, thus became vivid and beautiful. The difference between the room as I saw it then and the appearance it usually presents to me was the difference one may often observe between the picture of a room and the actual room. The shadows I saw were the shadows which the artist puts in, but which are not visible in the actual scene under normal conditions of casual inspection. I was reminded of the paintings of Claude Monet, and as I gazed at the scene it occurred to me that mescal perhaps produces exactly the same conditions of visual hyperesthesia, or rather exhaustion, as may be produced on the artist by the influence of prolonged visual attention. I wished to ascertain how the subdued and steady electric light would influence vision, and passed into the next room; but here the shadows were little marked, although walls and floor seemed tremulous and insubstantial, and the texture of everything was heightened and enriched.

About 3.30 a. m. I felt that the phenomena were distinctly diminishing—though the visions, now chiefly of human figures, fantastic and Chinese in character, still continued—and I was able to settle myself to sleep, which proved peaceful and dreamless. I awoke at the usual hour and experienced no sense of fatigue nor other unpleasant reminiscence of the experience I had undergone. Only my eyes seemed unusually sensitive to color, especially to blue and violet; I can, indeed, say that ever since this experience I have been more aesthetically sensitive than I was before to the more delicate phenomena of light and shade and color.

It occurred to me that it would be interesting to have the experiences of an artist under the influence of mescal, and I induced an artist friend to make a similar experiment. Unfortunately no effects whatever were produced at the first attempt, owing, as I have since discovered, to the fact that the buttons had only been simply infused and their virtues not extracted. To make sure of success the experiment was repeated with four buttons, which proved to be an excessive and unpleasant dose. There were paroxysmal attacks of pain at the heart and a sense of imminent death, which naturally alarmed the subject, while so great was the dread of light and dilatation of the pupils that the eyelids had to be kept more or less closed, though it was evident that a certain amount of vision was still possible. The symptoms came on very suddenly, and when I arrived they were already at their height. As the experiences of this subject were in many respects very unlike mine, I will give them in his own words: "I noticed first that as I happened to turn my eyes away from a blue enamel kettle at which I had been unconsciously looking, and which was standing in the fender of the fireplace, with no fire in it, it seemed to me that I saw a spot of the same blue in the black coals of the grate, and that this spot appeared again, farther off, a little brighter in hue. But I was in doubt whether I had not imagined these blue spots. When, however, I lifted my eyes to the mantelpiece, on which were scattered all sorts of odds and ends, all doubt was over. I saw an intensely vivid blue light begin to play around every object. A square cigarette box, violet in color, shone like an amethyst. I turned my eyes away and beheld this time, on the back of a polished chair, a bar of color glowing like a ruby. Although I was expecting some such manifestation as one of the first symptoms of the intoxication, I was nevertheless somewhat alarmed when this phenomenon took place. Such a silent and sudden illumination of all things around, where a moment before I had seen nothing uncommon, seemed like a kind of madness beginning from outside me, and its strangeness affected me more than its beauty. A desire to escape from it led me to the door, and the act of moving had, I noticed, the effect of dispelling the colors. But a sudden difficulty in breathing and a sensation of numbness at the heart brought me back to the arm-chair from which I had risen. From this moment I had a series of attacks or paroxysms, which I can only describe by saying that I felt as though I were dying. It was impossible to move, and it seemed almost impossible to breathe. My speedy dissolution, I half imagined, was about to take place, and the power of making any resistance to the violent sensations that were arising within was going, I felt, with every second.

"The first paroxysms were the most violent. They would come on with tinglings in the lower limbs, and with the sensation of a nauseous and suffocating gas mounting up into my head. Two or three times this was accompanied by a color vision of the gas bursting into flame as it passed up my throat. But I seldom had visions during the paroxysms; these would appear in the intervals. They began with a spurting up of colors; once, of a flood of brightly illuminated green water covering the field of vision, and effervescing in parts, just as when fresh water with all the air bubbles is pumped into a swimming bath. At another time my eye seemed to be turning into a vast drop of dirty water in which millions of minute creatures resembling tadpoles were in motion. But the early visions consisted mostly of a furious succession of colored arabesques, arising and descending or sliding at every possible angle into the field of view. It would be as difficult as to give a description of the whirl of water at the bottom of a waterfall as to describe the chaos of color and design which marked this period."

"Now also began another series of extraordinary sensations. They set in with bewildering suddenness and followed one another in rapid succession. These I now record as they occur to my mind at haphazard: 1. My right leg became suddenly heavy and solid; it seemed, indeed, as if the entire weight of my body had shifted into one part, about the thigh and knee, and that the rest of my body had lost all substantiality. 2. With the suddenness of a neuralgic pang, the back of my head seemed to open and emit streams of bright color; this was immediately followed by the feeling as of a draft blowing like a gale through the hair in the same region. 3. At one moment the color, green, acquired a taste in my mouth; it was sweetish and somewhat metallic; blue again would have a taste that seemed to recall phosphorus; these are the only colors that seemed to be connected with taste. 4. A feeling of delightful relief and preternatural lightness about my forehead, succeeded by a growing sensation of contraction. 5. Singing in one of my ears. 6. A sensation of burning heat in the palm of my left hand. 7. Heat about both eyes. The last continued throughout the whole period, except for a moment when I had a sensation of cold upon the eyelids, accompanied with a color vision of the wrinkled lid, of the skin disappearing from the brow, of dead flesh, and finally of a skull."

"Throughout these sensations and visions my mind remained not only perfectly clear, but enjoyed, I believe, an unusual lucidity. Certainly I was conscious of an odd contrast in hearing myself talk rationally with H. E., who had entered the room a short time before, and experiencing at the same moment the wild and extraordinary pranks that were taking place in my body. My reason appeared to be the sole survivor of my being. At times I felt that this, too, would go, but the sound of my own voice would establish again the communication with the outer world of reality."

"Tremors were more or less constant in my lower limbs. Persistent, also, was the feeling of nausea. This, when attended by a feeling of suffocation and a pain at the heart, was relieved by taking brandy, coffee, or biscuit. For muscular exertion I felt neither the wish nor the power. My hands, however, retained their full strength."

"It was painful for me to keep my eyes open above a few seconds; the light of day seemed to fill the room with a blinding glare. Yet every object, in the brief glimpse I caught, appeared normal in color and shape. With my eyes closed, most of the visions, after the first chaotic display, represented parts of the whole of my body undergoing a variety of marvelous changes, of metamorphoses or illumination. They were more often than not comic and grotesque in character, though often beautiful in color. At one time I saw my right leg filling up with delicate heliotrope; at another, the sleeve of my coat changed into a dark green material, in which was worked a pattern in red braid, and the whole bordered at the cuff with sable. Scarcely had my new sleeve taken shape than I found myself attired in a complete costume of the same fashion, medieval in character, but I could not say to what precise period it belonged. I noted that a chance movement—of my hand, for instance—would immediately call up a color vision of the part exerted, and that this again would pass, by a seemingly natural transition, into another wholly dissimilar. Thus, pressing my fingers accidentally against my temples, the fingertips became elongated, and then grew into the ribs of a vaulting or of a dome-shaped roof. But most of the visions were of a more personal nature. I happened once to lift a spoonful of coffee to my lips, and as I was in the act of raising my arm for that purpose a vision dashed before my closed (or nearly closed) eyes, in all the hues of the rainbow, of my arm separated from my body, and serving me with coffee from out of dark and indefinite space. On another occasion, as I was seeking to relieve slight nausea by taking a piece of biscuit passed to me by H. E., it suddenly streamed out into blue flame. For an instant I held the biscuit close to my leg. Immediately my trousers caught alight, and then the whole of the right side of my body, from the foot to the shoulder, was enveloped in waving blue flame. It was a sight of wonderful beauty. But this was not all. As I placed the biscuit in my mouth it burst out again into the same colored fire and illuminated the interior of my mouth, casting a blue resection on the roof. The light in the Blue Grotto at Capri, I am able to affirm, is not nearly as blue as seemed for a short space of time the interior of my mouth. There were many visions of which I could not trace the origin."

"There were spirals and arabesques and flowers, and sometimes objects more trivial and prosaic in character. In one vision I saw a row of small white flowers, one against the other like pearls of a necklace, begin to revolve in the form of a spiral. Every flower, I observed, had the texture of porcelain. It was at a moment when I had the sensation of my cheeks growing hot and feverish that I experienced the strangest of all the color visions. It began with feeling that the skin of my face was becoming quite thin and of no stouter consistency than tissue paper, and the feeling was suddenly enhanced by a vision of my face, paper-like and semitransparent and somewhat reddish in color. To my amazement I saw myself as though I were inside a Chinese lantern, looking out through my cheek into the room. Not long after this I became conscious of a change in the visions. Their tempo was more moderate, they were less frequent, and they were losing somewhat in distinctness. At the same time the feeling of nausea and of numbness was departing. A short period followed in which I had no visions at all, and experienced merely a sensation of heaviness and torpor. I found that I was able to open my eyes again and keep them fixed on any object in the room without observing the faintest blue halo or prism, or bar of glowing color, and that, moreover, no visions appeared on closing them. It was now twilight, but beyond the fact of not seeing light or color, either without or within, I had a distinct feeling that the action of the drug was at an end and that my body had become sober suddenly. I had no more visions, though I was not wholly free from abnormal sensations, and I retired to rest. I lay awake till the morning, and with the exception of the following night I scarcely slept for the next three days, but I cannot say that I felt any signs of fatigue, unless, perhaps, on one of the days when my eyes, I noticed, became very susceptible to any indications of blue in an object. Of color visions, or of any approach to color visions, there was no further trace; but all sorts of odd and grotesque images passed in succession through my mind during part of the first night. They might have been the dreams of a Baudelaire or of an Aubrey Beardsley. I would see figures with prodigious limbs, or strangely dwarfed and curtailed, or impossible combinations such as five or six fish, the color of canaries, floating about in air in a gold wire cage. But these were purely mental images, like the visions seen in a dream by a distempered brain."

"Of the many sensations of which my body had been the theater during three hours, not the least strange was the feeling I experienced on coming back into a normal condition. The recovery did not proceed gradually, but the whole outer and inner world of reality came back, as it were, with a bound. And for a moment it seemed strange. It was the sensation—only much intensified—which everyone has known on coming out into the light of day from an afternoon performance at a theater, where one has sat in an artificial light of gas and lamps, the spectator of a fictitious world of action. As one pours out with the crowd into the street, the ordinary world, by force of contrast with the sensational scenes just witnessed, breaks in upon one with almost a sense of unreality. The house, the aspects of the street, even the light of day appear a little foreign for a few moments. During these moments everything strikes the mind as odd and unfamiliar, or at least with a greater degree of objectivity. Such was my feeling with regard to my old and habitual self. During the period of intoxication the connection between the normal condition of my body and my intelligence had broken—my body had become in a manner a stranger to my reason—so that now on reasserting itself it seemed, with reference to my reason, which had remained perfectly sane and alert, for a moment sufficiently unfamiliar for me to become conscious of its individual and peculiar character. It was as if I had unexpectedly attained an objective knowledge of my own personality. I saw, as it were, my normal state of being with the eyes of a person who sees the street on coming out of the theater in broad day."

"This sensation also brought out the independence of the mind during the period of intoxication. It alone appeared to have escaped the ravages of the drug; it alone remained sane during a general delirium, vindicating, so it seemed, the majesty of its own impersonal nature. It had reigned for a while, I now felt, as an autocrat, without ministers and their officiousness. Henceforth I should be more or less conscious of the interdependence of body and brain; a slight headache, a touch of indigestion, or what not, would be able to effect what a general intoxication of my senses and nerves could not touch."

I next made experiments on two poets, whose names are both well known. One is interested in mystical matters, an excellent subject for visions, and very familiar with various vision-producing drugs and processes. His heart, however, is not very strong. While he obtained the visions, he found the effects of mescal on his breathing somewhat unpleasant; he much prefers hasheesh, though recognizing that its effects are much more difficult to obtain. The other enjoys admirable health, and under the influence of mescal he experienced scarcely the slightest unpleasant reaction, but, on the contrary, a very marked state of well being and beatitude. He took somewhat less than three buttons, so that the results were rather less marked than in my case, but they were perfectly definite. He writes: "I have never seen a succession of absolutely pictorial visions with such precision and such unaccountability. It seemed as if a series of dissolving views were carried swiftly before me, all going from right to left, none corresponding with any seen reality. For instance, I saw the most delightful dragons, puffing out their breath straight in front of them like rigid lines of steam, and balancing white balls at the end of their breath! When I tried to fix my mind on real things, I could generally call them up, but always with some inexplicable change. Thus, I called up a particular monument in Westminster Abbey, but in front of it, to the left, knelt a figure in Florentine costume, like someone out of a picture of Botticelli; and I could not see the tomb without also seeing this figure. Late in the evening I went out on the Embankment and was absolutely fascinated by an advertisement of 'Bovril,' which went and came in letters of light on the other side of the river. I cannot tell you the intense pleasure this moving light gave me and how dazzling it seemed to me. Two girls and a man passed me, laughing loudly, and lolling about as they walked. I realized, intellectually, their coarseness, but visually I saw them, as they came under a tree, fall into the lines of a delicate picture; it might have been an Albert Moore. After coming in I played the piano with closed eyes and got waves and lines of pure color, almost always without form, though I saw one or two appearances which might have been shields or breastplates—pure gold, studded with small jewels in intricate patterns. All the time I had no unpleasant feelings whatever, except a very slight headache, which came and went. I slept soundly and without dreams."

The results of music in the case just quoted—together with the habit of the Indians to combine the drum with mescal rites, and my own observation that very slight jarring or stimulation of the scalp would affect the visions—suggested to me to test the influence of music on myself. I therefore once more put myself under the influence of mescal (taking a somewhat smaller dose than on the first occasion), and lay for some hours on a couch with my head more or less in contact with the piano, and with closed eyes directed toward a subdued light, while a friend played, making various tests, of his own devising, which were not explained to me until afterwards. I was to watch the visions in a purely passive manner, without seeking to direct them, nor was I to think about the music, which, so far as possible, was unknown to me. The music stimulated the visions and added greatly to my enjoyment of them. It seemed to harmonize with them, and, as it were, support and bear them up. A certain persistence and monotony of character in the music was required in order to affect the visions, which then seemed to fall into harmony with it, and any sudden change in the character of the music would blur the visions, as though clouds passed between them and me. The chief object of the tests was to ascertain how far a desire on the composer's part to suggest definite imagery would affect my visions. In about half the cases there was no resemblance, in the other half there was a distinct resemblance, which was sometimes very remarkable. This was especially the case with Schumann's music, for example, with his Waldscenen and Kinderscenen; thus "The Prophet Bird" called up vividly a sense of atmosphere and of brilliant feathery bird-like forms passing to and fro, "A Flower Piece" provoked constant and persistent images of vegetation, while "Scheherazade" produced an effect of floating white raiment, covered by glittering spangles and jewels. In every case my description was, of course, given before I knew the name of the piece. I do not pretend that this single series of experiments proves much, but it would certainly be worthwhile to follow up this indication and to ascertain if any light is hereby thrown on the power of a composer to suggest definite imagery, or the power of a listener to perceive it.

It would be out of place here to discuss the obscure question as to the underlying mechanism by which mescal exerts its magic powers. It is clear from the foregoing descriptions that mescal intoxication may be described as chiefly a saturnalia of the specific senses, and, above all, an orgy of vision. It reveals an optical fairyland, where all the senses now and again join the play, but the mind itself remains a self-possessed spectator. Mescal intoxication thus differs from the other artificial paradises which drugs procure. Under the influence of alcohol, for instance, as in normal dreaming, the intellect is impaired, although there may be a consciousness of unusual brilliance; hasheesh, again, produces an uncontrollable tendency to movement and bathes its victim in a sea of emotion. The mescal drinker remains calm and collected amid the sensory turmoil around him; his judgment is as clear as in the normal state; he falls into no oriental condition of vague and voluptuous reverie. The reason why mescal is of all this class of drugs the most purely intellectual in its appeal is evidently because it affects mainly the most intellectual of the senses. On this ground it is not probable that its use will easily develop into a habit. Moreover, unlike most other intoxicants, it seems to have no special affinity for a disordered and unbalanced nervous system; on the contrary, it demands organic soundness and good health for the complete manifestation of its virtues. Further, unlike the other chief substances to which it may be compared, mescal does not wholly carry us away from the actual world, or plunge us into oblivion; a large part of its charm lies in the halo of beauty which it casts around the simplest and commonest things. It is the most democratic of the plants which lead men to an artificial paradise. If it should ever chance that the consumption of mescal becomes a habit, the favorite poet of the mescal drinker will certainly be Wordsworth. Not only the general attitude of Wordsworth, but many of his most memorable poems and phrases cannot—one is almost tempted to say—be appreciated in their full significance by one who has never been under the influence of mescal. On all these grounds it may be claimed that the artificial paradise of mescal, though less seductive, is safe and dignified beyond its peers.

At the same time it must be remembered that at present we are able to speak on a basis of but very small experience, so far as civilized men are concerned. The few observations recorded in America and my own experiments in England do not enable us to say anything regarding the habitual consumption of mescal in large amounts. That such consumption would be gravely injurious I cannot doubt. Its safeguard seems to lie in the fact that a certain degree of robust health is required to obtain any real enjoyment from its visionary gifts. It may at least be claimed that for a healthy person to be once or twice admitted to the rites of mescal is not only an unforgettable delight, but an educational influence of no mean value.

# Ayahuasca

*Eugenio Buona*

I RECOGNIZED MY mother and my grandfather Ramon at the same time. My grandfather Ramon came towards me leaping over my father, as if he had broken the link of a chain no one else could see. My father was swallowed up by the trees and, finally, by the stars. Everything which had lived before or never had been was reeling in the heavens. For this reason, I have taught myself to pray with my eyes uplifted, though my grandfather Ramon prays looking downward. This is mostly so as to ward off the spirits.

Our house, made of lumber rejected by the sawmill, is about a kilometer from the highway and very close to the airstrip. Because of this, my grandfather almost never sleeps. He watches the smoke of the torch which is planted in the soil, while my mother lies on one side of the cot, and my sister and I lie on the other, cuddled against her shoulder, with our eyes shut tight, until at last our eyelids loosen, and luminous penumbra melts into dream. We don't hear the airplanes as they wrinkle the air around us, sometimes droning loud and close, later, farther off, then nearing again with a roar, but this time going, going, until their place is taken by the crowing of the roosters.

Around our house the ground is firm and white. Not even the heaviest rain can soften it. On clear nights it glitters in the encircling thickets like a ring of light from a lantern. A path which curves among the mangos, vines, and tall grass, ends at a deep, narrow spring whose waters are always cloudy.

This is the only place I remember ever having lived. My grandfather Ramon says the same thing, but in a different way. He says that he has been in this same spot for forty years. Since long before I was born. It's really all the same. Forty years are to me life and death put together.

My mother reaps what my grandfather sows. It's as if the abundant earth is more generous the farther away it is from people. My mother is happiest when picking the plump, porous lemons, and gathering the warm eggs freshly left by the hens.

My sister knows how to talk without words. She understands the ducks and the hens and can imitate the rattling of the vipers, and even the buzzing of the mosquitoes which she finishes with a crescendo, like the noise made by the airplanes, before breaking into a senseless laugh. I have never been able to do this, but perhaps that is because she was born a woman like my mother and I, like my grandfather, was born a man.

My grandfather makes long journeys. He goes. My mother limits herself to saying to the people who come in the night: "The maestro is not at home". I often think that my grandfather Ramon has died many times, that by dying he has learned to live, and never to die again. That's why, when he arrives, it never seems as if he is returning, but as if he is only visiting from the other side.

My grandfather has no age. When those who go looking for him cannot find him, I have the impression that it is the flickering torch which wrinkles his face as he blows and blows, now whistling, now not, upon the lip of the glass that vibrates between his hands. Inclining the plastic jug and filling the glasses, one at a time; closing the stopcock with a half-turn, and setting it to one side; blowing softly on the glass, sometimes only briefly, sometimes much longer, he knows how much, and offering it to whomever asks, just like a priest offering communion. I think that my grandfather must be a saint fallen from heaven. I have only seen the saints in supplication this way, so humble and so silent.

My grandfather has made a hoop carved out of dark wood and lashed with a taut cord at points fitted with silver studs. When everyone is sitting or stretched out, waiting for the emancipation, and all they can hear is the noise of the stars blazing all around them, my grandfather plucks the cord and begins to pray or chant with his mouth closed. I can never understand what words he is saying, because he doesn't speak in words; his voice struggles from his throat as if it, too, had a cord fastened around it.

A gringa with long legs and bushy eyebrows has already gone to vomit twice, and complains of the taste. My grandfather Ramon goes to check on her, and the lady, who is dressed like a cowboy, begins to tell him that she is seeing green snakes and lizards and that the stars, too, are green, and that they are flaring all around like rockets which come down at the same time as they go up and that she feels as if she were nailed to the ground, and that her body is filled with holes of light.

My grandfather, crouching now and almost crawling, murmurs things to the spirits which have crowded together under the bench where the engineer with arms dangling from either side, tries to scare off the bats with wings like spider webs which come flitting past like a flock of flying mustaches. Then my grandfather undoes the umbilicus of the child with the swollen stomach and begins to blow into the hole, to blow and to suck, to suck and to blow, seeking to put evil to flight, and the mother winces and squints her eyes when she notices the crimson of blood, and her face resembles that of an injured, frightened cow and meanwhile her clenched fists open and close, fuss and fret over the head of the little boy, crackling, rustling like leaves underfoot in springtime.

Here is your dose, Señor, says my grandfather Ramon to the man lying on the ground next to a little mother-of-pearl crucifix, and the man protests no, Maestro, I don't want a dose I don't believe in this I vomited like a beast, but I can't see or feel anything please take away your torch the smoke makes me sick I don't want a dose it scares me Maestro the only thing I can hear is the crowing of the roosters one after another, and I know that the last one is crowing now in Aguaytia and I hear it as if his head with its blaring beak and its colored comb were right inside my ear. I repeat that this cross is not mine it must belong to the gringa's friend I only want to get away from here because I've been here three nights without seeing daylight and my handkerchief is full of drivel and cold sweat they told me

I could see Rosita nude and that's all I could think about but instead all I see are women with the bodies of trees I want to go the spring which you told us about a while ago but the path is blocked by big soft fish with lacy red sleeves on their cheeks and they won't let me pass and there is a village in ruins farther along on the other side which made me very frightened so I urinated on the burning logs lifting my leg like a dog.

I remembered that it was Agucho who introduced my grandfather to the poet-gentleman I recognized along the road. He was wearing a big, billowy shirt which hung down to his pant legs with embroidery which had been unraveling until it was torn with holes and he wanted to talk with the dead but the only one who could help there was God and he didn't want to talk with God only with the dead and then he ripped open his soiled shirt showing his fuzzy white chest and his ribs protruding as if they were going to break through his skin. He was in the middle of the circle of hard white dirt and he started to run through the ruins and the fish towards the narrow, deep spring with the always-cloudy water and he dove in shouting I am a big phallus! All of me is a big phallus! and he rose from the water and submerged again, and did this many times until it seemed as if he were actually copulating with the well and when he came up he was flopping, like a fish, and when he submerged, he was like a man, and he did this again and again for many hours, until he ended up bathed in sweat, with his head resting between the legs of the gringa with long legs and bushy eyebrows.

My grandfather Ramon has returned. The torch is faltering, but just the same I can see him crouching, with his eyes closed and his head bowed, listening to the respirations of a dozen lungs; just the same I can see his fine short silvery hair illuminated, as if from below. I could swear that at this moment during which my grandfather is looking within himself, he is able to see the womb of the stones washed by the most hidden rivers and pinpoint the most sequestered desires; I could swear that, during his sidereal travels, he knows which portion of the eternal ages each one is touched by, he knows which fires burn the wings of men, he knows how to see life in the worms of death.

My mother and my sister sleep without being heard, perhaps because they do not dream, they don't need to, because the greatest happiness of my mother is when she is awake, gathering plump lemons from the trees, and that of my sister is knowing how to talk with the animals. Therefore they stop living when they sleep, and will live longer than others, or simply die later.

* * *

My grandfather Ramon has taken a trip again. He has been gone so long that my mother has grown tired of saying "the maestro is not at home". The nights are empty and now I, like my mother and my sister, have stopped living when asleep, and I am afraid that if all this continues I am going to live longer than a tortoise, and I will live out my days until I am old, on the edge of the airstrip, selling pine nuts, yams, and manioc root, condemned to never being inside the planes, but only to frame them lovingly with my hands, to be like the dust which is raised from the roadway and falls only a little farther on, and is ground under the tires of escaping cars.

All the time, fewer and fewer people come looking for my grandfather. And once again I think that my grandfather Ramon has died many times, and through dying has learned how to live, never to die again, and that one day he will return like always, not as if he were coming back, but only as if he were visiting from the other side. But this time, it strikes me that he has really died, that my mother has said "the maestro is not at home" so often, that it has finally killed him, that the day will come when it will no longer be necessary to say it, because no one will come to ask about my grandfather, not even Agucho, who spends more and more time searching farther and farther for skeletons among the frog ponds in the marsh. And if the day comes when my mother no longer has to say "the maestro is not at home" and my sister continues to talk by herself with the snakes and my grandfather stays imprisoned in my head and neither the dogs nor the fish remember him, I hope it will be said that my grandfather Ramon chose to die, that he didn't want to leave the other side, that he definitely didn't want to return to us anymore. And I, the only one who can understand him, I am the only one who will know that my grandfather Ramon decided to remain on the other side, crouching forever at the back of things …

*—Translated from the Spanish*
*by Gilbert Alter-Gilbert*

# The New Accelerator

*H. G. Wells*

CERTAINLY, IF EVER a man found a guinea when he was looking for a pin it is my good friend Professor Gibberne. I have heard before of investigators overshooting the mark, but never quite to the extent that he has done. He has really, this time at any rate, without any touch of exaggeration in the phrase, found something to revolutionise human life. And that when he was simply seeking an all-round nervous stimulant to bring languid people up to the stresses of these pushful days. I have tasted the stuff now several times, and I cannot do better than describe the effect the thing had on me. That there are astonishing experiences in store for all in search of new sensations will become apparent enough.

Professor Gibberne, as many people know, is my neighbour in Folkestone. Unless my memory plays me a trick, his portrait at various ages has already appeared in The Strand Magazine—I think late in 1899; but I am unable to look it up because I have lent that volume to someone who has never sent it back. The reader may, perhaps, recall the high forehead and the singularly long black eyebrows that give such a Mephistophelian touch to his face. He occupies one of those pleasant detached houses in the mixed style that make the western end of the Upper Sandgate Road so interesting. His is the one with the Flemish gables and the Moorish portico, and it is in the room with the mullioned bay window that he works when he is down here, and in which of an evening we have so often smoked and talked together. He is a mighty jester, but, besides, he likes to talk to me about his work; he is one of those men who find a help and stimulus in talking, and so I have been able to follow the conception of the New Accelerator right up from a very early stage. Of course, the greater portion of his experimental work is not done in Folkestone, but in Gower Street, in the fine new laboratory next to the hospital that he has been the first to use.

As everyone knows, or at least as all intelligent people know, the special department in which Gibberne has gained so great and deserved a reputation among physiologists is the action of drugs upon the nervous system. Upon soporifics, sedatives, and anæsthetics he is, I am told, unequalled. He is also a chemist of considerable eminence, and I suppose in the subtle and complex jungle of riddles that centres about the ganglion cell and the axis fibre there are little cleared places of his making, glades of illumination, that, until he sees fit to publish his results, are inaccessible to every other living man. And in the last few years he has been particularly assiduous upon this question of nervous stimulants, and already, before the discovery of the New Accelerator, very successful with them. Medical science has to thank him for at least three distinct and absolutely safe invigorators of unrivaled value to practising men. In cases of exhaustion the preparation known as Gibberne's

B Syrup has, I suppose, saved more lives already than any lifeboat round the coast.

"But none of these things begins to satisfy me yet," he told me nearly a year ago. "Either they increase the central energy without affecting the nerves or they simply increase the available energy by lowering the nervous conductivity; and all of them are unequal and local in their operation. One wakes up the heart and viscera and leaves the brain stupefied, one gets at the brain champagne fashion and does nothing good for the solar plexus, and what I want—and what, if it's an earthly possibility, I mean to have—is a stimulant that stimulates all round, that wakes you up for a time from the crown of your head to the tip of your great toe, and makes you go two—or even three to everybody else's one. Eh? That's the thing I'm after."

"It would tire a man," I said.

"Not a doubt of it. And you'd eat double or treble—and all that. But just think what the thing would mean. Imagine yourself with a little phial like this"—he held up a bottle of green glass and marked his points with it—"and in this precious phial is the power to think twice as fast, move twice as quickly, do twice as much work in a given time as you could otherwise do."

"But is such a thing possible?"

"I believe so. If it isn't, I've wasted my time for a year. These various preparations of the hypophosphites, for example, seem to show that something of the sort....Even if it was only one and a half times as fast it would do."

"It would do," I said.

"If you were a statesman in a corner, for example, time rushing up against you, something urgent to be done, eh?"

"He could dose his private secretary," I said.

"And gain—double time. And think if you, for example, wanted to finish a book."

"Usually," I said, "I wish I'd never begun 'em."

"Or a doctor, driven to death, wants to sit down and think out a case. Or a barrister—or a man cramming for an examination."

"Worth a guinea a drop," said I, "and more—to men like that."

"And in a duel again," said Gibberne, "where it all depends on your quickness in pulling the trigger."

"Or in fencing," I echoed.

"You see," said Gibberne, "if I get it as an all-round thing it will really do you no harm at all—except perhaps to an infinitesimal degree it brings you nearer old age. You will just have lived twice to other people's once ..."

"I suppose," I meditated, "in a duel—it would be fair?"

"That's a question for the seconds," said Gibberne;

I harked back further. "And you really think such a thing is possible?" I said.

"As possible," said Gibberne, and glanced at something that went throbbing by the window, "as a motorbus. As a matter of fact—"

He paused and smiled at me deeply, and tapped slowly on the edge of his desk with the green phial. "I think I know the stuff.... Already I've got something coming." The nervous smile upon his face betrayed the gravity of his revelation. He rarely talked of his actual experimental work unless things were very near the end. "And it may be—I shouldn't be surprised—it may even do the thing at a greater rate than twice."

"It will be rather a big thing," I hazarded.

"It will be, I think, rather a big thing."

But I don't think he quite knew what a big thing it was to be, for all that.

I remember we had several subsequent talks about the stuff. "The New Accelerator" he called it, and his tone about it grew more confident on each occasion. Sometimes he talked nervously of unexpected physiological results its use might have, and then he would get a bit unhappy; at others he was frankly mercenary, and we debated long and anxiously how the preparation might be turned to commercial account. "It's a good thing," said Gibberne, "a tremendous thing. I know I'm giving the world something, and I think it only reasonable we should expect the world to pay. The dignity of science is all very well, but I think somehow I must have the monopoly of the stuff for, say, ten years. I don't see why all the fun in life should go to the dealers in ham."

My own interest in the coming drug certainly did not wane in the time. I have always had a queer twist towards metaphysics in my mind. I have always been given to paradoxes about space and time, and it seemed to me that Gibberne was really preparing no less than the absolute acceleration of life. Suppose a man repeatedly dosed with such a preparation: he would live an active and record life indeed, but he would be an adult at eleven, middle-aged at twenty-five, and by thirty well on the road to senile decay.

It seemed to me that so far Gibberne was only going to do for anyone who took his drug exactly what Nature has done for the Jews and Orientals, who are men in their teens and aged by fifty, and quicker in thought and act than we are all the time. The marvel of drugs has always been great to my mind; you can madden a man, calm a man, make him incredibly strong and alert or a helpless log, quicken this passion and allay that, all by means of drugs, and here was a new miracle to be added to this strange armoury of phials the doctors use! But Gibberne was far too eager upon his technical points to enter very keenly into my aspect of the question.

It was the 7th or 8th of August, when he told me the distillation that would decide his failure or success for a time was going forward as we talked, and it was on the 10th that he told me the thing was done and the New Accelerator a tangible reality in the world. I met him as I was going up the Sandgate Hill towards Folkestone—I think I was going to get my hair cut; and he came hurrying down to meet me—I suppose he was coming to my house to tell me at once of his success. I remember that his eyes were unusually bright and his face flushed, and I noted even then the swift alacrity of his step. "It's done," he cried, and gripped my hand, speaking very fast; "it's more than done. Come up to my house and see."

"Really?"

"Really!" he shouted. "Incredibly! Come up and see!"

"And it does—twice!"

"It does more, much more. It scares me. Come up and see the stuff. Taste it! Try it! It's the most amazing stuff on earth!" He gripped my arm and, walking at such a pace that he forced me into a trot, went shouting with me up the hill. A whole charabancful of people turned and stared at us in unison after the manner of people in charabancs. It was one of those hot, clear days that Folkestone sees so much of, every color incredibly bright and every outline hard. There was a breeze, of course, but not so much breeze as sufficed under these conditions to keep me cool and dry. I panted for mercy.

"I'm not walking fast, am I?" cried Gibberne, and slackened his pace to a quick march.

"You've been taking some of this stuff," I puffed.

"No," he said. "At the utmost a drop of water that stood in a beaker from which I had washed out the last traces of the stuff. I took some last night, you know. But that is ancient history now."

"And it goes twice?" I said, nearing his doorway in a grateful perspiration. "It goes a thousand times, many thousand times!" cried Gibberne, with a dramatic gesture, flinging open his Early English carved oak gate.

"Phew!" said I, and followed him to the door.

"I don't know how many times it goes," he said, with his latch-key in his hand.

"And you—"

"It throws all sorts of light on nervous physiology, it kicks the theory of vision into a perfectly new shape!... Heaven knows how many thousand times. We'll try all that after—The thing is to try the stuff now."

"Try the stuff?" I said, as we went along the passage.

"Rather," said Gibberne, turning on me in his study. "There it is in that little green phial there! Unless you happen to be afraid?"

I am a careful man by nature, and only theoretically adventurous. I was afraid. But on the other hand there is pride.

"Well," I haggled. "You say you've tried it?"

"I've tried it," he said, "and I don't look hurt by it, do I? I don't even look livery and I feel—"

I sat down. "Give me the potion," I said. "If the worst comes to the worst it will save having my hair cut, and that I think is one of the most hateful duties of a civilised man. How do you take the mixture?"

"With water," said Gibberne, whacking down a carafe.

He stood up in front of his desk and regarded me in his easy chair; his manner was suddenly affected by a touch of the Harley Street specialist. "It's rum stuff, you know," he said.

I made a gesture with my hand.

"I must warn you in the first place as soon as you've got it put down to shut your eyes, and open them very cautiously in a minute or so's time. One still sees. The sense of vision is a question of length of vibration, and not of multitude of impacts; but there's a kind of shock to the retina, a nasty giddy confusion just at the time if the eyes are open. Keep 'em shut."

"Shut," I said. "Good!"

"And the next thing is, keep still. Don't begin to whack about. You may fetch something a nasty rap if you do. Remember you will be going several thousand times faster than you ever did before, heart, lungs, muscles, brain—everything—and you will hit hard without knowing it. You won't know it, you know. You'll feel just as you do now. Only everything in the world will seem to be going ever so many thousand times slower than it ever went before. That's what makes it so deuced queer."

"Lor'," I said. "And you mean—"

"You'll see," said he, and took up a measure. He glanced at the material on his desk. "Glasses," he said, "water. All here. Mustn't take too much for the first attempt."

The little phial glucked out its precious contents. "Don't forget what I told you," he said, turning the contents of the measure into a glass in the manner of an Italian waiter measuring whisky. "Sit with the eyes tightly shut and in absolute stillness for two minutes," he said. "Then you will hear me speak."

He added an inch or so of water to the dose in each glass.

"By-the-bye," he said, "don't put your glass down. Keep it in your hand and rest your hand on your knee. Yes—so. And now—"

He raised his glass.

"The New Accelerator," I said.

"The New Accelerator," he answered, and we touched glasses and drank, and instantly I closed my eyes.

You know that blank non-existence into which one drops when one has taken "gas." For an indefinite interval it was like that. Then I heard Gibberne telling me to wake up, and I stirred and opened my eyes. There he stood as he had been standing, glass still in hand. It was empty, that was all the difference.

"Well?," said I.

"Nothing out of the way?"

"Nothing. A slight feeling of exhilaration, perhaps. Nothing more."

"Sounds?"

"Things are still," I said. "By Jove! yes! They are still. Except the sort of faint pat, patter, like rain falling on different things. What is it?"

"Analysed sounds," I think he said, but I am not sure. He glanced at the window. "Have you ever seen a curtain before a window fixed in that way before?"

I followed his eyes, and there was the end of the curtain, frozen, as it were, corner high, in the act of flapping briskly in the breeze.

"No," said I; "that's odd."

"And here," he said, and opened the hand that held the glass. Naturally I winced, expecting the glass to smash. But so far from smashing it did not even seem to stir; it hung in mid-air—motionless. "Roughly speaking," said Gibberne, "an object in these latitudes falls 16 feet in the first second. This glass is falling 16 feet in a second now. Only, you see, it hasn't been falling yet for the hundredth part of a second. That gives you some idea of the pace of my Accelerator." And he waved his hand round and round, over and under the slowly sinking glass. Finally he took it by the bottom, pulled it down and placed it very carefully on the table. "Eh?" he said to me, and laughed.

"That seems all right," I said, and began very gingerly to raise myself from my chair. I felt perfectly well, very light and comfortable, and quite confident in my mind. I was going fast all over. My heart, for example, was beating a thousand times a second, but that caused me no discomfort at all. I looked out of the window. An immovable cyclist, head down and with a frozen puff of dust behind his driving-wheel, scorched to overtake a galloping char-à-banc that did not stir. I gaped in amazement at this incredible spectacle. "Gibberne," I cried, "how long will this confounded stuff last?"

"Heaven knows!" he answered. "Last time I took it, I went to bed and slept it off. I tell you, I was frightened. It must have lasted some minutes, I think—it seemed like hours. But after a bit it slows down rather suddenly, I believe."

I was proud to observe that I did not feel frightened—I suppose because there were two of us. "Why shouldn't we go out?" I asked.

"Why not?"

"They'll see us."

"Not they. Goodness, no! Why, we shall be going a thousand times faster than the quickest conjuring trick that was ever done. Come along! Which way shall we go? Window or door?"

And out by the window we went.

Assuredly of all the strange experiences that I have ever had, or imagined, or read of other people having or imagining, that little raid I made with Gibberne on the Folkestone Leas, under the influence of the New Accelerator, was the strangest and maddest of all. We went out by his gate into the road, and there we made a minute examination of the statuesque passing traffic. The tops of the wheels and some of the legs of the horses of this char-à-banc, the end of the whip-lash and the lower jaw of the conductor—who was just beginning to yawn—were perceptibly in motion, but all the rest of the lumbering conveyance seemed still. And quite noiseless except for a faint rattling that came from one man's throat! And as parts of this frozen edifice there were a driver, you know, and a conductor, and eleven people! The effect as we walked about the thing began by being madly queer and ended by being—disagreeable. There they were, people like ourselves and yet not like ourselves, frozen in careless attitudes, caught in mid-gesture. A girl and a man smiled at one another, a leering smile that threatened to last forevermore; a woman in a floppy capelline rested her arm on the rail and stared at Gibberne's house with the unwinking stare of eternity; a man stroked his mustache like a figure of wax, and another stretched a tiresome stiff hand with extended fingers towards his loosened hat. We stared at them, we laughed at them, we made faces at them, and then a sort of disgust of them came upon us, and we turned away and walked round in front of the cyclist towards the Leas.

"Goodness!" cried Gibberne, suddenly; "look there!"

He pointed, and there at the tip of his finger and sliding down the air with wings flapping slowly and at the speed of an exceptionally languid snail—was a bee.

And so we came out upon the Leas. There the thing seemed madder than ever. The band was playing in the upper stand, though all the sound it made for us was a low-pitched, wheezy rattle, a sort of prolonged last sigh that passed at times into a sound like the slow, muffled ricking of some monstrous clock. Frozen people stood erect; strange, silent, self-conscious-looking dummies hung unstably in mid-stride, promenading upon the grass. I passed close to a poodle dog suspended in the act of leaping, and watched the slow movement of his legs as he sank to earth. "Lord, look here!" cried Gibberne, and we halted for a moment before a magnificent person in white faint-striped flannels, white shoes, and a Panama hat, who turned back to wink at two gaily-dressed ladies he had passed. A wink, studied with such leisurely deliberation as we could afford, is an unattractive thing. It loses any quality of alert gaiety, and one remarks that the winking eye does not completely close, that under its drooping lid appears the lower edge of an eyeball and a line of white. "Heaven give me memory," said I, "and I will never wink again."

"Or smile," said Gibberne, with his eye on the lady's answering teeth.

"It's infernally hot, somehow," said I. "Let's go slower."

"Oh, come along!" said Gibberne.

We picked our way among the Bath chairs in the path. Many of the people sitting in the chairs seemed almost natural in their passive poses, but the contorted scarlet of the bandsmen was not a restful thing to see. A purple-faced gentleman was frozen in the midst of a violent struggle to refold his newspaper against the wind; there were many evidences that all these people in their sluggish way were exposed to a considerable breeze, a breeze that had no existence so far as our sensations went. We came out and walked a little way from the crowd, and turned and regarded it. To see all that multitude changed to a picture, smitten rigid, as it were, into the semblance of realistic wax, was impossibly wonderful. It was absurd, of course; but it filled me with an irrational, an exultant sense of superior advantage. Consider the wonder of it! All that I had said and thought and done since the stuff had begun to work in my veins had happened, so far as those people, so far as the world in general went, in the twinkling of an eye. "The New Accelerator—," I began, but Gibberne interrupted me.

"There's that infernal old woman!" he said.

"What old woman?"

"Lives next door to me," said Gibberne. "Has a lapdog that yaps. Gods! The temptation is strong!"

There is something very boyish and impulsive about Gibberne at times. Before I could expostulate with him he had dashed forward, snatched the unfortunate animal out of visible existence, and was running violently with it towards the cliff of the Leas. It was most extraordinary. The little brute, you know, didn't bark or wriggle or make the slightest sign of vitality. It kept quite stiffly in an attitude of somnolent repose, and Gibberne held it by the neck. It was like running about with a dog of wood. "Gibberne," I cried, "put it down!" Then I said something else. "If you run like that, Gibberne," I cried, "you'll set your clothes on fire. Your linen trousers are going brown as it is!"

He clapped his hand on his thigh and stood hesitating on the verge. "Gibberne," I cried, coming up, "put it down. This heat is too much! It's our running so! Two or three miles a second! Friction of the air!"

"What?" he said, glancing at the dog.

"Friction of the air," I shouted. "Friction of the air. Going too fast. Like meteorites and things. Too hot. And, Gibberne! Gibberne! I'm all over pricking and a sort of perspiration. You can see people stirring slightly. I believe the stuff's working off! Put that dog down."

"Eh?" he said.

"It's working off," I repeated. "We're too hot and the stuff's working off! I'm wet through."

He stared at me. Then at the band, the wheezy rattle of whose performance was certainly going faster. Then with a tremendous sweep of the arm he hurled the dog away from him and it went spinning upward, still inanimate, and hung at last over the grouped parasols of a knot of chattering people. Gibberne was gripping my elbow. "By Jove!" he cried. "I believe it is! A sort of hot pricking and—yes. That man's moving his pocket-handkerchief! Perceptibly. We must get out of this sharp."

But we could not get out of it sharply enough. Luckily, perhaps! For we might have run, and if we had run we should, I believe, have burst into flames. Almost certainly we should have burst into flames! You know we had neither of us thought of that.... But before we could even begin to run the action of the drug had ceased. It was the business of a minute fraction of a second. The effect of the New Accelerator passed like the drawing of a curtain, vanished in the movement of a hand. I heard Gibberne's voice in infinite alarm. "Sit down," he said, and flop, down upon the turf at the edge of the Leas I sat—scorching as I sat. There is a patch of burnt grass there still where I sat down. The whole stagnation seemed to wake up as I did so, the disarticulated vibration of the band rushed together into a blast of music, the promenaders put their feet down and walked their ways, the papers and flags began flapping, smiles passed into words, the winker finished his wink and went on his way complacently, and all the seated people moved and spoke.

The whole world had come alive again, was going as fast as we were, or rather we were going no faster than the rest of the world. It was like slowing down as one comes into a railway station. Everything seemed to spin round for a second or two, I had the most transient feeling of nausea, and that was all. And the little dog which had seemed to hang for a moment when the force of Gibberne's arm was expended fell with a swift acceleration clean through a lady's parasol!

That was the saving of us. Unless it was for one corpulent old gentleman in a Bath chair, who certainly did start at the sight of us and afterwards regarded us at intervals with a darkly suspicious eye, and finally, I believe, said something to his nurse about us, I doubt if a solitary person remarked our sudden appearance among them. Plop! We must have appeared abruptly. We ceased to smolder almost at once, though the turf beneath me was uncomfortably hot. The attention of everyone—including even the Amusements Association band, which on this occasion, for the only time in its history, got out of tune—was arrested by the amazing fact, and the still more amazing yapping and uproar caused by the fact, that a respectable, over-fed lapdog sleeping quietly to the east of the bandstand should suddenly fall through the parasol of a lady on the west—in a slightly singed condition due to the extreme velocity of its movements through the air. In these absurd days, too, when we are all trying to be as psychic and silly and superstitious as possible! People got up and trod on other people, chairs were overturned, the Leas policeman ran. How the matter settled itself, I do not know—we were much too anxious to disentangle ourselves from the affair and get out of range of the eye of the old gentleman in the Bath chair to make minute inquiries. As soon as we were sufficiently cool and sufficiently recovered from our giddiness and nausea and confusion of mind to do so we stood up and, skirting the crowd, directed our steps back along the road below the Metropole towards Gibberne's house. But amidst the din I heard very distinctly the gentleman who had been sitting beside the lady of the ruptured sunshade using quite unjustifiable threats and language to one of those chair-attendants who have "Inspector" written on their caps. "If you didn't throw the dog," he said, "who did?"

The sudden return of movement and familiar noises, and our natural anxiety about ourselves (our clothes were still dreadfully hot, and the fronts of the thighs of Gibberne's white trousers were scorched a drabbish brown), prevented the minute observations I should have liked to make on all these things. Indeed, I really made no observations of any scientific value on that return. The bee, of course, had gone. I looked for that cyclist, but he was already out of sight as we came into the Upper Sandgate Road or hidden from us by traffic; the charabanc, however, with its people now all alive and stirring, was clattering along at a spanking pace almost abreast of the nearer church.

We noted, however, that the window-sill on which we had stepped in getting out of the house was slightly singed, and that the impressions of our feet on the gravel of the path were unusually deep.

So it was I had my first experience of the New Accelerator. Practically we had been running about and saying and doing all sorts of things in the space of a second or so of time. We had lived half an hour while the band had played, perhaps, two bars. But the effect it had upon us was that the whole world had stopped for our convenient inspection. Considering all things, and particularly considering our rashness in venturing out of the house, the experience might certainly have been much more disagreeable than it was. It showed, no doubt, that Gibberne has still much to learn before his preparation is a manageable convenience, but its practicability it certainly demonstrated beyond all cavil.

Since that adventure he has been steadily bringing its use under control, and I have several times, and without the slightest bad result, taken measured doses under his direction; though I must confess I have not yet ventured abroad again while under its influence. I may mention, for example, that this story has been written at one sitting and without interruption, except for the nibbling of some chocolate, by its means. I began at 6:25, and my watch is now very nearly at the minute past the half-hour. The convenience of securing a long, uninterrupted spell of work in the midst of a day full of engagements cannot be exaggerated. Gibberne is now working at the quantitative handling of his preparation, with especial reference to its distinctive effects upon different types of constitution. He then hopes to find a Retarder with which to dilute its present rather excessive potency. The Retarder will, of course, have the reverse effect to the Accelerator; used alone it should enable the patient to spread a few seconds over many hours of ordinary time, and so to maintain an apathetic inaction, a glacierlike absence, of alacrity, amidst the most animated or irritating surroundings. The two things together must necessarily work an entire revolution in civilised existence. It is the beginning of our escape from that Time Garment of which Carlyle speaks. While this Accelerator will enable us to concentrate ourselves with tremendous impact upon any moment or occasion that demands our utmost sense and vigour, the Retarder will enable us to pass in passive tranquillity through infinite hardship and tedium. Perhaps I am a little optimistic about the Retarder, which has indeed still to be discovered, but about the Accelerator there is no possible sort of doubt whatever. Its appearance upon the market in a convenient, controllable, and assimilable form is a matter of the next few months. It will be obtainable of all chemists and druggists, in small green bottles, at a high but, considering its extraordinary qualities, by no means excessive price. Gibberne's Nervous Accelerator it will be called, and he hopes to be able to supply it in three strengths: one in 200, one in 900, and one in 2000, distinguished by yellow, pink, and white labels respectively.

No doubt its use renders a great number of very extraordinary things possible; for, of course, the most remarkable and, possibly, even criminal proceedings may be effected with impunity by thus dodging, as it were, into the interstices of time. Like all potent preparations it will be liable to abuse. We have, however, discussed this aspect of the question very thoroughly, and we have decided that this is purely a matter of medical jurisprudence and altogether outside our province. We shall manufacture and sell the Accelerator, and, as for the consequences—we shall see.

# The Elixir of Life

*Nathaniel Hawthorne*

"Be secret!" and he kept his stern eye fixed upon him, as the coach began to move.

"Be secret," repeated the apothecary. "I know not any secret that he has confided to me thus far, and as for his nonsense (as I will be bold to style it now he is gone) about a medicine of long life, it is a thing I forget in spite of myself, so very empty and trashy it is. I wonder, by the by, that it never came into my head to give the Colonel a dose of the cordial whereof I partook last night. I have no faith that it is a valuable medicine—little or none—and yet there has been an unwonted briskness in me all the morning."

Then a simple joy broke over his face—a flickering sunbeam among his wrinkles—as he heard the laughter of the little girl, who was running rampant with a kitten in the kitchen.

"Pansie! Pansie!" cackled he, "grandpapa has sent away the ugly man now. Come, let us have a frolic in the garden."

And he whispered to himself again, "That is a cordial yonder, and I will take it according to the prescription, knowing all the ingredients." Then, after a moment's thought, he added, "All, save one."

So, as he had declared to himself his intention, that night, when little Pansie had long been asleep, and his small household was in bed, and most of the quiet, old-fashioned townsfolk likewise, this good apothecary went into his laboratory, and took out of a cupboard in the wall a certain ancient-looking bottle, which was cased over with a net-work of what seemed to be woven silver, like the wicker-woven bottles of our days. He had previously provided a goblet of pure water. Before opening the bottle, however, he seemed to hesitate, and pondered and babbled to himself; having long since come to that period of life when the bodily frame, having lost much of its value, is more tenderly cared for than when it was a perfect and inestimable machine.

"I triturated, I infused, I distilled it myself in these very rooms, and know it—know it all—all the ingredients," save one. They are common things enough—comfortable things—some of them a little queer—one or two that folks have a prejudice against—and then there is that one thing that I don't know. It is foolish in me to be dallying with such a mess, which I thought was a piece of quackery, while that strange visitor bade me do it—and yet, what a strength has come from it! He said it was a rare cordial, and, methinks, it has brightened up my weary life all day, so that Pansie has found me the fitter playmate. And then the dose—it is so absurdly small I will try it again."

He took the silver stopple from the bottle, and with a practised hand, tremulous as it was with age, so that one would have thought it must have shaken the liquor into a perfect shower of misapplied drops, he dropped—I have heard it said—only one single drop into the goblet of water.

It fell into it with a dazzling brightness, like a spark of ruby flame, and subtly diffusing itself through the whole body of water, turned it into a rosy hue of great brilliancy. He held it up between his eyes and the light, and seemed to admire and wonder at it.

"It is very odd," said he, "that such a pure, bright liquor should have come out of a parcel of weeds that mingled their juices here. The thing is a folly—it is one of those compositions in which the chemists—the cabalists, perhaps—used to combine what they thought the virtues of many plants, thinking that something would result in the whole, which was not in either of them, and a new efficacy be created. Whereas, it has been the teaching of my experience that one virtue counteracts another, and is the enemy of it. I never believed the former theory, even when that strange madman bade me do it. And what a thick, turbid matter it was, until that last ingredient—that powder which he put in with his own hand! Had he let me see it, I would first have analyzed it, and discovered its component parts. The man was mad, undoubtedly, and this may have been poison. But its effect is good. Poh! I will taste again, because of this weak, agued, miserable state of mine; though it is a shame in me, a man of decent skill in my way, to believe in a quack's nostrum. But it is a comfortable kind of thing."

Meantime, that single drop (for good Dr. Dolliver had immediately put a stopper into the bottle) diffused a sweet odor through the chamber, so that the ordinary fragrances and scents of apothecaries' stuff seemed to be controlled and influenced by it, and its bright potency also dispelled a certain dimness of the antiquated room.

The Doctor, at the pressure of a great need, had given incredible pains to the manufacture of this medicine; so that, reckoning the pains rather than the ingredients (all except one, of which he was not able to estimate the cost, nor value), it was really worth its weight in gold. And, as it happened, he had bestowed upon it the hard labor of his poor life, and the time that was necessary for the support of his family, without return; for the customers, after playing off this cruel joke upon the old man, had never come back; and now, for seven years, the bottle had stood in a corner of the cupboard. To be sure, the silver-cased bottle was worth a trifle for its silver, and still more, perhaps, as an antiquarian knickknack. But, all things considered, the honest and simple apothecary thought that he might make free with the liquid to such small extent as was necessary for himself. And there had been something in the concoction that had struck him; and he had been fast breaking lately, and so, in the dreary fantasy and lonely recklessness of his old age, he had suddenly bethought himself of this medicine (cordial—as the strange man called it, which had come to him by long inheritance in his family) and he had determined to try it. And again, as the night before, he took out the receipt—a roll of antique parchment, out of which, provokingly, one fold had been lost—and put on his spectacles to puzzle out the passage.

Guttam unicam in aquam puram, two gills. "If the Colonel should hear of this," said Dr. Dolliver, "he might fancy it his nostrum of long life, and insist on having the bottle for his own use. The foolish, fierce old gentleman! He has grown very earthly, of late, else he would not desire such a thing. And a strong desire it must be to make him feel it desirable. For my part, I only wish for something that, for a short time, may clear my eyes, so that I may see little Pansie's beauty, and quicken my ears, that I may hear her sweet voice, and give me nerve, while God keeps me here, that I may live longer to earn bread for dear Pansie. She provided for, I would gladly lie down yonder with Bessie and our children. Ah! the vanity of desiring lengthened days!—There!—I have drunk it, and methinks its final, subtle flavor hath strange potency in it."

The old man shivered a little, as those shiver who have just swallowed good liquor, while it is permeating their vitals. Yet he seemed to be in a pleasant state of feeling, and, as was frequently the case with this simple soul, in a devout frame of mind. He read a chapter in the Bible, and said his prayers for Pansie and himself, before he went to bed, and had much better sleep than usually comes to people of his advanced age; for, at that period, sleep is diffused through their wakefulness, and a dim and tiresome half-perception through their sleep, so that the only result is weariness.

Nothing very extraordinary happened to Dr. Dolliver or his small household for some time afterwards. He was favored with a comfortable winter, and thanked Heaven for it, and put it to a good use (at least he intended it so) by concocting drugs; which perhaps did a little towards peopling the graveyard, into which his windows looked; but that was neither his purpose nor his fault. None of the sleepers, at all events, interrupted their slumbers to upbraid him. He had done according to his own artless conscience and the recipes of licensed physicians, and he looked no further, but pounded, triturated, infused, made electuaries, boluses, juleps, or whatever he termed his productions, with skill and diligence, thanking Heaven that he was spared to do so, when his contemporaries generally were getting incapable of similar efforts. It struck him with some surprise, but much gratitude to Providence, that his sight seemed to be growing rather better than worse. He certainly could read the crabbed handwriting and hieroglyphics of the physicians with more readiness than he could a year earlier. But he had been originally near-sighted, with large, projecting eyes; and nearsighted eyes always seem to get a new lease of light as the years go on. One thing was perceptible about the Doctor's eyes, not only to himself in the glass, but to everybody else; namely, that they had an unaccustomed gleaming brightness in them; not so very bright either, but yet so much so, that little Pansie noticed it, and sometimes, in her playful, roguish way, climbed up into his lap, and put both her small palms over them; telling Grandpapa that he had stolen somebody else's eyes, and given away his own, and that she liked his old ones better. The poor old Doctor did his best to smile through his eyes, and so to reconcile Pansie to their brightness: but still she continually made the same silly remonstrance, so that he was fain to put on a pair of green spectacles when he was going to play with Pansie, or took her on his knee. Nay, if he looked at her, as had always been his custom, after she was asleep, in order to see that all was well with her, the little child would put up her hands, as if he held a light that was flashing on her eyeballs; and unless he turned away his gaze quickly, she would wake up in a fit of crying.

On the whole, the apothecary had as comfortable a time as a man of his years could expect. The air of the house and of the old graveyard seemed to suit him. What so seldom happens in man's advancing age, his night's rest did him good, whereas, generally, an old man wakes up ten times as nervous and dispirited as he went to bed, just as if, during his sleep he had been working harder than ever he did in the daytime. It had been so with the Doctor himself till within a few months. To be sure, he had latterly begun to practise various rules of diet and exercise, which commended themselves to his approbation. He sawed some of his own fire-wood, and fancied that, as was reasonable, it fatigued him less day by day. He took walks with Pansie, and though, of course, her little footsteps, treading on the elastic air of childhood, far outstripped his own, still the old man knew that he was not beyond the recuperative period of life, and that exercise out of doors and proper food can do somewhat towards retarding the approach of age. He was inclined, also, to impute much good effect to a daily dose of Santa Cruz rum (a liquor much in vogue in that day), which he was now in the habit of quaffing at the meridian hour. All through the Doctor's life he had eschewed strong spirits: "But after seventy," quoth old Dr. Dolliver, "a man is all the better in head and stomach for a little stimulus"; and it certainly seemed so in his case. Likewise, I know not precisely how often, but complying punctiliously with the recipe, as an apothecary naturally would, he took his drop of the mysterious cordial.

He was inclined, however, to impute little or no efficacy to this, and to laugh at himself for having ever thought otherwise. The dose was so very minute! and he had never been sensible of any remarkable effect on taking it, after all. A genial warmth, he sometimes fancied, diffused itself throughout him, and perhaps continued during the next day. A quiet and refreshing night's rest followed, and alacritous waking in the morning; but all this was far more probably owing, as has been already hinted, to excellent and well-considered habits of diet and exercise. Nevertheless he still continued the cordial with tolerable regularity—the more, because on one or two occasions, happening to omit it, it so chanced that he slept wretchedly, and awoke in strange aches and pains, torpors, nervousness, shaking of the hands, blearedness of sight, lowness of spirits and other ills, as is the misfortune of some old men—who are often threatened by a thousand evil symptoms that come to nothing, foreboding no particular disorder, and passing away as unsatisfactorily as they come. At another time, he took two or three drops at once, and was alarmingly feverish in consequence. Yet it was very true, that the feverish symptoms were pretty sure to disappear on his renewal of the medicine. "Still it could not be that," thought the old man, a hater of empiricism (in which, however, is contained all hope for man), and disinclined to believe in anything that was not according to rule and art. And then, as aforesaid, the dose was so ridiculously small!

Sometimes, however, he took, half laughingly, another view of it, and felt disposed to think that chance might really have thrown in his way a very remarkable mixture, by which, if it had happened to him earlier in life, he might have amassed a larger fortune, and might even have raked together such a competency as would have prevented his feeling much uneasiness about the future of little Pansie. Feeling as strong as he did nowadays, he might reasonably count upon ten more years of life, and in that time the precious liquor might be exchanged for much gold. "Let us see!" quoth he, "by what attractive name shall it be advertised? 'The old man's cordial?' That promises too little. Poh, poh! I would stain my honesty, my fair reputation, the accumulation of a lifetime, and befool my neighbor and the public, by any name that would make them imagine I had found that ridiculous talisman that the alchemists have sought. The old man's cordial—that is best. And five shillings sterling the bottle. That surely were not too costly, and would give the medicine a better reputation and higher vogue (so foolish is the world) than if I were to put it lower. I will think further of this. But pshaw, pshaw!"

"What is the matter, Grandpapa," said little Pansie, who had stood by him, wishing to speak to him at least a minute, but had been deterred by his absorption; "why do you say 'Pshaw'?"

"Pshaw!" repeated Grandpa, "there is one ingredient that I don't know."

So this very helpful design was necessarily given up, but that it had occurred to Dr. Dolliver was perhaps a token that his mind was in a very vigorous state; for it had been noted of him through life, that he had little enterprise, little activity, and that, for the want of these things, his very considerable skill in his art had been almost thrown away, as regarded his private affairs, when it might easily have led him to fortune. Whereas, here in his extreme age, he had first bethought himself of a way to grow rich. Sometimes this latter spring causes—as blossoms come on the autumnal tree—a spurt of vigor, or untimely greenness, when Nature laughs at her old child, half in kindness and half in scorn. It is observable, however, I fancy, that after such a spurt, age comes on with redoubled speed, and that the old man has only run forward with a show of force, in order to fall into his grave the sooner.

Sometimes, as he was walking briskly along the street, with little Pansie clasping his hand, and perhaps frisking rather more than became a person of his venerable years, he had met the grim old wreck of Colonel Dabney, moving goutily, and gathering wrath anew with every touch of his painful foot to the ground; or driving by in his carriage, showing an ashen, angry, wrinkled face at the window, and frowning at him—the apothecary thought—with a peculiar fury, as if he took umbrage at his audacity in being less broken by age than a gentleman like himself. The apothecary could not help feeling as if there were some unsettled quarrel or dispute between himself and the Colonel, he could not tell what or why. The Colonel always gave him a haughty nod of half-recognition; and the people in the street, to whom he was a familiar object, would say, "The worshipful Colonel begins to find himself mortal like the rest of us. He feels his years." "He'd be glad, I warrant," said one, "to change with you, Doctor. It shows what difference a good life makes in men, to look at him and you. You are half a score of years his elder, methinks, and yet look what temperance can do for a man. By my credit, neighbor, seeing how brisk you have been lately, I told my wife you seemed to be growing younger. It does me good to see it. We are about of an age, I think, and I like to notice how we old men keep young and keep one another in heart. I myself—ahem—ahem—feel younger this season than for these five years past."

"It rejoices me that you feel so," quoth the apothecary, who had just been thinking that this neighbor of his had lost a great deal, both in mind and body, within a short period, and rather scorned him for it. "Indeed, I find old age less uncomfortable than I supposed. Little Pansie and I make excellent companions for one another."

And then, dragged along by Pansie's little hand, and also impelled by a certain alacrity that rose with him in the morning, and lasted till his healthy rest at night, he bade farewell to his contemporary, and hastened on; while the latter, left behind, was somewhat irritated as he looked at the vigorous movement of the apothecary's legs.

"He need not make such a show of briskness neither," muttered he to himself. "This touch of rheumatism troubles me a bit just now, but try it on a good day, and I'd walk with him for a shilling. Pshaw! I'll walk to his funeral yet."

One day, while the Doctor, with the activity that bestirred itself in him nowadays, was mixing and manufacturing certain medicaments that came in frequent demand, a carriage stopped at his door, and he recognized the voice of Colonel Dabney, talking in his customary stern tone to the woman who served him. And, a moment afterwards, the coach drove away, and he actually heard the old dignitary lumbering up stairs, and bestowing a curse upon each particular step, as if that were the method to make them soften and become easier when he should come down again. "Pray, your worship," said the Doctor from above, "let me attend you below stairs."

"No," growled the Colonel, "I'll meet you on your own ground. I can climb a stair yet, and be hanged to you."

So saying, he painfully finished the ascent, and came into the laboratory, where he let himself fall into the Doctor's easy-chair, with an anathema on the chair, the Doctor, and himself; and, staring round through the dusk, he met the wide-open, startled eyes of little Pansie, who had been reading a gilt picture-book in the corner.

"Send away that child, Dolliver," cried the Colonel, angrily. "Confound her, she makes my bones ache. I hate everything young."

"Lord, Colonel," the poor apothecary ventured to say, "there must be young people in the world as well as old ones. 'Tis my mind, a man's grandchildren keep him warm round about him."

"I have none, and want none," sharply responded the Colonel; "and as for young people, let me be one of them, and they may exist, otherwise not. It is a cursed bad arrangement of the world, that there are young and old here together."

When Pansie had gone away, which she did with anything but reluctance, having a natural antipathy to this monster of a Colonel, the latter personage tapped with his crutch-handled cane on a chair that stood near, and nodded in an authoritative way to the apothecary to sit down in it. Dr. Dolliver complied submissively, and the

Colonel, with dull, unkindly eyes, looked at him sternly, and with a kind of intelligence amid the aged stolidity of his aspect, that somewhat puzzled the Doctor. In this way he surveyed him all over, like a judge, when he means to hang a man, and for some reason or none, the apothecary felt his nerves shake, beneath this steadfast look.

"Aha! Doctor!" said the Colonel at last, with a doltish sneer, "you bear your years well."

"Decently well, Colonel; I thank Providence for it," answered the meek apothecary.

"I should say," quoth the Colonel, "you are younger at this moment than when we spoke together two or three years ago. I noted then that your eyebrows were a handsome snow-white, such as befits a man who has passed beyond his threescore years and ten, and five years more. Why, they are getting dark again, Mr. Apothecary."

"Nay, your worship must needs be mistaken there," said the Doctor, with a timorous chuckle. "It is many a year since I have taken a deliberate note of my wretched old visage in a glass, but I remember they were white when I looked last."

"Come, Doctor, I know a thing or two," said the Colonel, with a bitter scoff; "and what's this, you old rogue? Why, you've rubbed away a wrinkle since we met. Take off those infernal spectacles, and look me in the face. Ha! I see the devil in your eye. How dare you let it shine upon me so?"

"On my conscience, Colonel," said the apothecary, strangely struck with the coincidence of this accusation with little Pansie's complaint, 'I know not what you mean. My sight is pretty well for a man of my age. We near-sighted people begin to know our best eyesight, when other people have lost theirs."

"Ah! ah! old rogue," repeated the insufferable Colonel, gnashing his ruined teeth at him, as if, for some incomprehensible reason, he wished to tear him to pieces and devour him. "I know you. You are taking the life away from me, villain! and I told you it was my inheritance. And I told you there was a Bloody Footstep, bearing its track down through my race."

"I remember nothing of it," said the Doctor, in a quake, sure that the Colonel was in one of his mad fits. "And on the word of an honest man, I never wronged you in my life, Colonel."

"We shall see," said the Colonel, whose wrinkled visage grew absolutely terrible with its hardness; and his dull eyes, without losing their dullness, seemed to look through him.

"Listen to me, sir. Some ten years ago, there came to you a man on a secret business. He had an old musty bit of parchment, on which were written some words, hardly legible, in an antique hand—an old deed, it might have been—some family document, and here and there the letters were faded away. But this man had spent his life over it, and he had made out the meaning, and he interpreted it to you, and left it with you, only there was one gap—one torn or obliterated place. Well, sir—and he bade you, with your poor little skill at the mortar, and for a certain sum—ample repayment for such a service—to manufacture this medicine—this cordial. It was an affair of months. And just when you thought it finished, the man came again, and stood over your cursed beverage, and shook a powder, or dropped a lump into it, or put in some ingredient, in which was all the hidden virtue—or, at least, it drew out all the hidden virtue of the mean and common herbs, and married them into a wondrous efficacy. This done, the man bade you do certain other things with the potation, and went away"—the Colonel hesitated a moment—"and never came back again."

"Surely, Colonel, you are correct," said the apothecary; much startled, however, at the Colonel's showing himself so well acquainted with an incident which he had supposed a secret with himself alone. Yet he had a little reluctance in owning it, although he did not exactly understand why, since the Colonel had, apparently, no rightful claim to it, at all events.

"That medicine, that receipt," continued his visitor, "is my hereditary property, and I challenge you, on your peril, to give it up."

"But what if the original owner should call upon me for it," objected Dr. Dolliver.

"I'll warrant you against that," said the Colonel, and the apothecary thought there was something ghastly in his look and tone. "Why, 'tis ten year, you old fool; and do you think a man with a treasure like that in his possession would have waited so long?"

"Seven years it was ago," said the apothecary, "Septem annis passatis: so says the Latin."

"Curse your Latin," answers the Colonel. "Produce the stuff. You have been violating the first rule of your trade—taking your own drugs—your own, in one sense; mine by the right of three hundred years. Bring it forth, I say!"

"Pray excuse me, worthy Colonel," pleaded the apothecary; for though convinced that the old gentleman was only in one of his insane fits, when he talked of the value of this concoction, yet he really did not like to give up the cordial, which perhaps had wrought him some benefit. Besides, he had at least a claim upon it for much trouble and skill expended in its composition. This he suggested to the Colonel, who scornfully took out of his pocket a net-work purse, with more golden guineas in it than the apothecary had seen in the whole seven years, and was rude enough to fling it in his face. "Take that," thundered he, "and give up the thing, or I will have you in prison before you are an hour older. Nay," he continued, growing pale, which was his mode of showing terrible wrath; since all through life, till extreme age quenched it, his ordinary face had been a blazing red, "I'll put you to death, you villain, as I've a right!" And thrusting his hand into his waistcoat-pocket, the madman took a small pistol from it, which he cocked, and presented at the poor apothecary. The old fellow quaked and cowered in his chair, and would indeed have given his whole shopful of better concocted medicines than this, to be out of this danger. Besides, there were the guineas; the Colonel had paid him a princely sum for what was probably worth nothing.

"Hold! hold!" cried he as the Colonel, with stern eye pointed the pistol at his head. "You shall have it."

So he rose all trembling, and crept to that secret cupboard, where the precious bottle—since precious it seemed to be—was reposited. In all his life, long as it had been, the apothecary had never before been threatened by a deadly weapon; though many as deadly a thing had he seen poured into a glass, without winking. And so it seemed to take his heart and life away, and he brought the cordial forth feebly, and stood tremulously before the Colonel, ashy pale, and looking ten years older than his real age, instead of five years younger, as he had seemed just before this disastrous interview with the Colonel.

"You look as if you needed a drop of it yourself," said Colonel Dabney, with a great scorn. "But not a drop shall you have. Already have you stolen too much;" said he, lifting up the bottle, and marking the space to which the liquor had subsided in it in consequence of the minute doses with which the apothecary had made free. "Fool, had you taken your glass like a man, you might have been young again. Now, creep on, the few months you have left, poor, torpid knave, and die! Come—a goblet! quick!"

He clutched the bottle meanwhile voraciously, miserly, eagerly, furiously, as if it were his life that he held in his grasp; angry, impatient, as if something long sought were within his reach, and not yet secure—with longing thirst and desire; suspicious of the world and of fate; feeling as if an iron hand were over him, and a crowd of violent robbers round about him, struggling for it. At last, unable to wait longer, just as the apothecary was tottering away in quest of a drinking-glass, the Colonel took out the stopple, and lifted the flask itself to his lips.

"For Heaven's sake, no!" cried the Doctor. "The dose is one single drop!—one drop, Colonel, one drop!"

"Not a drop to save your wretched old soul," responded the Colonel; probably thinking that the apothecary was pleading for a small share of the precious liquor. He put it to his lips, and, as if quenching a lifelong thirst, swallowed deep draughts, sucking it in with desperation, till, void of breath, he set it down upon the table. The rich, poignant perfume spread itself through the air.

The apothecary, with an instinctive carefulness that was rather ludicrous under the circumstances, caught up the stopper, which the Colonel had let fall, and forced it into the bottle to prevent any further escape of virtue. He then fearfully watched the result of the madman's potation.

The Colonel sat a moment in his chair, panting for breath; then started to his feet with a prompt vigor that contrasted widely with the infirm and rheumatic movements that had heretofore characterized him. He struck his forehead violently with one hand, and smote his chest with the other: he stamped his foot thunderously on the ground; then he leaped up to the ceiling, and came down with an elastic bound. Then he laughed, a wild, exulting ha! ha! with a strange triumphant roar that filled the house and re-echoed through it; a sound full of fierce, animal rapture—enjoyment of sensual life mixed up with a sort of horror. After all, real as it was, it was like the sounds a man makes in a dream. And this, while the potent draught seemed still to be making its way through his system; and the frightened apothecary thought that he intended a revengeful onslaught upon himself. Finally, he uttered a loud unearthly screech, in the midst of which his voice broke, as if some unseen hand were throttling him, and, starting forward, he fought frantically, as if he would clutch the life that was being rent away—and fell forward with a dead thump upon the floor.

"Colonel! Colonel!" cried the terrified Doctor.

The feeble old man, with difficulty, turned over the heavy frame, and saw at once, with practised eye, that he was dead. He set him up, and the corpse looked at him with angry reproach. He was so startled, that his subsequent recollections of the moment were neither distinct nor steadfast; but he fancied, though he told the strange impression to no one, that on his first glimpse of the face, with a dark flush of what looked like rage still upon it, it was a young man's face that he saw—a face with all the passionate energy of early manhood—the capacity for furious anger which the man had lost half a century ago, crammed to the brim with vigor till it became agony. But the next moment, if it were so (which it could not have been), the face grew ashen, withered, shrunken, more aged than in life, though still the murderous fierceness remained, and seemed to be petrified forever upon it.

# Dark Angel

*Gaston Danville*

A FLIGHT OF roseate flamingos sailed through fantastic silver clouds embroidered on turquoise silk. Next to this exotic hanging a tiny Japanese skeleton, dazzlingly white, spun slowly, suspended from the chandelier by a thin wire, which was invisible to Pierre from the divan where he lay. The velvety, quivering glow of the candle, which he had lit when he came in, was reflected in the dual diamonds of his starched shirt front and poured a gleaming glaze of liquid gold onto his coat, its lapel pinned with a sprig of withered heather. The flickering flame died at the threshold of darkness where it crossed the young man's face.

On a scarlet cushion before the hearth sat a cat in a serious, sacerdotal pose, its luminous eyes—emerald crescents streaked with jade—fixed on the pale crimson of the dying embers. In the floating dimness, striped with faint, diffused light, the chiffon shade of a tall lamp lay a broad, lilac stroke, bright with sulfur accents. Outside, the wind entoned the tremulous, lugubrious symphony of the night, frenzied with lengthy passages of chromatic scales, its fierce breath inspiring the organ pipes of grave chimneys which responded to the call of its plaintive harmony, evoking sad, feeble, painful thoughts, and suffering, too.

Pierre is suddenly seized by the oppressive grip which only moments before tore at his heart with the persistent clenching of awful tongs whose closed teeth never meet. His breast burns with intense, excruciating pain as his muscles are slowly shredded, fiber by fiber. He daren't move, for fear of exacerbating this horrible torture. His head, unbearably heavy, flashes with endless, unsteady needles that jab him, aggressively assailing him with their delicate bite. The mask contracted, he suffers in silent stillness; his teeth bite into the bloodless pallor of his lips, and his fingernails dig into the palms of his clenched fists. Blood spurts in sporadic, torrid waves beneath his damp, shivering skin, flooding his face, invading his forehead, streaming beneath his skull and furiously drowning his brain, while at his temples the unbearable arterial pendulum sounds the charge like the steady beating of a gong. His head teems with myriad beasts whose snapping jaws and terrified muzzles rummage through his brain. Will his head split open? He must lower the opaque, bloody veil of his eyelids between himself and the outer, so painfully do the slightest vibrations of light shatter his battered being, increased tenfold by the tiring tension of his exacerbated, hypersensitive nerves at this moment of supreme, indeed, infinite anguish.

The trance-like crisis was followed by a relative well being, punctuated, however, with sudden, shooting pains reminiscent of the gaping chasm crossed, the last lightning flashes of a calming storm ploughing the now purer sky, still streaked with somber shreds of clouds.

The fleeting memory of the evening, spent without a single ill-omen at the home of Madame de Prezilles, is sketchy in his dim, yet reeling memory; an insignificant evening, embellished with the usual young women, the accustomed procession of black clothing—not one unpleasant incident recalling itself to the mind. The fabric of painful sensations wears thin, tears away, and finally disappears. Pierre breathes deeply, stretches out, as if delivered from a bad nightmare, happily relieved.

Emboldened by the tranquillity of his calmed nerves and now serene body he stands, walks to a bureau modeled with an odd inlay of malachite and jasper, and slides open a drawer: letters. He gently closes it, then finds the tobacco he seeks and fastidiously rolls a cigarette between his still trembling fingers. Capricious arabesques curl and uncurl; moireed spirals, milky blue, rise up and are lost in a changing design, stairways of candid dreams, set in azure. Pierre listens to the gusts of wind as they run their tremulous course. Their clamor is attenuated by the closed blinds and window panes, outlined in hardened lead. Stiff brown curtains, half-veiling the window with their armor of coppery humps and folds gleam with the silky, warm sheen of polished bronze. The sound of the squall drones into a chant, entoning the sweet, melancholy distances and seemingly repeating the moaning of the waves to the evening's ebb and flow. The feeble, sad melody embroiders its groaning arpeggios onto the monotonous purring of the dozing feline, whose tufted, gray ball stains the crimson satin with its now paler color, suggesting an uncertain ellipse.

The cracking of dry wood streaks the resonant breaches of the half-silence.

Struck down, not by a refreshing weariness, that herald of sleep, but by the onslaught of discouragement, by the fear felt on emerging from danger, and overwhelmed by an unstable and dreary muddle of troubling ideas, the young man resolves not to go to bed, for he suspects a bout of cruel insomnia in which his trembling limbs would refuse rest, his eyes would sail through the darkness, and his mind would wander through the ghostly night. So he lies, struck numb by an insidious, treacherous, somnolent torpor. He tries to avoid it, fearing the torments of terrifying apparitions, with their attendant fears, suffocation, withdrawal, annihilation vis-a-vis a derisory, vain peril every bit as dangerous as a real one, perhaps even more so.

The reverie recedes, limp and uncertain; it flees through clearings in the vast field of memories, sidestepping unexpected associative traps, which would only send it flying down multifarious paths. Trifles are encountered and immediately abandoned. The fictitious landscape then comes alive, is peopled by characters who assume the completed life of a posthumous person. Shadows, having strayed in the deepest recesses of memory, step out into light. One face now emerges from the confused groups, the divergent coexistences—a black braid, pearly shoulders of ideal curve, and a fleeting female torso complete it. Who was she? Ah, the letters in the drawer! Pierre unknowingly moves his lips—a name is pronounced, then, unbeknownst to him, he mutters incoherent words, unaware that they unconsciously translate his inner thoughts.

"She must be dead ... I feel she is dead ... When? Perhaps tonight! Ha, what a strange premonition: I'm frozen to the very marrow of my bones ..."

"Why does this absurd idea come to me, and at a time when, through some odd coincidence—very odd, indeed—her image haunts me, as clear in its form as on the day it first appeared, when in hours of intoxication she silently entered this chamber?"

"Why would she not be dead? I can see her now, so pale! too pale for a living person. I particularly dislike the dull, colorless tresses that cover her neck: she had such beautiful hair."

"What?... Someone has just spoken, here, and something has entered the room, something cold, fluid ... yes, something ... the cat awakens, meows, hisses; its fur stands on end. Something strange indeed occurs, but what?"

"I see nothing ... nothing ..."

"Not a sound."

"The supernatural force of this deathly conviction frightens me. I don't want to believe in this glacial revelation, which appeared suddenly and of its own accord, but I simply cannot shake off the odd evidence it heaps on me."

"In winter, the day is slow to break, the heavy hours to take flight, and I remain alone, alone, always alone, with only my wicked thoughts to keep me company! Oh, had I not been so cowardly, cruel, and unkind when the stupid voice of pride spoke in me. I let her leave, nearly one month ago ... and after a futile scene that I could have stopped with a word. That word burned my lips, and in my foolish pride I would not utter it. I could have kept her with a kiss, a gesture—she was so good, so kind to my fragile soul. My arms, that should have opened, hung limp at my sides, my mouth closed, my eyes hard. At the fatal moment she stopped at the door, half turning around, still uncertain, the very notion of a tomorrow without her, of my lowly behavior, frightened me. Yet I let her go.... One month ago already! Why, only yesterday I sought her svelte form next to me, I thought I heard the familiar rustle of her skirt, the delicate sound of her step?... Never have I seen her again, except in the fanciful lands of dream.... Dead!"

In his desire to free himself from the grip of fruitless regret, Pierre decides to take ether.

Soon enough, under the influence of the toxin, he smiles at the fantastically exaggerated marvels that loom in the swirling mists of the Imaginary. A whirlwind passes, cradling its dull, gray vapor over the immense abyss of the Infinite that stretches to the mauve horizon, so far off that the enormous Space emanates a delirious vertigo, a superstitious, yet attractive terror. The ground, strewn with fleecy feathers, rumbles with slow convulsions. Pustules well up out of the ground, swell to the point of bursting, then shrink down into adorable bubbles and vanish. Massive shapes stir, crawl, move with sinuously curved deformations, a hearth-like glow hovers over the chaos, which becomes clearer.

"You see," he murmurs, "the crystal lamps with their glistening chandeliers will twinkle up above, dropping a sparkling cascade of green and red pendants. The painted bayaderes, like fragile idols whose pointed limbs might be draped in muslin, run in mosaic frescoes around the gleaming vault. On the square, strong, powerful pillars bristling with brass nails, stand cinnabar columns, surmounted by the holy image of the Good Goddess!"

"You see, friend, how the whirling swarm of supple ballerinas takes flight, provocative wasps in shadowy damascene corselets—how light they are! Tambourines tinkle, flutes spill out their harmonious modulations. Ah! my limbs have shaken off their earthly shackles before this spectacle, and I feel an inexpressible pleasure, free from the burden of life as I hover over the forgotten fields of human ugliness!"

"Stay by me, friend ... Ah, I once felt you enter without a sound, I called out to you ... you didn't respond. You were cold, for the rustle of your fluid garb touched me ... you did not sit by the hearth.... Stay by me still; tell me you've forgotten the fateful moment of my cruelty?... If only you knew, my love, how I've suffered, cried, and cursed my absurd, ill-fated anger. Now I shall be so humble, submissive, and tender that you'll love me. We were once so happy! Please, forgive me. Beautiful! You are still beautiful! Your long, long hair—how long your hair is!—it still gleams with an uncertain hint of amethyst or sapphire whose sheen I so loved. And your eyes, your black eyes—in truth are they not darker!—they again refresh my soul with the repose that once it found there. You glow with the virginal, allicient color that your ivory skin once possessed ... But, how shall I see your skin?... It has grown dark, yes, very dark; and in the darkness I see only vague, whitish stains."

"Why won't you speak to me? I adore your voice, I adore its fresh, melodious timbre. You don't say a word ... and this veil that enfolds you?..."

"Will you remove it and reveal your dazzling radiance, dressed as for a ball.... And what ball could be more joyous than this one! For you've come back to me, haven't you, you've forgotten, you forgive me? Say something; kiss me ..."

"Ah, a bit of light, this moon beam seeping discreetly through the closed curtain is more precious to me than myriad blazing suns, for it allows me to gaze upon you ..."

"You laugh, it seems, you laugh, and your tiny, pearly teeth echo the light which illuminates them.... Heavens! How horrible! Am I dreaming! No, no, she's hurting me.... Those nails, those pointy nails, the nails of a dead woman, dig into my neck ... and that emaciated, bony head stares at me with its hollow sockets.... Ah!"

Pierre seizes a dagger from a trophy and, haggard, slashes at the phantom ...

*—Translated from the French*
*by Guy Bennett*

# Dreams

*Guy de Maupassant*

Five old friends had been dining together—an author, a doctor, and three wealthy bachelors of independent means.

All available topics of conversation had been exhausted, and that feeling of weariness which heralds the breaking up of such a gathering was already settling upon those present. One of the party, who for five minutes had been silently contemplating the lighted boulevard, with its noise and bustle, suddenly remarked:

"The days seem long when one has nothing to do from morning till night."

"And the nights also," added his neighbor. "I hardly sleep at all, amusements bore me and conversation is always the same. I never come across a new idea, and before talking to anybody I always have to struggle with a violent desire to remain quite silent and not listen to anyone. I don't know what to do in the evenings."

"I would give anything," the third idler said, "for some means of spending even two pleasant hours every day."

The author, who had just thrown his overcoat over his arm, came towards them and said:

"Anybody who could find a new vice and could pass it on to his fellow creatures, even though it might shorten life by half, would do a far greater service to humanity than anyone who might discover a means of securing perpetual health and youth."

The doctor began to laugh, and, biting off the end of his cigar, he said:

"Yes, but it is not found so easily as that. Ever since the beginning of the world the problem has been vigorously attacked. Primitive man instantly attained perfection in that line, but we can scarcely equal him."

One of the three idlers murmured:

"What a pity!"

A moment later he added:

"If only one could sleep, could sleep well, without feeling too warm or too cold, sleep with that exhaustion which comes from an evening of intense fatigue, sleep without dreaming!"

"Why without dreaming?" inquired his neighbor.

"Because dreams are not always pleasant," the other replied, "because they are always strange, improbable and incoherent, and while asleep we cannot even enjoy the best ones to the full. You must dream while awake."

"Who prevents you from doing so?" asked the author.

The doctor threw away his cigar.

"My dear fellow, daydreaming requires the exercise of great will power, and therefore leaves one very tired. Now one of the most delightful things in the world is a real dream—the mind wandering through pleasant visions—but it must come naturally, not under painful stimulation, and it should be accompanied by complete physical comfort. That kind of dream I can offer you, if you will promise not to abuse it."

The author shrugged his shoulders.

"Oh, yes," he said, "I know all about that; hashish, opium, green jam, the paradis artificiels. I have read Baudelaire's books and I have even tasted his famous drug, which made me very ill."

The doctor sat down again.

"No, I mean ether, simply ether; and I might add that you literary men ought to use it sometimes."

The three rich men came nearer, and one of them asked him to explain its effect.

"Let us come down to facts," the doctor replied; "I am leaving medicine and morality out of the question; I am only concerned at the moment with pleasure. You are indulging every day in excesses which are shortening your lives. I will bring a new sensation to your notice, possibly only for men of intelligence—that is to say, of considerable intelligence—dangerous, like everything which overexcites us, but none the less exquisite. I should add that a certain amount of preparation is required, that is to say, it is necessary to become accustomed to it, in order to experience to the full the singular effects of ether.

"They are different from the effects of hashish, opium and morphine, and they cease as soon as you stop inhaling it, while the other dream producers continue their action for hours.

"I will try to analyze as clearly as possible the feelings experienced by the use of ether, but so delicate and fleeting are those sensations that it is not an easy task.

"I first tried this remedy when I was suffering from violent neuralgia, and I have perhaps rather abused it since. I had sharp pains in the head and neck, and my skin became unbearably hot and feverish. I took a large flask of ether, and, lying down, I began slowly to inhale it. After a few minutes, I thought I heard a vague murmur, which soon became a kind of drone, and it seemed to me that the inside of my body was getting lighter—as light as air—and dissolving in vapor.

"Then came a sort of stupor, a drowsy feeling of comfort, in spite of the pains, which were still present but were no longer acute. They were pains such as one could endure with resignation, and no longer that terrible excruciating agony against which the whole tortured body protests.

"Soon that curious and delightful feeling of buoyancy spread from my body to my limbs, which in turn became light as a feather, as if the flesh and bones had disappeared and had left only the skin to enable me to feel the pleasure of living and resting in such comfort. I then realized that I was no longer in agony, the pain had vanished, melted away. I heard four voices, as if two conversations were going on at the same time, but I could not understand a single word; sometimes there was a confused jumble of sounds; sometimes I could distinguish words; but it was evident that what I heard was nothing but the intensified drumming in my ears. Far from being asleep, I was very much awake; my ideas, my sensations and my thoughts were marvelously clear and strong, aided by a feeling of exhilaration, a curious intoxication arising from a tenfold increase in my mental powers.

"It was not like the dreams produced by hashish, or the morbid illusions of opium; it was a wonderful clearness of thought, a new way of regarding and appreciating the important things in life, with the absolute certainty that this way was the right one.

"And I suddenly remembered the old Biblical idea. It seemed to me that I had eaten of the tree of knowledge and that all mysteries were solved, so powerful and irrefutable was this strange new logic. Arguments, reasons, and proofs crowded upon me, only to be upset by still stronger ones. My brain became a battlefield of ideas; I saw myself as a superior being, armed with an invincible intelligence, and I experienced a fierce joy in the discovery of my power.

"All this lasted a very long time, while I continued to inhale the ether in my flask. Suddenly I realized that it was empty, and felt most terribly grieved."

The four men spoke together:

"Doctor, give me a prescription for a pint of ether!"

But the doctor put on his hat and retorted:

"Certainly not! Go and be poisoned by somebody else!"

And he went out.

Ladies and gentlemen, if you feel inclined to try?—

# The Possessed

*Jean Lorrain*

"YES," SERGE ANNOUNCED to me, "I must go away, I can no longer stay here; and it isn't because I am shivering, my whole organism forever chilled from the pints of blood that the surgeons have been removing for months. My body is still sound, thank God, and with precautions I am relatively certain that my lungs will hold out; but I can no longer winter here because, with the first gusts of November, I become hallucinatory, half-crazy, prey to a really frightful obsession, in a word: because I am afraid of this place."

And under the steadfastness of my gaze, he added, "Oh! Don't jump to the conclusion that I am suffering from ether problems. I am cured, radically cured; although somehow still intoxicated. The ether, which barely two years ago spread through all my being with the swiftness of the most intense air, with I can't say what delicious, imponderable sensation, now distills a poison that crushes my arms and legs. The last time, about a year ago, that I inhaled some of it, I had a murderous ache in all my limbs for three days.

"Besides, why would I take any of it? I have neither insomnia nor constrictions of the heart. These swellings and this spongy heaviness in my left side, these atrocious sensations of agony, which had me suddenly sitting straight up in bed, skin clammy, trembling with a little death—all that is no longer any more to me than a distant nightmare, like a vague memory of the tales of Edgar Allan Poe that one would have read during one's childhood, and really, when I think about that sad period of my existence, I believe I lived it less than I dreamed it.

"And yet I must leave, or I will fall ill again in this ghostly Paris, haunted by November; because what is mysterious about my case is that I am no longer terrified of the invisible, but of reality." "Of reality?" And as I was intentionally leaning on the words, a little disconcerted by this last confession: "Of reality!" Serge repeated, stressing each syllable. "It's with reality that I become visionary. It's the beings of flesh and bone met in the street—it's the man in the street, the woman in the street, the same anonymous ones brushed past in the crowd—which would appear to me in the guise of spectres. It's the ugliness, the banality even, of modern life that freezes my blood and immobilizes me with terror."

And sitting down suddenly on the corner of the table: "It's not just recently, you know, that I have become a visionary. When I was miserable, damned by ether, you would have seen me change apartments three times in two years to escape the persecution of my dreams. I literally populated the rooms with phantoms. They were inside me and as soon as I would find myself alone in some closed room, the ambient atmosphere completely crawling with larvæ—like a drop of water seen under the microscope swarming with germs and infusoria—would reveal to my eyes frightening, shadowy faces. It was the period of time when I could not let my gaze wander in the solitude of my cubicle without seeing dubious, naked feet materialize level with the door curtain or strange, pale hands in the gap between the curtains; that terrible time, finally, when the air I breathed was polluted with horrible presences and when I was dying of exhaustion from endless battles against the unknown, half crazed with anguish in the middle of pale creepings of shadows and unnameable touches.

But isn't all of that far away? I am cured, thank God! I have regained my appetite and my ability to sleep like a twenty-year-old. I sleep like a dormouse; I eat like an ogre; and all this summer I ran in the mountains with the gusto of a schoolboy. And yet, I must go away, and as quickly as possible, because the ignoble nervous condition is watching and waiting for me; the fear is in me, and I know myself, I am afraid of this fear."

Serge had gotten up. He was now pacing the room with great strides, hands crossed behind his back, forehead stubborn, eyes on the deep wool carpeting; suddenly he came to a halt. "Have you noticed how the ugliness of people you meet in the street—especially the little people, workers going to their jobs, functionaries to their offices, housewives and domestics—exacerbates itself and takes on semi-fantastic aspects in the interior of the omnibus! With the first winter chill, it becomes terrible. Is it the daily worry of lowly tasks, the depressing weight of petty preoccupations, or the terror of the ends of the months, of failures and of debts that they will never pay? Is it the weariness of all these penniless people in the grip of life, a rancid life without surprises, or all the sadness of an existence without a slightly higher thought under the cranium or a slightly larger dream in the heart? It always appears that I have never seen anywhere more ignoble caricatures of the human face! It becomes hallucinatory. Is it suddenly being put face to face with the feeling of their ugliness, the sudden relaxation of the organism that forgets itself for a minute on the warmth of the benches, or is it the deleterious influence of the stinking atmosphere? A sudden limpness seems to take over all of the beings piled up there; those who are standing struggle, with animal preoccupation, not to fall from the platform; but the fat ladies collapsed in the four corners of the interior, the old workers with knotted fingers, whose napes are turned ham-like by the cold, with pitifully few hairs, the sly-looking physiognomy of maids in flight, the chlorotic and vicious look, eyes oblique, the whites showing from one corner to the other under flaccid lids, shady men buttoned up to the neck, whose undershirts you never see. Can there exist, my dear sir, under the dim light of a November day, a more mournful and repugnant spectacle than that of the inside of a tramway? The outside cold has hardened all these traits, frozen all these eyes and contracted these foreheads with bowl-cuts; the glassy stares, expressionless, are the stares of crazy men or of sleepwalkers. If they have a thought, it's worse, because the thought is ignoble or sordid and the gazes are criminal; you can only see the glow and passing flashes of lucre-madness and the impulse to thievery. Lust, whenever it appears, is venal and despoiled; each person, in his heart of hearts, thinks of nothing but ways to rob and trick his neighbor.

Modern life, luxurious and hard, has given to these men and to these women, souls of muggers or of prison guards; envy, hatred, and the despair of being poor gives them an ill-tempered aspect to match their flattened heads, pointy faces and snarls of shrew-mice and vipers; avarice and egotism gives to others the snouts of old pigs with shark's jaws. It's a bestiary, where each lowly instinct is stamped with animal traits. Since the beginning of the month I have traveled and circulated in a rolling cage full of wild beasts and amphibians quizzically dressed like people of the big city, in pants, in shawls, and in modern dresses.

"Because I only have 25,000 francs income, I take the tramway, just like my concierge. Well! this perspective of cohabiting, even if it is only for an hour a day, with piglet-headed men and women with fowl profiles, lawyers who look like blackbirds, delinquents with lynx eyes, and fashionable errand girls with flattened, lizard faces, this forced promiscuity with all the human soul's ignoble, unnameable things, suddenly brought to skin depth—all of that is beyond my strength. I am afraid, do you understand the word? I am afraid.

"The other day, no later than Saturday, the nightmare feeling was so strong (it was in the tramway from the Louvre to Sèvres, and the stress of the suburban landscape, the deserted quays of the Avenue Versailles perhaps further exacerbated by the anguished ugliness of all these faces), that I had to make a stop and get off in the middle of nowhere on the banks of the Point-du-Jour. I couldn't stand it anymore; I had, so severely that I wanted to beg for mercy, the feeling that all these people, seated in front of and around me, were beings of another race, half beasts, half men, a species of living spectres, ignoble by-products of I know not what monstrous couplings, a species of anthropoids closer to animals than to men and each one embodying a lowly and evil instinct of stinking beasts, of great carnivores, of ophidians or of rodents.

"Among others, there was just in front of me a flat and dry middle class woman with a long and granular neck like that of a swan, with little sharp teeth hard and gapped in a yawning fish mouth and whose membranous eyelids, extraordinarily dilated and vacuous pupils, alarmed me. This woman was stupidity itself. She embodied it and identified it definitively, and a growing terror hit me, the terror that she would open her mouth and say something. She would have, I was certain, clucked like a hen. This woman was from the barnyard, and a great sadness, an infinite sorrow took hold of me in front of this degeneration of a human being.

"A cameo brooch was pinned to the two strings of her mauve velveteen hat. I wanted to get off; and every day, in the tramway, in the omnibus, in the coach, even, where the hideousness of the ghostly faces becomes horrifying by the light of the nocturnal lamps, the same animal profiles slowly come forth from the faces, and all of this for me alone, only for me. I'm possessed, what can I tell you?

"So, I've made up my mind. I'm fleeing this hell. I'm leaving without delay."

*—Translated from the French*
*by Jordan Jones*

# The Effects of Nitrous Oxide

*Peter Mark Roget*

"The effect of the inspirations of the nitrous oxide was that of making me vertiginous, and producing a tingling sensation in my hands and feet: as these feelings increased, I seemed to lose the sense of my own weight, and imagined I was sinking into the ground. I then felt a drowsiness gradually steal upon me, and a disinclination to motion; even the actions of inspiring and expiring were not performed without effort: and it also required some attention of mind to keep my nostrils closed with my fingers. I was gradually roused from this torpor by a kind of delirium, which came on so rapidly that the air-bag dropped from my hands. This sensation increased for about a minute after I had ceased to breathe, to a much greater degree than before, and I suddenly lost sight of all the objects around me, they being apparently obscured by clouds, in which were many luminous points, similar to what is often experienced on rising suddenly and stretching out the arms, after sitting long in one position.

"I felt myself totally incapable of speaking, and for some time lost all consciousness of where I was, or who was near me. My whole frame felt as if violently agitated: I thought I panted violently: my heart seemed to palpitate, and every artery to throb with violence; I felt a singing in my ears; all the vital motions seemed to be irresistibly hurried on, as if their equilibrium had been destroyed, and everything was running headlong into confusion. My ideas succeeded one another with extreme rapidity, thoughts rushed like a torrent through my mind, as if their velocity had been suddenly accelerated by the bursting of a barrier which had before retained them in their natural and equable course. This state of extreme hurry, agitation, and tumult, was but transient. Every unnatural sensation gradually subsided; and in about a quarter of an hour after I had ceased to breathe the gas, I was nearly in the same state in which I had been at the commencement of the experiment."

# The Anesthetic Revelation

*Benjamin Paul Blood*

"THE ANESTHETIC REVELATION is the Initiation of Man into the Immemorial Mystery of the Open Secret of Being, revealed as the Inevitable Vortex of Continuity. Inevitable is the word. Its motive is inherent—it is what has to be. It is not for any love or hate, nor for joy nor sorrow, nor good nor ill. End, beginning, or purpose, it knows not of.

"It affords no particular of the multiplicity and variety of things; but it fills appreciation of the historical and the sacred with a secular and intimately personal illumination of the nature and motive of existence, which then seems reminiscent—as if it should have appeared, or shall yet appear, to every participant thereof.

"Although it is at first startling in its solemnity, it becomes directly such a matter of course—so old fashioned, and so akin to proverbs, that it inspires exultation rather than fear, and a sense of safety, as identified with the aboriginal and the universal. But no words may express the imposing certainty of the patient that he is realizing the primordial, Adamic surprise of Life.

"Repetition of the experience finds it ever the same, and as if it could not possibly be otherwise. The subject resumes his normal consciousness only to partially and fitfully remember its occurrence, and to try to formulate its baffling import,—with only this consolatory after thought: that he has known the oldest truth, and that he has done with human theories as to the origin, meaning or destiny of the race. He is beyond instruction in 'spiritual things.'

"The lesson is one of central safety: the Kingdom is within. All days are judgment days: but there can be no climacteric purpose of eternity, nor any scheme of the whole. The astronomer abridges the row of bewildering figures by increasing his unit of measurement: so we may reduce the distracting multiplicity of things to the unity for which each of us stands.

"This has been my moral sustenance since I have known of it. In my first printed mention of it I declared: "The world is no more the alien terror that was taught me. Spurning the cloud-grimed and still sultry battlements whence so lately Jehovan thunders boomed, my gray gull lifts her wing against the nightfall, and takes the dim leagues with a fearless eye." And now, after twenty-seven years of this experience, the wing is grayer, but the eye is fearless still, while I renew and doubly emphasize that declaration. I know—as having known—the meaning of Existence: the sane centre of the universe—at once the wonder and the assurance of the soul—for which the speech of reason has as yet no name but the Anesthetic Revelation."

By the Anesthetic Revelation I mean a certain survived condition, (or uncondition) in which is the satisfaction of philosophy by an appreciation of the genius of being, which appreciation cannot be brought out of that condition into the normal sanity of sense—cannot be formally remembered, but remains informal, forgotten until we return to it.

As here we find in trances, men
Forget the dream that happens then,
Until they fall in trance again.

Of this condition, although it may have been attained otherwise, I know only by the use of anesthetic agents. After experiments ranging over nearly fourteen years I affirm—what any man prove at will—that there is an invariable and reliable condition (or uncondition) ensuing about the instant of recall from anesthetic stupor to sensible observation, or "coming to," in which the genius of being is revealed; but because it cannot be remembered in the normal condition it is lost altogether through the infrequency of the anesthetic treatment in any individual's case ordinarily, and buried, amid the hum of returning common sense, under the epitaph of all illumination "this is a queer world." Yet I have warned others to expect this wonder on entering the anesthetic slumber, and none so cautioned has failed to report of it in terms which assured me of its realization. I have spoken with various persons also who induce anesthesia professionally (dentists, surgeons, etc.) who had observed that many patients at the moment of recall seem as having made a startling yet somehow matter-of-course (and even grotesque) discovery in their own nature, and try to speak of it, but invariably fail in a lost mood of introspection. Of what astonishes them it is hard to give or receive intimation; but I think most persons who have tested it will accept this as the central point of the illumination: That sanity is not the basic quality of intelligence, but it is a mere condition which is variable, and like the humming of a wheel, goes up or down the musical gamut according to a physical activity; and that only in sanity is formal or contrasting thought, while the naked life is realized only outside of sanity altogether; and it is the instant contrast of this "tasteless water of souls" with formal thought as we "come to", that leaves in the patient an astonishment that the awful mystery of Life is at last but a homely and a common thing, and that aside from mere formality the majestic and the absurd are of equal dignity. The astonishment is aggravated as at a thing of course, missed by sanity in overstepping, as in too foreign a search, or with too eager an attention: as in finding one's spectacles on one's nose, or in making in the dark a step higher than the stair. My first experiences of this revelation had many varieties of emotion; but as a man grows calm and determined by experience in general, so am I now not only firm and familiar in this weird condition, but triumphant—divine. To minds of sanguine imagination there will be a sadness in the tenor of the mystery, as if the key-note of the Universe were low,—for no poetry, no emotion known to the normal sanity of man can furnish a hint of its primeval prestige and its all but appalling solemnity; but for such as have felt sadly the instability of temporal things there is a comfort of serenity and ancient peace; while for the resolved and imperious spirit there are majesty and supremacy unspeakable. Nor can it be long until all who enter the anesthetic condition (and there are hundreds every secular day) will be taught to expect this revelation, and will date from its experience their initiation into the secret of Life.

Men and brethren, into this pervading genius we pass, forgetting and forgotten, and thenceforth each is all, in God. There is no higher, no deeper, no other than the life in which we are founded. "The One remains, the many change and pass." And each and every of us is the One that remains. Listen, then, to the charming of the Prince of Peace, who takes away the sin from the world, and say, each for himself, "My father and I are one." Mourn not for the dead, who have awoke in the bosom of God. They care not, they think not, and when we are what they are, we too shall think of them no-more. Much might I say of the good of this discovery, if it were, as it soon may be, generally known of. Now for the first time, the ancient problem is referred to empirical resolution, when the expert and the novice may meet equally on the same ground. My worldly tribulation reclines on its divine composure; and though not in haste to die, I "care not to be dead," but look into the future with serene and changeless cheer. This world is no more than that alien terror which was taught me. Spurning the cloud-grimed and still sultry battlements whence so lately Jehovan thunders boomed, my gray gull lifts her wing against the nightfall, and takes the dim leagues with a fearless eye.

By this revelation we enter to the sadness and majesty of Jesus—to the solemn mystery which inspired the prophets of every generation. By some accident of being they entered into this condition. This is "the voice of One crying in the wilderness, Make straight the way of the Lord: 'He that hath ears to hear let him hear.'" Heed not for themselves the voice nor the hand, which ever deny themselves; remember only how many inspired times it is spoken and written: I AM—that God whom faltering spirits seek in far-off courts of Heaven, while behold! the kingdom of God is neither lo! here nor lo! there but within you; it is the Soul. Thou shalt vanish, but the soul is eternal: I speak not of souls. And behold, I say unto you, the Supreme Genius does not factualize; the glory is not what it does but what it is; it hath no old nor new, no here nor there; it stays not to remember, to wonder, to compare; to the whim of the patrician Presence, omniscience were an idle labor and delay, and prophecy is forestalled and bootless in the sole sufficiency whose paean hath no echo.

This is the Ultimatum. It is no glance between conditions, as if in passing from this sphere of existence we might catch a glimpse of

> the Gods, who haunt
> the lucid interspace of world and world,
> Where never creeps a cloud, or moves a wind
> Nor ever falls the least white star of snow.

and lose them again as we pass onto another orb and organization. This thick net of space containing all worlds—this fate of being which contains both gods and men, is the capacity of the Soul, and can be claimed as greater than us only by claiming a greater than the greatest, and denying God and safety. As sure as being—whence is all our care—so sure is content, beyond duplexity, antithesis, or trouble, where I have triumphed in a solitude that God is not above.

It is written that "there was war in heaven," that aeons of dominion, as absolute as any, beheld the banners of Lucifer streaking with silver and crimson the mists of the morning, and heard the heavy guns of Moloch and Belial beating on the heights of the mind; and I read that dead men have appeared as human forms;—nought of this can I deny, more or better than I can deny myself. The tales, whether they be true or false, are as substantial as the things of which they tell.

"We are such stuff
As dreams are made of, and our little life
Is rounded with a sleep."

# Under the Knife

*H. G. Wells*

"What if I die under it!" The thought recurred again and again as I walked home from Haddon's. It was a purely personal question. I was spared the deep anxieties of a married man, and I knew there were few of my intimate friends but would find my death troublesome chiefly on account of the duty of regret. I was surprised indeed, and perhaps a little humiliated, as I turned the matter over, to think how few could possibly exceed the conventional requirement. Things came before me stripped of glamor, in a clear dry light, during that walk from Haddon's house over Primrose Hill. There were the friends of my youth: I perceived now that our affection was a tradition, which we foregathered rather laboriously to maintain. There were the rivals and helpers of my later career. I suppose I had been cold-blooded or undemonstrative—one perhaps implies the other. It may be that even the capacity for friendship is a question of physique. There had been a time in my own life when I had grieved bitterly enough at the loss of a friend; but as I walked home that afternoon the emotional side of my imagination was dormant. I could not pity myself, nor feel sorry for my friends, nor conceive of them as grieving for me.

I was interested in this deadness of my emotional nature—no doubt a concomitant of my stagnating physiology; and my thoughts wandered off along the line it suggested. Once before, in my hot youth, I had suffered a sudden loss of blood, and had been within an ace of death. I remembered now that my affections as well as my passions had drained out of me, leaving scarce anything but a tranquil resignation and the faintest dreg of self-pity. It had been weeks before the old ambitions, and tendernesses, and all the complex moral interplay of a man had reasserted themselves. It occurred to me that the real meaning of this numbness might be a gradual slipping away from the pleasure-pain guidance of the animal man. It has been proven, I take it, as thoroughly as anything can be proven in this world, that the higher emotions, the moral feelings, even the subtle tenderness of love, are evolved from the elemental desires and fears of the simple animal: they are the harness in which man's mental freedom goes. And, it may be that, as death overshadows us, as our possibility of acting diminishes, this complex growth of balanced impulse, propensity, and aversion, whose interplay inspires our acts, goes with it. Leaving what?

I was suddenly brought back to reality by an imminent collision with a butcher-boy's tray. I found that I was crossing the bridge over the Regent's Park Canal which runs parallel with the bridge in the Zoological Gardens. The boy in blue had been looking over his shoulder at a black barge advancing slowly, towed by a gaunt white horse. In the Gardens a nurse was leading three happy little children over the bridge. The trees were bright green; the spring hopefulness was still unstained by the dusts of summer; the sky in the water was bright and clear, but broken by long waves, by quivering bands of black, as the barge drove through. The breeze was stirring; but it did not stir me as the spring breeze used to do.

Was this dullness of feeling in itself an anticipation? It was curious that I could reason and follow out a network of suggestion as clearly as ever; so, at least, it seemed to me. It was calmness rather than dullness that was coming upon me. Was there any ground for the belief in the presentiment of death? Did a man near to death begin instinctively to withdraw himself from the meshes of matter and sense, even before the cold hand was laid upon his? I felt strangely isolated—isolated without regret—from the life and existence about me. The children playing in the sun and gathering strength and experience for the business of life, the park-keeper gossiping with a nurse-maid, the nursing mother, the young couple intent upon each other as they passed me, the trees by the wayside spreading new pleading leaves to the sunlight, the stir in their branches—I had been part of it all, but I had nearly done with it now.

Some way down the Broad Walk I perceived that I was tired, and that my feet were heavy. It was hot that afternoon, and I turned aside and sat down on one of the green chairs that line the way. In a minute I had dozed into a dream, and the tide of my thoughts washed up a vision of the Resurrection. I was still sitting in the chair, but I thought myself actually dead, withered, tattered, dried, one eye (I saw) pecked out by birds. "Awake!" cried a voice, and incontinently the dust of the path and the mould under the grass became insurgent. I had never before thought of Regent's Park as a cemetery, but now, through the trees, stretching as far as eye could see, I beheld a flat plain of writhing graves and heeling tombstones. There seemed to be some trouble, the rising dead appeared to stifle as they struggled upward, they bled in their struggles, the red flesh was tattered away from the white bones. "Awake!" cried a voice; but I determined I would not rise to such horrors. "Awake!" They would not let me alone. "Wike up!" said an angry voice. A cockney angel! The man who sells the tickets was shaking me, demanding my penny.

I paid my penny, pocketed my ticket, yawned, stretching my legs, and feeling now rather less torpid, got up and walked on towards Langham Place. I speedily lost myself again in a shifting maze of thoughts about death. Going across Marylebone Road into that crescent at the end of Langham Place, I had the narrowest escape from the shaft of a cab, and went on my way with a palpitating heart and a bruised shoulder. It struck me that it would have been curious if my meditations on my death on the morrow had led to my death that day.

But I will not weary you with more of my experiences that day and the next. I knew more and more certainly that I should die under the operation; at times I think I was inclined to pose to myself. The doctors were coming at eleven, and I did not get up. It seemed scarce worth while to trouble about washing and dressing, and, though I read my newspapers and the letters that came by the first post, I did not find them very interesting. There was a friendly note from Addison, my old school friend, calling my attention to two discrepancies and a printer's error in my new book; with one from Langridge, venting some vexation over Minton. The rest were business communications. I breakfasted in bed. The glow of pain at my side seemed more massive. I knew it was pain, and yet, if you can understand, I did not find it very painful. I had been awake and hot and thirsty in the night, but in the morning bed felt comfortable. In the nighttime I had lain thinking of things that were past; in the morning I dozed over the question of immortality. Haddon came, punctual to the minute, with a neat black bag; and Mowbray soon followed. Their arrival stirred me up a little. I began to take a more personal interest in the proceedings. Haddon moved the little octagonal table close to the bedside, and with his broad black back to me began taking things out of his bag. I heard the light click of steel upon steel. My imagination, I found, was not altogether stagnant. "Will you hurt me much?" I said, in an offhand tone.

"Not a bit," Haddon answered over his shoulder. "We shall chloroform you. Your heart's as sound as a bell." And, as he spoke, I had a whiff of the pungent sweetness of the anæsthetic.

They stretched me out, with a convenient exposure of my side, and, almost before I realized what was happening, the chloroform was being administered. It stings the nostrils and there is a suffocating sensation, at first. I knew I should die—that this was the end of consciousness for me. And suddenly I felt that I was not prepared for death; I had a vague sense of a duty overlooked—I knew not what. What was it I had not done? I could think of nothing more to do, nothing desirable left in life; and yet I had the strangest disinclination to death. And the physical sensation was painfully oppressive. Of course the doctors did not know they were going to kill me. Possibly I struggled. Then I fell motionless, and a great silence, a monstrous silence, and an impenetrable blackness, came upon me.

There must have been an interval of absolute unconsciousness, seconds or minutes. Then, with a chilly, unemotional clearness, I perceived that I was not yet dead. I was still in my body; but all the multitudinous sensations that come sweeping from it to make up the background of consciousness had gone, leaving me free of it all. No, not free of it all; for as yet something still held me to the poor stark flesh upon the bed, held me, yet not so closely that I did not feel myself external to it, independent of it, straining away from it. I do not think I saw, I do not think I heard; but I perceived all that was going on, and it was as if I both heard and saw. Haddon was bending over me, Mowbray behind me; the scalpel—it was a large scalpel—was cutting my flesh at the side under the flying ribs. It was interesting to see myself cut like cheese, without a pang, without even a qualm. The interest was much of a quality with that one might feel in a game of chess between strangers. Haddon's face was firm, and his hand steady; but I was surprised to perceive (how I know now) that he was feeling the gravest doubt as to his own wisdom in the conduct of the operation.

Mowbray's thoughts, too, I could see. He was thinking that Haddon's manner showed too much of the specialist.

New suggestions came up like bubbles through a stream of frothing meditation, and burst one after another in the little bright spot of his consciousness. He could not help noticing and admiring Haddon's swift dexterity, in spite of his envious quality and his disposition to detract. I saw my liver exposed. I was puzzled at my own condition. I did not feel that I was dead, but I was different in some way from my living self. The gray depression that had weighed on me for a year or more, and colored all my thoughts, was gone. I perceived and thought without any emotional tint at all. I wondered if every one perceived things in this way under chloroform, and forgot it again when he came out of it. It would be inconvenient to look into some heads, and not forget.

Although I did not think that I was dead, I still perceived, quite clearly, that I was soon to die. This brought me back to the consideration of Haddon's proceedings. I looked into his mind, and saw that he was afraid of cutting a branch of the portal vein. My attention was distracted from details by the curious changes going on in his mind. His consciousness was like the quivering little spot of light which is thrown by the mirror of a galvanometer. His thoughts ran under it like a stream, some through the focus bright and distinct, some shadowy in the half-light of the edge. Just now the little glow was steady; but the least movement on Mowbray's part, the slightest sound from outside, even a faint difference in the slow movement of the living flesh he was cutting, set the light-spot shivering and spinning. A new sense-impression came rushing up through the flow of thoughts; and lo! the light-spot jerked away towards it, swifter than a frightened fish. It was wonderful to think that upon that unstable, fitful thing depended all the complex motions of the man, that for the next five minutes, therefore, my life hung upon its movements. And he was growing more and more nervous in his work. It was as if a little picture of a cut vein grew brighter, and struggled to oust from his brain another picture of a cut falling short of the mark. He was afraid: his dread of cutting too little was battling with his dread of cutting too far.

Then, suddenly, like an escape of water from under a lock gate, a great uprush of horrible realization set all his thoughts swirling, and simultaneously I perceived that the vein was cut. He started back with a hoarse exclamation, and I saw the brown-purple blood gather in a swift bead, and run trickling. He was horrified. He pitched the red-stained scalpel onto the octagonal table; and instantly both doctors flung themselves upon me, making hasty and ill-conceived efforts to remedy the disaster. "Ice," said Mowbray, gasping. But I knew that I was killed, though my body still clung to me.

I will not describe their belated endeavors to save me, though I perceived every detail. My perceptions were sharper and swifter than they had ever been in life; my thoughts rushed through my mind with incredible swiftness, but with perfect definition. I can only compare their crowded clarity to the effects of a reasonable dose of opium. In a moment it would all be over, and I should be free. I knew I was immortal, but what would happen I did not know. Should I drift off presently, like a puff of smoke from a gun, in some kind of half-material body, an attenuated version of my material self? Should I find myself suddenly among the innumerable hosts of the dead, and know the world about me for the phantasmagoria it had always seemed? Should I drift to some spiritualistic séance, and there make foolish, incomprehensible attempts to affect a purblind medium? It was a state of unemotional curiosity, of colorless expectation. And then I realized a growing stress upon me, a feeling as though some huge human magnet was drawing me upward out of my body. The stress grew and grew. I seemed an atom, for which monstrous forces were fighting. For one brief, terrible moment sensation came back to me. That feeling of falling headlong which comes in nightmares, that feeling a thousand times intensified, that and a black horror swept across my thoughts in a torrent. Then the two doctors, the naked body with its cut side, the little room, swept away from under me, and vanished, as a speck of foam vanishes down an eddy.

I was in mid air. Far below was the West End of London, receding rapidly—for I seemed to be flying swiftly upward—and, as it receded, passing westward like a panorama. I could see through the faint haze of smoke the innumerable roofs chimney-set, the narrow roadways stippled with people and conveyances, the little specks of squares, and the church steeples like thorns sticking out of the fabric. But it spun away as the earth rotated on its axis, and in a few seconds (as it seemed) I was over the scattered clumps of town about Ealing, the little Thames a thread of blue to the south, and the Chiltern Hills and the North Downs coming up like the rim of a basin, far away and faint with haze. Up I rushed.

And at first I had not the faintest conception what this headlong upward rush could mean.

Every moment the circle of scenery beneath me grew wider and wider, and the details of town and field, of hill and valley, got more and more hazy and pale and indistinct, a luminous gray was mingled more and more with the blue of the hills and the green of the open meadows; and a little patch of cloud, low and far to the west, shone ever more dazzlingly white. Above, as the veil of atmosphere between myself and outer space grew thinner, the sky, which had been a fair springtime blue at first, grew deeper and richer in color, passing steadily through the intervening shades, until presently it was as dark as the blue sky of midnight, and presently as black as the blackness of a frosty starlight, and at last as black as no blackness I had ever beheld. And first one star, and then many, and at last an innumerable host, broke out upon the sky: more stars than any one has ever seen from the face of the earth. For the blueness of the sky is the light of the sun and stars sifted and spread abroad blindingly; there is diffused light even in the darkest skies of winter, and we do not see their light by day because of the dazzling irradiation of the sun. But now I saw things—I know not how; assuredly with no mortal eyes—and that defect of bedazzlement blinded me no longer. The sun was incredibly strange and wonderful. The body of it was a disc of blinding white light; not yellowish as it seems to those who live upon the earth, but livid white, all streaked with scarlet streaks, and rimmed about with a fringe of writhing tongues of red fire. And, shooting halfway across the heavens from either side of it, and brighter than the Milky Way, were two pinions of silver-white, making it look more like those winged globes I have seen in Egyptian sculpture, than anything else I can remember upon earth. These I knew for the solar corona, though I had never seen anything of it but a picture during the days of my earthly life.

When my attention came back to the earth again, I saw that it had fallen very far away from me. Field and town were long since indistinguishable, and all the varied hues of the country were merging into a uniform bright gray, broken only by the brilliant white of the clouds that lay scattered in flocculent masses over Ireland and the west of England. For now I could see the outlines of the north of France and Ireland, and all this island of Britain, save where Scotland passed over the horizon to the north, or where the coast was blurred or obliterated by cloud. The sea was a dull gray, and darker than the land; and the whole panorama was rotating slowly towards the east.

All this had happened so swiftly that, until I was some thousand miles or so from the earth, I had no thought for myself. But now I perceived I had neither hands nor feet, parts nor organs, and that I felt neither alarm nor pain. All about me, I perceived that the vacancy (for I had already left the air behind) was cold beyond the imagination of man; but it troubled me not. The sun's rays shot through the void, powerless to light or heat until they should strike on matter in their course. I saw things with a serene self-forgetfulness, even as if I were God. And down below there, rushing away from me,—countless miles in a second—where a little dark spot on the gray marked the position of London, two doctors were struggling to restore life to the poor hacked and outworn shell I had abandoned. I felt then such release, such serenity, as I can compare to no earthly delight I have ever known.

It was only after I had perceived all these things that the meaning of that headlong rush of the earth grew into comprehension. Yet it was so simple, so obvious, that I was amazed at my never anticipating the thing that was happening to me. I had suddenly been cut adrift from matter: all that was material of me was there upon earth, whirling away through space, held to the earth by gravitation, partaking of the earth-inertia, moving in its wreath of epicycles round the sun, and with the sun and the planets on their vast march through space. But the immaterial has no inertia, feels nothing of the pull of matter for matter: where it parts from its garment of flesh there it remains (so far as space concerns it any longer) immovable in space. I was not leaving the earth: the earth was leaving me, and not only the earth but the whole solar system was streaming past. And about me in space, invisible to me, scattered in the wake of the earth upon its journey, there must be an innumerable multitude of souls, stripped like myself of the material, stripped like myself of the passions of the individual and the generous emotions of the gregarious brute, naked intelligences, things of newborn wonder and thought, marveling at the strange release that had suddenly come on them!

As I receded faster and faster from the strange white sun in the black heavens, and from the broad and shining earth upon which my being had begun, I seemed to grow, in some incredible manner, vast: vast as regards this world

I had left, vast as regards the moments and periods of a human life. Very soon I saw the full circle of the earth, slightly gibbous, like the moon when she nears her full, but very great; and the silvery shape of America was now in the noonday blaze, wherein (as it seemed) little England had been basking but a few minutes ago. At first the earth was large, and shone in the heavens, filling a great part of them; but every moment she grew smaller and more distant. As she shrunk, the broad moon in its third quarter crept into view over the rim of her disc. I looked for the constellations. Only that part of Aries directly behind the sun and the Lion which the earth covered were hidden. I recognized the tortuous, tattered band of the Milky Way, with Vega very bright between sun and earth; and Sirius and Orion shone splendid against the unfathomable blackness in the opposite quarter of the heavens. The Polestar was overhead, and the Great Bear hung over the circle of the earth. And away beneath and beyond the shining corona of the sun were strange groupings of stars I had never seen in my life; notably a dagger-shaped group that I knew for the Southern Cross. All these were no larger than when they had shone on earth; but the little stars that one scarce sees shone now as brightly as the first magnitudes had done, while the larger worlds were points of indescribable glory and color. Aldebaran was a spot of blood-red fire, and Sirius condensed to one point the light of a world of sapphires. And they shone steadily: they did not scintillate, they were calmly glorious. My impressions had an adamantine hardness and brightness; there was no blurring softness, no atmosphere, nothing but infinite darkness set with the myriads of these acute and brilliant points and specks of light. Presently, when I looked again, the little earth seemed no bigger than the sun, and it dwindled and turned as I looked, until, in a second's space (as it seemed to me), it was halved; and so it went on swiftly dwindling. Far away in the opposite direction a little pinkish pin's head of light, shining steadily, was the planet Mars. I swam motionless in vacancy, and without a trace of terror or astonishment, watched the speck of cosmic dust we call the world fall away from me.

Presently it dawned upon me that my sense of duration had changed: that my mind was moving not faster, but infinitely slower; that between each separate impression there was a period of many days. The moon spun once round the earth as I noted this; and I perceived, clearly, the motion of Mars in his orbit. Moreover it appeared as if the time between thought and thought grew steadily greater, until at last a thousand years was but a moment in my perception.

At first the constellations had shone motionless against the black background of infinite space; but presently it seemed as though the group of stars about Hercules and the Scorpion was contracting, while Orion and Aldebaran and their neighbors were scattering apart. Flashing suddenly out of the darkness, there came a flying multitude of particles of rock, glittering like dust-specks in a sunbeam and encompassed in a faintly luminous haze. They swirled all about me and vanished again in a twinkling far behind. And then I saw that a bright spot of light, that shone a little to one side of my path, was growing very rapidly larger, and perceived that it was the planet Saturn rushing towards me. Larger and larger it grew, swallowing up the heavens behind it, and hiding every moment a fresh multitude of stars. I perceived its flattened whirling body, its disclike belt, and seven of its little satellites. It grew and grew, till it towered enormous, and then I plunged amid a streaming multitude of clashing stones and dancing dust-particles and gas-eddies, and saw for a moment the mighty triple belt like three concentric arches of moonlight above me, its shadow black on the boiling tumult below. These things happened in one tenth of the time it takes to tell of them. The planet went by like a flash of lightning; for a few seconds it blotted out the sun, and there and then became a mere black, dwindling, winged patch against the light. The earth, the mother mote of my being, I could no longer see.

So with a stately swiftness, in the profoundest silence, the solar system fell from me, as it had been a garment, until the sun was a mere star amid the multitude of stars, with its eddy of planet-specks lost in the confused glittering of the remoter light. I was no longer a denizen of the solar system: I had come to the Outer Universe, I seemed to grasp and comprehend the whole world of matter. Ever more swiftly the stars closed in about the spot where Antares and Vega had vanished in a luminous haze, until that part of the sky had the semblance of a whirling mass of nebulæ, and ever before me yawned vaster gaps of vacant blackness, and the stars shone fewer and fewer. It seemed as if I moved towards a point between Orion's belt and sword; and the void about that region opened vaster and vaster every second, an incredible gulf of nothingness into which I was falling. Faster and ever faster the universe rushed by, a hurry of whirling motes at last, speeding silently into the void. Stars, glowing brighter and brighter, with their circling planets catching the light in a ghostly fashion as I neared them, shone out and vanished again into inexistence; faint comets, clusters of meteorites, winking specks of matter, eddying light points whizzed past, some perhaps a hundred millions of miles or so from me at most, few nearer, traveling with unimaginable rapidity, shooting constellations, momentary darts of fire through the black night. More than anything else it was like a dusty draught, sunbeam-lit. Broader and wider and deeper grew the starless space, the vacant Beyond, into which I was being drawn. At last a quarter of the heavens was black and blank, and the whole headlong rush of stellar universe closed in behind me like a veil of light that is gathered together. It drove away from me like a monstrous Jack-o'-lantern driven by the wind. I had come out into the wilderness of space. Even the vacant blackness grew broader, until the hosts of the stars seemed only like a swarm of fiery specks hurrying away from me, inconceivably remote, and the darkness, the nothingness and emptiness, was about me on every side. Soon the little universe of matter, the cage of points in which I had begun to be, was dwindling, now to a whirling disc of luminous glittering, and now to one minute disc of hazy light. In a little while it would shrink to a point, and at last would vanish altogether.

Suddenly feeling came back to me: feeling in the shape of over-whelming terror—such a dread of those dark vastitudes as no words can describe, a passionate resurgence of sympathy and social desire. Were there other souls, invisible to me as I to them, about me in the blackness? or was I indeed, even as I felt, alone? Had I passed out of being into something that was neither being nor not-being? The covering of the body, the covering of matter had been torn from me, and the hallucinations of companionship and security. Everything was black and silent. I had ceased to be. I was nothing. There was nothing, save only that infinitesimal dot of light that dwindled in the gulf. I strained myself to hear and see, and for a while there was naught but infinite silence, intolerable darkness, horror, and despair.

Then I saw that about the spot of light into which the whole world of matter had shrunk, there was a faint glow. And in a band on either side of that the darkness was not absolute. I watched it for ages, as it seemed to me, and through the long waiting the haze grew imperceptibly more distinct. And then about the band appeared an irregular cloud of the faintest, palest brown. I felt a passionate impatience; but the things grew brighter so slowly that they scarce seemed to change. What was unfolding itself? What was this strange reddish dawn in the interminable night of space?

The cloud's shape was grotesque. It seemed to be looped along its lower side into four projecting masses, and, above, it ended in a straight line. What phantom was it? I felt assured I had seen that figure before; but I could not think what, nor where, nor when it was. Then the realization rushed upon me. It was a clenched Hand. I was alone, in space, alone with this huge, shadowy Hand, upon which the whole Universe of Matter lay like an unconsidered speck of dust. It seemed as though I watched it through vast periods of time. On the forefinger glittered a ring; and the universe from which I had come was but a spot of light upon the ring's curvature. And the thing that the Hand gripped had the likeness of a black rod. Through a long eternity I watched the Hand, with the ring and the rod, marveling and fearing and waiting helplessly on what might follow. It seemed as though nothing could follow: that I should watch forever, seeing only the Hand and the thing it held, and understanding nothing of its import. Was the whole universe but a refracting speck upon some greater Being? Were our worlds but the atoms of another universe, and those again of another, and so on through an endless progression? And what was I? Was I indeed immaterial? A vague persuasion of a body gathering about me came into my suspense. The abysmal darkness about the Hand filled with impalpable suggestions, with uncertain, fluctuating shapes.

Then, suddenly, came a sound, like the sound of a tolling bell: faint, as if infinitely far; muffled, as though heard through thick swathings of darkness,—a deep vibrating resonance with vast gulfs of silence between each stroke. And the Hand appeared to tighten on the rod. And I saw far above the Hand, towards the apex of the darkness, a circle of dim phosphorescence, a ghostly sphere whence these sounds came throbbing; and at the last stroke the Hand vanished, for the hour had come, and I heard a noise of many waters. But the black rod remained as a great band across the sky. And then a voice, which seemed to run to the uttermost parts of space, spoke, saying: "There will be no more pain."

At that an almost intolerable gladness and radiance rushed in upon me, and I saw the circle shining white and bright, and the rod black and shining, and many other things else distinct and clear. And the circle was the face of the clock, and the rod the rail of my bed. Haddon was standing at the foot, against the rail, with a small pair of scissors on his fingers; and the hands of my clock on the mantel over his shoulder were clasped together over the hour of twelve. Mowbray was washing something in a basin at the octagonal table, and at my side I felt a subdued feeling that could scarce be spoken of as pain.

The operation had not killed me. And I perceived suddenly that the dull melancholy of half a year was lifted from my mind.

# Under Chloroform

*Maurice Level*

"As for me," declared pretty young Madame Chaligny, "if ever I were obliged to have an operation and it was absolutely necessary to give me an anæsthetic, I would not place myself in the hands of any doctor I didn't know personally.... When I come to think of it, it seems to me that it would be ideal to be chloroformed by a man who was in love with you."

At this the old doctor, who had been sitting listening in silence, probably because they were speaking of his profession, shook his head.

"No, Madame, no. You are quite wrong there. That is the very last man you ought to choose."

"Why? With a man who loved her a woman would feel completely at ease; her thoughts would be concentrated, on him, and she would not run the risk of having her mind distracted in a way that might prove dangerous at such a moment. There must be even a sort of rare voluptuousness in sinking into unconsciousness with beloved eyes gazing into yours.... Then, think of the enchantment of coming to ... of the return to consciousness ..."

"Don't make any mistake about that return," smiled the doctor. "There's very little poetry about it. The sick person emerges painfully from the heaviest of all intoxications, and at such a moment the prettiest woman in the world lacks charm and runs the risk of disenchanting the most ardent lover."

After a little silence, he added gravely:

"She runs a still more terrible risk—that of never returning at all."

As every one protested he went on:

"I will tell you a story to illustrate what I mean, an old and very sad story. I am the tragic hero of it, and if I am able to speak of it to-day, it is because the telling can no longer compromise any one. I am the only one left of those who played a part in it, and you will lose your time if you try to discover the names of people who are now in their graves. I am seventy years old; I was twenty-four then, so you see ...

"I was house-surgeon at a hospital when I first met the woman who was the great and only love of my life. I would have done the maddest things to be able to see her; to keep her happy, out of the reach of any trouble, I was capable of making any and every sacrifice; I would have killed myself without regret rather than have a breath of suspicion touch her.

"We were very young. They had married her to a man twenty years older than herself, and I can say with truth, though the words sound strange from the mouth of an old man, that she loved me as much as I loved her.

"We had found complete happiness in each other for some months, discreetly, and without causing the slightest remark, when one morning I received a hasty line from the husband begging me to come and see his wife who was ill. I rushed to the house. I found her in bed, very pale, with the anxious face, blue-circled eyes, pinched nose and lifeless hair I had so often seen at the hospital. The night before she had been seized with violent pains in the side; they had put her to bed, and since then she had lain there moaning, hiccoughing between her sobs, warding off with terrified gestures any hand that approached her, her appealing eyes begging no one to touch her.

"There was not an hour, not a minute to lose. "We sent for my Chief, and it was decided to operate there and then.

"You must have been through it to understand the difference between calmly preparing to operate on people you don't know, and the horror of doing it for some one very dear to you.

"While they were getting the next room ready for the operation, my poor little darling beckoned to me, and trying to keep the pain out of her voice whispered:

"'I'm not afraid.... Don't worry about me ... you will put me to sleep, won't you?...'

"I protested with a gesture, but she persisted:

"'I beg you to do it. You must.... No one but you ...'

"I had neither the time nor the strength to say no. They came and carried her away.

"Then began my Calvary.

"While my Chief and the other doctors and nurses moved about the room, I took the bottle of chloroform and the compress.

"She started back as she inhaled the first few drops, then smiled at me and gave herself up without further resistance. But she did not go off properly. Perhaps it was that, too moved to measure it carefully, I gave too little chloroform, letting too much air pass between the handkerchief and her lips. Also I could not help thinking of all the accidents that might happen, of the cases of syncope I had seen or heard of, and it was not astonishing that my eyes were not as sharp as usual, my fingers uncertain ...

"My Chief, his sleeves turned up, his streaming hands stretched out; came up:

"'Has she gone off?"

"The sound of his voice braced me. It took my mind to the hospital, and I pulled myself together as I replied:

"'No, Sir, not yet.'

"'Hurry ...'

"I bent over her asking:

"'Can you hear me?...'

"She opened her eyes and lowered the lids twice to say 'yes.'

"'Is there a buzzing in your ears?... What can you hear?'

"She murmured:

"'Bells ...'

"As she spoke she seemed to shrink a little. One of her arms fell inert on the table; her breathing grew even, her face paler, and little blue veins appeared at the side of the nose. I bent over her: her breath was sibilant, and heavy with the smell of chloroform: she was asleep.

"'You can begin now, Sir,' I said to my Chief.

"'But when I saw the knife move along the white body, leaving behind it a red line, my agitation returned. As I watched them cut and pinch her flesh, it seemed to me that they were cutting and pinching my own. My hand stole up mechanically and stroked her face. Suddenly her legs moved with an instinctive gesture of defense, and she moaned.

"My Chief straightened himself:

"'But you haven't got her under.'

"I poured some drops of chloroform on the compress; they made a large gray stain on the fine batiste.

"The operator bent over her again.

"But again she moaned and began to mutter incoherent syllables.

"How I longed for it all to be over; longed to see her come to herself, to have done with the awful nightmare! She was now motionless but she continued to moan and mutter, and suddenly among the murmurings she pronounced distinctly a name, mine: Jean.

"A shudder ran through me. Speaking as if in a dream she went on:

"'Don't worry ... I'm not afraid ..."

"Great God, it was I who was afraid!

"Not so much afraid that she would never come to, that she would die in my arms, but afraid that in her delirium she would betray our secret.

"She began to stammer words that increased my fear. Hardly knowing what I was doing, I said:

"'Sir, she is not completely under ...'

"'Because she chatters?... What does that matter so long as she doesn't move?...'

"At that moment her voice rose clearly, every word distinct:

"'I'm not afraid … You are with me.… You put me to sleep …'

"There was no knowing what she might say next, and terrified, I administered more chloroform … Four, five times, tilt on tilt, I poured it on the compress and held it to her face. Her voice, now uneven, came to me muffled by the handkerchief I held against her mouth.

"'I am asleep.… I can hear the bells.… When I am well again we will go for walks together like we used to …'

"I lost my head. I thought that her husband, who was in the next room and probably near the door, would hear, that the others would understand. She, so proud, she whom no suspicion had ever touched, who till then had been above all suspicion, would be dishonored.

"To get her quite under, to try to keep her silent, I tilted the bottle, I tilted it again. The compress became heavy in my hand.

"'We shall be together … at night,' chanted the voice. 'And you will take me in your arms again … you will …'

"I lost my reason. What would the next words be? I poured … I poured … I no longer knew what I was doing.

"Then came the moment when I found that the bottle was empty. I realized that I had given too much. Terrified, I flung the compress away; with a hasty finger I lifted one of her eyelids and saw that the pupil of the eye was fixed, dilated so that there was nothing left of the iris but a transparent ring. I wanted to shout: 'stop!…'

"The word was strangled by the contraction in my throat.

"At the same moment I heard the voice of my Chief, short and anxious:

"'What's this.... What ... the blood-pressure is low.'

"With a violent movement he pushed me away:

"'But she's not breathing ... Some oxygen ... some ether ... quick ...'

"Alas! Too late.

"Her poor head rolled lifeless; her blue eye, the eyelid still up, was glazed and looked at me with an empty stare ...

"We tried everything, but nothing was any good. Syncope, the horrible white syncope, as we call it, had taken her from me."

For a few moments he sat lost in thought, then went on:

"I know perfectly well that such accidents happen frequently; that no one is safe from the treachery of chloroform. But I also know that if I had not loved her and had done my work with cold indifference; if I had not been overwhelmed by the double anguish of holding her life in my hands and hearing her unconsciously betraying the secret that would ruin her, I should not have to reproach myself with causing her death ..."

He was silent. A wave of sadness passed through the room as if it had been carried in on the chilly autumn wind that blew against the damp window.

Madame Chaligny, her head on the back of her armchair, sat gazing into space like a person lost in a dream.

The party broke up early that night.

# Artificial Hell

*Horacio Quiroga*

On moonlit nights, the gravedigger steps among the graves with a singularly stiff gait. He is naked to the waist but wears a straw hat. His fixed smile gives the impression of being stuck to his face with glue. If he didn't have shoes on, we could see the deformity of his feet, the big toes bent downwards.

None of this need cause any surprise, for the gravedigger abuses chloroform. His professional duties have led him to try this anesthetic, and once chloroform sinks its teeth into a man, he can't shake it loose without a fight. Our friend waits until nightfall before he uncorks his bottle. Being no fool, he chooses the cemetery as the place to play out his intoxicated fantasies, for there's no fear of interruption here.

At the first inhalation chloroform dilates the chest; the second floods the mouth with saliva; the third makes the extremities tingle; the fourth swells the lips, and one's ideas along with them, and that's when bizarre events begin.

The gravedigger's journey into fantasy has brought him to an open tomb from which the bones were being removed that afternoon, a job left incomplete when time ran out. Behind the ironwork gate a coffin has remained open, and beside it, on sandy ground, lies the skeleton of the man once confined in it.

What was that noise? Our friend slides back the bolt, steps inside, and after warily circling the skeleton, kneels down and applies his eyes to the eye-sockets of the skull.

There, at the back, slightly above the base of the cranium, supported on a ledge formed by the occipital bone, is crouched a shivering mannikin, yellow, his face a mass of creases. His lips are bluish, the eyes sunk deep into his head, his expression one of insane longing.

It is all that remains of a cocaine addict.

"Cocaine! Please, a little cocaine!"

The gravedigger calmly acknowledges that he'd manage to dissolve the glass of his bottle with his own saliva, if it were the only way to get at the forbidden chloroform. Hence it is his duty to help the shivering mannikin.

He leaves and comes back with a full syringe, courtesy of the cemetery's medical cabinet. But how does one inject a mannikin?

"Through the fissures of the cranium! Hurry up!"

Of course! Why hadn't he thought of it himself? Getting down on his knees, the gravedigger injects into the fissures the entire contents of the syringe which seep through the cracks and disappear.

Without a doubt something has reached the fissure to which the mannikin clings desperately. After eight years of abstinence, what molecule of cocaine could fail to ignite a delirium of strength, youth, and beauty?

The gravedigger returned his eyes to the sockets of the skull. He didn't recognize the dying mannikin. The skin, now firm and smooth, had not the slightest wrinkle. The lips, full of red vitality, were drawn close against each other with a lazy voluptuousness which would be hard to explain in a man, if we didn't know that almost every drug has something womanly in it. But especially those eyes! Previously glassy and burnt out, they were now shining with such passionate life that the gravedigger was seized with an unexpected envy.

"So it's like that? Cocaine?" he murmured.

The voice from inside the skull rang out with a delight beyond words.

"Ah, you'd first have to know what eight years of agony were! Eight years of frozen despair, pinned to eternity by the mere hope of one drop! Yes, that's what cocaine is! And what about you? I recognize that smell. Is it chloroform?"

"Yes," replied the gravedigger, embarrassed by the pettiness of his artificial paradise. "Chloroform likewise. I'd kill myself before I'd give it up."

The voice took on a mocking tone.

"Kill yourself! O yes, you'd end the business for sure. You'd become like any one of my neighbors around here. In three hours you'd be a rotten pulp, both you and your addiction."

"It's true," thought the gravedigger. "It'd be all over with me in no time." But this cocaine-addict still hadn't quit. Eight years dead, he still burned with a passion which had defied the absence of its vessel of delight, which had outlived the death of the organism that had created and sustained it. Nothing had been able to destroy that passion. It survived in monstrous form solely by itself, defiantly proclaiming its destructive longing as its supreme joy, holding fast in the face of eternity itself to the cranny of an aged skull.

The voice, drawling with warm voluptuousness, mocked on.

"You'd kill yourself. How charming! Well, I killed myself. Want to hear about it? Really? But you and I, we're not in the same league. Still, go fetch your chloroform, sniff some more, and listen to me. Then you'll appreciate how far your drug falls short of cocaine. Yes indeed."

The gravedigger returned and lying chest down on the ground, propped himself on his elbows, passed the bottle under his nose, and waited.

"Your chloroform. It's small-time stuff, eh? Even morphine isn't that—. Are you familiar with an addiction to perfumes? No? Not to Jicky by Guerlain? Listen then. At the age of thirty I got married. I had three children. With money to burn, an adorable wife, and three healthy children, I was quite happy. The only thing was, the house was far too big for us. You know the sort of place. No, I suppose, you don't. Anyway, those luxuriously appointed rooms appear rather solitary and useless. Solitary, more than anything. In that silence our whole palatial house lived out its barren and dreary splendor.

One day, in less than 18 hours, we lost our oldest boy to diphtheria. The following afternoon our second son went the way of his brother. My wife threw herself desperately on the only child remaining to us, a girl of four months. What did we care if we caught diphtheria or anything else? The doctor warned her not to breastfeed our daughter, but she ignored him, and before long the child was twisting convulsively. She died eight hours later, poisoned by her mother's milk.

Do the arithmetic: 18 plus 24 plus 9. In 51 hours, a little more than two days, our house lapsed into total silence. We had nothing to do. My wife was in her room, I paced up and down beside her. Apart from that, nothing. Not a sound. And only two days before we'd had three children.

So, my wife spent four days scratching at the sheets with a brain hemorrhage, and I resorted to morphine.

"Cut that out," the doctor told me. "That isn't for you."

"So, what is?" I replied. I gestured to the gloomy splendor of my house which had kindled one catastrophe after another, like rubies.

The doctor had to sympathize.

"Try sulfonal, or something. But your nerves won't stand up to much."

Sulfonal, brional, Jimson weed ... bah! But cocaine! How much heavenly delight there is in a single drop of it! We lie in wretched ashes at the foot of a sleepless bed, and then cocaine comes racing to the glorious rescue of our maimed delight! One minute we are suffering a measureless grief; an astonishing moment later we are bursting with lively confidence. At once hopes blossom forth and bring the future toward our opened souls, as close as ten centimeters away. All this hurtles into our veins through a platinum needle. Don't talk to me about chloroform.

My wife, she died. In two years I spent more money on cocaine than you could ever imagine. Do you know anything about drug-tolerances? Five centigrams of morphine can kill a robust individual. De Quincey ended up taking two grams daily for 15 years. That's to say, 40 times the fatal dose.

But all that takes its toll. In my case, the truth about my sad state of affairs, a truth repressed by intoxication day after day, started to demand satisfaction. I was at the end of my tether, unable to fight off the revolting hallucinations that assailed me from all sides. I made unprecedented efforts to rid myself of the curse, but to no avail. Three times I tried to withdraw from cocaine for a month, yes a whole month. But I gave in each time. You don't know-but you will one day—what suffering, what agony, what agonizing sweats you experience, when you try to stay away from that drug even for a single day.

Finally, poisoned to my innermost being, laden with torturing fantasies, transformed into a quivering wreck of a man, bloodless, lifeless—a horror over which cocaine cast a glittering disguise ten times a day, only to sink me immediately in a stupor deeper than before—one last shred of dignity drove me into a sanatorium. Bound hand and foot, I was delivered over to my redemption.

There, my willpower subjected to another's, supervised nonstop to prevent me acquiring the drug, I reached, was forced to reach, a level of detoxification.

You know what happened? Along with my heroic decision to hand myself over to this torture had come a tiny bottle of cocaine that I carried hidden in a pocket. Now you've some idea how far addiction will go.

For an entire year, after this fiasco, I kept on injecting myself. I took a long trip and thanks to that, I can't say why or how, I recovered some of my old self, and I fell in love."

The voice fell silent. The gravedigger, with the fatuous smile still stuck on his face, put his eye closer and thought he detected in the eyes of the mannikin something dull and glassy lightly veiling them over. The skin too was visibly losing its glossy smoothness.

"Oh yes," conceded the voice, "it's started. Anyway, to finish my tale. I owe it to you, a colleague in addiction, to finish my tale."

The girl's parents tried everything they could to block a marriage to this morphine addict or whatever he was! But it was a girl of painful hypersensibility who'd crossed my path—to my ruin, to hers, to everybody's. And stunningly beautiful! Only 18 years old. The luxury that surrounded her was what cut glass is to a perfume: its natural container.

The first time I forgot to inject myself before visiting her, she saw me decaying abruptly in her presence, turning into a drooling, wrinkled idiot. Beautiful and horrified, her eyes stared into mine. But inquisitively horrified! Pale and jumpy, she watched me inject myself. All night she didn't take her eyes off me, not for an instant. Behind the dilated eyes that stared so intently, I in turn discerned the congenital defect that had already surfaced in her uncle shut up in an asylum and in her epileptic younger brother.

The next day I caught her sniffing Jicky, her favourite perfume. In twenty four hours she had read everything available to her about drugs.

So, there we are! All it takes for two people to understand each other intimately is for them to share an abnormal taste for pleasure, however strange its method of satisfaction. Immediately they form a a bond that overrides every other interest, so that they can isolate themselves in the illusionary happiness of an artificial paradise.

In twenty days that paragon of physical beauty, youth, and elegance was dependent on the intoxicating breath of a perfume. She began to live, like me with my cocaine, in the destructive heaven of her Jicky.

We eventually realized that it was asking for trouble to act out our mutual somnambulism, however fleeting it might be, in her family's house, and decided to create a paradise of our own. My old house was the perfect place for it. I'd touched nothing there. I'd not even been back to it. We had wide, sumptuous divans placed in the living room. There, in the habitual silence, in the same funereal luxury that had seen the death of my children, in the profound tranquility of the living room, with a lamp lit at one o'clock in the afternoon, in an atmosphere laden with perfume, we lived out, like brother and sister, the long hours of our wordless idyll, I stretched out motionless, my eyes open, deathly pale, and she lying on her divan, clasping under her nostrils, in a hand as still as ice, her bottle of perfume.

There was not the least trace of sexual desire in us—and yet how handsome she looked with her deeply shadowed eyes, her disordered hair, and her immaculate skirts, ablaze with costly luxury!

For three months without a break she hardly ever failed to arrive, though I'm baffled about what combinations of visits, weddings, and garden parties she concocted to avoid her parents' suspicions. On the rare occasions when she didn't come, she'd arrive the following day eaten up with anxiety. She'd come in without even looking at me, toss aside her hat with a careless gesture, and with no more ado stretch herself out, head back, eyes half-closed, with her sleepwalker's bottle of Jicky.

Anyway, to cut things short. One afternoon, for some inexplicable reason, my poisoned body launched a counter-attack against the drug—addicts will know what I'm talking about—and I became conscious of what delights existed—not in my cocaine—but in that 18-year old body, so admirably built to be desired. That afternoon, as never before, her beauty, pale and sensual, surged through me in the sumptuous quiet of the lamp-lit room. The shock was so unexpected that I found myself sitting on her divan, gazing at her. Eighteen years old, and such a beauty!

She did not react at all. When I bent over her, she stared back with a distant coldness.

"Yes," I murmured.

"No, no," she replied in a colorless voice, turning her mouth away, and tossing her masses of hair.

Finally, finally, she threw her head back, closed her eyes, and gave in to me.

What was the point of being my old self for a moment, if my manly prowess, if my pride in myself as a male could not live up to the moment? My manliness was dead once and for all, drowned, dissolved in a sea of cocaine. I dropped down by her side, and seated on the floor, buried my head in her skirts. For a whole hour I stayed that way, with never a word spoken, while she, very pale now, lay motionless, her eyes fixed on the ceiling.

The backlash that had kindled a brief flash of desire in my ruined body brought with it an awareness of my lost honor as a man and the agonizing shame that went with it. My farcical failure in the sanatorium, my daily losses in self-esteem—they were nothing, you understand, to that moment's defeat! Why bother living, if this artificial hell to which I'd consigned myself and could not get out of, was incapable of totally absorbing me. It had let me go for an instant, only to plunge me back into this!

I got up and went out into the rooms I'd known so well, to where I kept my revolver. When I came back, her eyelids were firmly shut.

"Let's kill ourselves," I said to her.

She half-opened her eyes. For a minute she did not take her gaze off me. Her flawless forehead shifted with its customary gesture of weary ecstasy.

"Let's kill ourselves," she murmured.

She glanced round at the room's gloomy luxury, at the brightly burning lamp, and frowned slightly.

"Not here," she said.

We left together, still weighed down with hallucinations, and crossed the echoing house, room after room. Finally she leaned against a door and closed her eyes. Down along the wall she fell. Then I turned the gun on myself and fired again.

The bullet shattered my jawbone. I felt an immeasurable tingling in my head. My heart gave two or three startled leaps and stopped dead. When my brain, my nerves, my blood showed not the least sign of life, I felt I'd paid my debt to cocaine. Yes, I'd killed myself, but in doing so, I'd killed the addiction.

How wrong I was! A moment later what did I see? Entering the room, hesitating, hand in hand, through the living room door, our two dead bodies stubbornly coming back for more ...

The voice gave way without warning.

"Cocaine, please. A little cocaine!"

*—Translated from the Spanish*
*by Geoff Hargreaves*

# *from* The Diary of a Drug Fiend

*Aleister Crowley*

I CAN'T REMEMBER any details of our first week in Paris. Details had ceased to exist. We whirled from pleasure to pleasure in one inexhaustible rush. We took everything in our stride. I cannot begin to describe the blind, boundless beatitude of love. Every incident was equally exquisite.

Of course, Paris lays herself out especially to deal with people in just that state of mind. We were living at ten times the normal voltage. This was true in more senses than one. I had taken a thousand pounds in cash from London, thinking as I did so how jolly it was to be reckless. We were going to have a good time, and damn the expense!

I thought of a thousand pounds as enough to paint Paris every colour of the spectrum for a quite indefinitely long period; but at the end of the week the thousand pounds was gone, and so was another thousand pounds for which I had cabled to London; and we had absolutely nothing to show for it except a couple of dresses for Lou, and a few not very expensive pieces of jewellery.

We felt that we were very economical. We were too happy to need to spend money. For one thing, love never needs more than a pittance, and I had never before known what love could mean.

What I may call the honeymoon part of the honeymoon seemed to occupy the whole of our waking hours. It left us no time to haunt Montmartre. We hardly troubled to eat, we hardly knew we were eating. We didn't seem to need sleep. We never got tired.

The first hint of fatigue sent one's hand to one's pocket. One sniff which gave us a sensation of the most exquisitely delicious wickedness, and we were on fourth speed again!

The only incident worth recording is the receipt of a letter and a box from Gretel Webster. The box contained a padded kimono for Lou, one of those gorgeous Japanese geisha silks, blue like a summer sky with dragons worked all over it in gold, with scarlet eyes and tongues.

Lou looked more distractingly, deliriously glorious than ever.

I had never been particularly keen on women. The few love affairs which had come my way had been rather silly and sordid. They had not revealed the possibilities of love; in fact, I had thought it a somewhat overrated pleasure, a brief and brutal blindness with boredom and disgust hard on its heels.

But with cocaine, things are absolutely different.

I want to emphasize the fact that cocaine is in reality a local anæsthetic. That is the actual explanation of its action. One cannot feel one's body. (As every one knows, this is the purpose for which it is used in surgery and dentistry.)

Now don't imagine that this means that the physical pleasures of marriage are diminished, but they are utterly etherealised. The animal part of one is intensely stimulated so far as its own action is concerned; but the feeling that this passion is animal is completely transmuted.

I come of a very refined race, keenly observant and easily nauseated. The little intimate incidents inseparable from love affairs, which in normal circumstances tend to jar the delicacy of one's sensibilities, do so no longer when one's furnace is full of coke. Everything soever is transmuted as by "heavenly alchemy" into a spiritual beatitude. One is intensely conscious of the body. But as the Buddhists tell us, the body is in reality an instrument of pain or discomfort. We have all of us a subconscious intuition that this is the case; and this is annihilated by cocaine.

Let me emphasize once more the absence of any reaction. There is where the infernal subtlety of the drug comes in. If one goes on the bust in the ordinary way on alcohol, one gets what the Americans call "the morning after the night before." Nature warns us that we have been breaking the rules; and Nature has given us common sense enough to know that although we can borrow a bit, we have to pay back.

We have drunk alcohol since the beginning of time; and it is in our racial consciousness that although "a hair of the dog" will put one right after a spree, it won't do to choke oneself with hair.

But with cocaine, all this caution is utterly abrogated. Nobody would be really much the worse for a night with the drug, provided that he had the sense to spend the next day in a Turkish bath, and build up with food and a double allowance of sleep. But cocaine insists upon one's living upon one's capital, and assures one that the fund is inexhaustible.

As I said, it is a local anæsthetic. It deadens any feeling which might arouse what physiologists call inhibition. One becomes absolutely reckless. One is bounding with health and bubbling with high spirits. It is a blind excitement of so sublime a character that it is impossible to worry about anything. And yet, this excitement is singularly calm and profound. There is nothing of the suggestion of coarseness which we associate with ordinary drunkenness. The very idea of coarseness or commonness is abolished. It is like the vision of Peter in the Acts of the Apostles in which he was told, "There is nothing common or unclean."

As Blake said, "Everything that lives is holy." Every act is a sacrament. Incidents which in the ordinary way would check one or annoy one, become merely material for joyous laughter. It is just as when you drop a tiny lump of sugar into champagne, it bubbles afresh.

Well, this is a digression. But that is just what cocaine does. The sober continuity of thought is broken up. One goes off at a tangent, a fresh, fierce, fantastic tangent, on the slightest excuse. One's sense of proportion is gone; and despite all the millions of miles that one cheerily goes out of one's way, one never loses sight of one's goal.

While I have been writing all this, I have never lost sight for a moment of the fact that I am telling you about the box and the letter from Gretel.

We met a girl in Paris, half a Red Indian, a lovely baby with the fascination of a fiend and a fund of the foulest stories that ever were told. She lived on cocaine. She was a more or less uneducated girl; and the way she put it was this: "I'm in a long, lovely garden, with my arms full of parcels, and I keep on dropping one; and when I stoop to pick it up, I always drop another, and all the time I am sailing along up the garden."

Lou threw the letter across the table to me. For some reason or no reason, I was irritated. I didn't want to hear from people like that at all. I didn't like or trust her.

"Queer fish," I said rather snappily.

It wasn't my own voice; it was, I fancy, some deep instinct of self-preservation speaking within me.

Lou, however, was radiant about it. I wish I could give you an idea of the sparkling quality of everything she said and did. Her eyes glittered, her lips twittered, her cheeks glowed like fresh blown buds in spring. She was the spirit of cocaine incarnate; cocaine made flesh. Her mere existence made the Universe infinitely exciting. Say, if you like, she was possessed of the devil!

Any good person, so-called, would have been shocked and scared at her appearance. She represented the siren, the vampire, Melusine, the dangerous, delicious devil that cowards have invented to explain their lack of manliness. Nothing would suit her mood but that we should dine up there in the room, so that she could wear the new kimono and dance for me at dinner.

We ate gray caviare, spoonful by spoonful. Who cared that it was worth three times its weight in gold? It's no use calling me extravagant; if you want to blame any one, blame the Kaiser. He started the whole fuss; and when I feel like eating gray caviare, I'm going to eat gray caviare.

We wolfed it down. It's silly to think that things matter.

Lou danced like a delirious demon between the courses. It pleased her to assume the psychology of the Oriental pleasure-making woman. I was her Pasha-with-three-tails, her Samurai warrior, her gorgeous Maharaja, with a scimitar across my knee, ready to cut her head off at the first excuse.

She was the Ouled Näil with tattooed cheeks and chin, with painted antimony eyebrows, and red smeared lips.

I was the masked Toureg, the brigand from the desert, who had captured her.

She played a thousand exquisite crazy parts.

I have very little imagination, my brain runs entirely to analysis; but I revel in playing a part that is devised for me. I don't know how many times during that one dinner I turned from a civilised husband in Bond Street pyjamas into a raging madman.

It was only after the waiters had left us with the coffee and liqueurs—which we drank like water without being affected—that Lou suddenly threw off her glittering garment.

She stood in the middle of the room, and drank a champagne glass half full of liqueur brandy. The entrancing boldness of her gesture started me screaming inwardly. I jumped up like a crouching tiger that suddenly sees a stag.

Lou was giggling all over with irrepressible excitement. I know "giggling all over" isn't English; but I can't express it any other way.

She checked my rush as if she had been playing full back in an International Rugger match.

"Get the scissors," she whispered.

I understood in a second what she meant. It was perfectly true—we had been playing it a bit on the heavy side with that snow. I think it must have been about five sniffs. If you're curious, all you have to do is to go back and count it up—to get me to ten thousand feet above the poor old Straits of Dover, God bless them! But it was adding up like the price of the nails in the horse's shoes that my father used to think funny when I was a kid. You know what I mean—Martingale principle and all that sort of thing. We certainly had been punishing the snow.

Five sniffs! it wasn't much in our young lives after a fortnight.

Don't imagine we had to spoil the kimono. It was just a tuck in the quilting. Out comes a dear little white silk bag; and we open that, and there's a heap of snow that I'd much rather see than Mont Blanc.

Well, you know, when you see it, you've got to sniff it. What's it for? Nobody can answer that. Don't tell me about "use in operations on the throat." Lou didn't need anything done to her throat. She sang like Melba, and she looked like a peach; and she was a Pêche-Melba, just like two and two makes four.

You bet we sniffed! And then we danced all round the suite for several years—probably as much as eight or nine minutes by the clock—but what's the use of talking about clocks when Einstein has proved that time is only another dimension of space? What's the good of astronomers proving that the earth wiggles round 1000 miles an hour, and wiggles on 1000 miles a minute, if you can't keep going?

It would be absolutely silly to hang about and get left behind, and very likely find ourselves on the moon, and nobody to talk to but Jules Verne, H. G. Wells, and that crowd.

Now I don't want you to think that that white silk packet was very big.

Lou stooped over the table, her long thin tongue shot out of her mouth like an ant-eater in the Dictionary of National Biography or whatever it is, and twiddled it round in that snow till I nearly went out of my mind.

I laughed like a hyena, to think of what she'd said to me. "Your kiss is bitter with cocaine." That chap Swinburne was always talking about bitter kisses. What did he know, poor old boy?

Until you've got your mouth full of cocaine, you don't know what kissing is. One kiss goes on from phase to phase like one of those novels by Balzac and Zola and Romain Rolland and D. H. Lawrence and those chaps. And you never get tired! You're on fourth speed all the time, and the engine purrs like a kitten, a big white kitten with the stars in its whiskers. And it's always different and always the same, and it never stops, and you go insane, and you stay insane, and you probably don't know what I'm talking about, and I don't care a bit, and I'm awfully sorry for you, and you can find out any minute you like by the simple process of getting a girl like Lou and a lot of cocaine.

# The Hop-Heads

*Fred V. Williams*

### *Coke Bugs*

As "SHOT" AFTER "shot" of cocaine made the rounds the company became talkative. The men openly boasted of the "jobs" they had pulled under the very eyes of the police, and the women chatted of the friends they had in hospitals and laboratories where "coke" could be had for a song.

Many of their stories were purely the figment of their drug inspired imaginations, but some of their tales rang true.

I heard the innermost gossip of the crime world, what this man and that woman was doing, how So-and-So was faring in jail, what "coppers" were honest and dishonest; their stories running to the Hall of Justice and "the fixers" that abound about the police courts.

The girl who had bared her shoulder to the "shot" mouthed her words and made horrible faces that transfixed me with horror whenever she looked at me.

One of the men arose from his seat and began to peep through the keyhole of the door to the adjoining room.

"What are yeh doing?" growled the man they called the "Pug."

"There's somebody in the next room," replied the man in a hoarse whisper.

"G'wan!"

"I tell yeh there is. I hear 'em whispering."

And with that he drew a pocket-knife and unleashed a long blade.

"Pug" sprang from his chair and threw open the door. The adjoining room was unoccupied.

"Now! See anybody? Hear anybody whispering now?" he asked.

The man made no reply, but returned to his chair, muttering to himself and pocketing his knife, to my intense relief.

The girl who was making the horrible faces got up and went into the hallway.

Dawson Sue and "Pug" exchanged significant glances.

"May'll be having bugs in a few minutes. She's gone out to hunt them now," explained Dawson Sue sweetly.

"Bugs?" I queried at the risk of showing gross ignorance.

"Coke bugs!" she exclaimed in surprise. "You've seen 'fiends' have them, of course. Imagine bugs are under their skin. Comes from seeing the shadow of the needle on your arm when you're taking a 'shot.'"

"Oh, yes; sure," I replied. But I wondered what May would do when she found them. I didn't have long to wait. May stumbled, swore and came into the room, digging at her wrist with a pin. Blood streamed from a fresh and open wound.

"Stop that!" ordered the "Pug."

May paid no attention to him, but continued to tear at her flesh.

"Her side is all tore up from digging at it with pins," Dawson Sue told me. "She's got her man's face all picked to pieces, too; jabs at him when he's asleep. Thinks there are bugs on him, too."

"Awful!" I exclaimed.

"Oh, well," said Dawson Sue, "we all see something, but thank heaven, I don't see bugs! Mine are rats."

"What?"

"Yes, rats! I'll see 'em in a couple of hours. But I hold off pretty well by taking a lot of 'm' along with my 'c'. That steadies you!"

With that, Dawson Sue reached for the 'c' and began to dissolve herself a "shot." Her eyes were bright now, and the fine lines at their corners deepening.

"How did you start on 'the habit?'" I asked.

"A man broke me in," she said. "I started on the pipe—smoking opium. It was great fun at first, and then one morning 1 woke up and realized that it was no longer play—that it was a habit.

"Then the law knocked over smoking and I took to heroin. I snuffed it and in 3 minutes I had the 'kick' that opium took 2 and 3 hours to give me.

"A lot of us didn't know really what heroin—sniff H—was, until after it was too late. And then the reaction was terrible. It takes your memory, you know. After a while you can't think. I got scared and quit and took up cocaine and morphine, I guess that's just as bad, though. Anyway it's cheaper and easier to get, though God knows the 'm' makes every cell in your body crave it."

"How about cocaine?" I asked.

"Oh, your legs and back don't ache and your stomach cramp for lack of 'c' like it does when you're without 'm.' 'C' is more of a mental craving; there's really no habit in it, but it gets your mind and soul if you have one! But 'm'—oh, boy, that just owns your body."

"And would you like to get off 'the habit' if you had a chance?" I asked.

"Would I?"

The girl's eyes were like stars. And she answered:

"Do I want to see my mother before she dies? Well, I can't go home until I'm rid of this, and they write me she hasn't much longer to live."

Unsteadily Dawson Sue reached for her "needle" and undid a "bindle" of the deadly grains of "c."

"I'm getting sentimental," she apologized. "This is the stuff that makes me forget."

### *Slaves of Dope*

The boy seized the safety pin again and jabbed it viciously into the flesh, widening the wound.

This time the point of the eye-dropper held its place and the last of the drug was driven into his veins.

Another person took his place before the light. He, too, was just a boy.

And he used a safety pin, the same pin.

I judged the boy to be 20 or 21. Like his predecessor, he also was in rags. He took only cocaine.

His jolt was a heavy one.

And he insisted on taking another one on top of it despite the protests of his fellows who crowded around and huskily demanded their turn.

"How did you fellows start?" I asked.

"Jail," said one of them out of the dark. "Got a jolt in the 'can.' They put me in with a lot of 'fiends.' I started with them."

"And you?" I asked of another shadowy figure at my side.

"Bad company. Knocking around under the sidewalks on the bum with birds like these."

"The pipe," said another. "Smoked just for fun. Had a good job then.

"All over now. Can't smoke. Cops smell it. Easier to shoot in out of the way joints like this."

"Why do you fellows use the safety pin?"

"Needles are expensive. When you get one the cops take it away from you when you're pinched."

I felt a light touch at my hip pocket. I sensed the presence of someone behind me.

And then a hand stole softly over my clothes.

The Rat, standing near me, snarled at the man behind.

"Aw, let him alone. I told you he wasn't a bull. He ain't got any gat on his hip."

The addicts circled me one by one. They kept up a constant succession of "shots" before the light in the keg.

The newspaper on which they knelt was red with their blood.

One of the boys showed me his shoes. They were worn and torn. He wore no socks, no underclothes.

Just a ragged cap, a dirty, torn shirt; a coat, a pair of pants, and the shoes falling to pieces on his feet.

"That's what the stuff is bringing me to," he said. "It costs me $6 and $8, and sometimes $10 a day to keep in the stuff. I don't have enough to live on or to dress myself on.

"God, what a life!"

"Why don't you take the cure?"

He looked up at me wistfully.

"The cure? The cure costs money. And the jails don't cure.

"If a guy could get reduced; if they could take him off the stuff gradually, so he wouldn't have to suffer, and then feed him up afterward—why, there would be a chance."

Another man mentioned the clinic in New York and New Orleans.

"Why, you can get your stuff at $1 or so a day," he said. "You can hold a job. And they cure you free, too."

An hour passed and still the boys feverishly shot themselves full of coke. The "m" was all gone now. It was "c," the most deadly of all drugs to which men and women are slaves.

And then, as the "c" ran riot in their blood and brains, strange things happened in the caverns beneath the sidewalks; scenes of which men in the world above the sidewalks know nothing and do not see.

The boy slaves of dope ceased to be human beings. They became creeping, crawling things without the power of connected speech or thought.

They wallowed in the filth and refuse under the sidewalks, suffering the dread illusions to which the slaves of cocaine are heir.

### *The Rat*

Cocaine first numbs, then quickens the senses.

It inspires either fear or courage.

The drug fires the brain and ravishes the body.

A thousand conflicting thoughts struggle on the moment for the supremacy of the mind.

The body is a willing slave to each and every one of them. The muscles are torn between their duties to each mad idea.

A man in a weakened physical condition may run miles under the influence of cocaine, and then fall in a faint as the power of the drug dies within him.

Charged with the deadly "c," an addict may show superhuman courage or abject cowardice; he may hold up a bank on a busy street in daylight, or he may cower in fear at the mere sight of a policeman's uniform and star.

It all depends on the peculiar twist the drug gives to the mind of the man or woman who uses the stuff.

A desire to be alone first sweeps over nearly every person who uses it to excess—an impulse to crawl away and hide in the darkness like a wounded animal.

And then, alone under the influence of his drug, the user suffers the illusions which cocaine invariably exacts from the minds of its victims.

The obsession, the apparition, is invariably the same, and it brings the cold sweat out all over him. Of course these are the most advanced cases, suffering from excessive use of the drug.

I describe their symptoms in detail so that you may understand the actions of my strange and weird companions of the night.

As the dope dragged them into mad delirium they stole away into the shadows to be alone with their fantasies.

At first, they stood like grim statutes in the dark; then their movements quickened, and they emitted curious little animal-like sounds.

One boy tore frantically at his sleeve in search of a rat! Another wrenched at his shirt, dropped to his knees, and whimpered pitifully.

His illusion was a snake coiling about his body. The Rat told me he actually felt the slimy body of the snake about his flesh, and would soon feel the very bite of its teeth!

A youngster who had doped himself freely with "c" during the night climbed high in the cone of the sidewalk roofing, muttering incoherently of water.

The Rat tried to call him down, but he refused to heed.

"That guy can hear water dripping all over this place," said the Rat. "I've been there myself; I know."

At our feet a boy groveled in the refuse of the lot and searched dumbly among the tin cans and the papers.

"He's got 'em, too," said the Rat. "But nobody has ever been able to find out what he hunts for."

A great pity arose in me for these youngsters who were slaves to the stuff which robbed them of their minds. It was an old sight and an older story to the Rat.

"You'll see 'em come to pretty soon," said the Rat. "And then they'll run all over town like race horses.

"I found myself up on Twin Peaks one morning. Ran all the way out there, during the night, without stopping, thinking a cop was chasing me."

Sure enough, in a few minutes the grim, ghastly figures about me began to shoot this way and that.

They raced out of the cavern and up the sides of the old foundation ruins; then into the street.

I watched them as they ran away.

"Where are they going?" I asked. "What are they going to do?"

The Rat chuckled.

"They don't know." He said. "Daylight will find them all over town, and then—"

"And what?"

"Folks will begin to miss things," laughed the Rat.

# Morbid Craving for Morphia

*Edward Levinstein*

HERE BEGINS THE history of the disease I am going to describe, and to which I have given the name of 'morbid craving for morphia.' The correctness of the name might be called in question, others having proposed to call it Morphinismus, Morphia-delirium, and Morphia-evil. Neither of these three designations sufficiently answer to the character of the disease as delineated by me. A patient who has for some months been treated with injections of morphia, on account of an acute and painful disease, may show all the symptoms of Morphinismus, i.e. of specific morphia poisoning; but if, on the termination of his illness, he does not feel any desire for more of the drug, he has no 'morbid craving for morphia.' On the other hand, an individual may for years have a craving for morphia without showing the least symptoms of Morphinismus. For this very reason, the name of Morphia-evil will be unacceptable, and still less the name of Morphio-mania, unless we desire to characterise the morbid craving for morphia as due to a diseased state of the mind; but the latter is only one of the symptoms which, when the drug is withheld, may or may not appear without in the least altering the character of the case.

Morbid craving for morphia means the uncontrollable desire of a person to use morphia as a stimulant and tonic, and the diseased state of the system caused by the injudicious use of the said remedy.

Under this head we do not include those cases which necessitate the use of morphia for special medical purposes. Its proper use in these cases prevents the patient getting accustomed to the drug, because the injections are discontinued as soon as the disease passes away. But this can only be decided by the medical man, who has himself administered the injections, and never by the patient, if perchance they have been left in his hands. All painful diseases accompanied with sleeplessness make the convalescents nervous and melancholy; they continually worry themselves about their bodily health, greatly magnifying the importance of every trifling bodily change, of which a healthy person would not have taken the slightest notice. If, then, they should have by them a remedy, such as injection of morphia, which has previously proved of great benefit to them, they will at once resort to its use, either to prevent pain coming on, or to avoid the recurrence of a restless night. Such are the causes of the habitual use of morphia, of the seeming impossibility of doing without it, and, finally, the morbid craving for it.

***Delirium Tremens, A Symptom of Morbid Craving for Morphia.***

The delirium tremens brought on by morbid craving for morphia is accompanied by a series of symptoms bearing more or less the character of alcoholic delirium. Consequently the choice of this name does not require any justification; the same may be said of the morbid state called intermittent fever in consequence of morbid craving for morphia, as referred to hereafter, its symptoms being nearly the same as those connected with true malarial fever.

According to my observation, we may discern two forms of delirium tremens in morbid craving for morphia: the chronic, and the acute.

The delirium tremens chronicum is due to chronic poisoning with morphia, continuing into the period of abstinence, and not producing any mental excitement.

The delirium tremens acutum is only a symptom of the deprivation, and is accompanied by the most intense mental irritation.

The temper is of a changeable nature in the chronic form of delirium tremens. The patients are mostly of a jovial disposition, only occasionally interrupted by a short period of oppression. With some individuals the mental condition in the daytime is depressed; in the evening they become somewhat excited, and sometimes suffer from delusions. Trembling of the hands and muscular quivering are a constant symptom of this kind of disease.

Notwithstanding this affliction, the patients are of sound mind, and perfectly conscious; they may be roused for a short or a long time from their depressed or excited condition, and are able to take part in conversation.

The acute delirium tremens of morbid craving for morphia shows itself in the course of from six to twelve hours after the administration of the drug is stopped.

The patient at first gets fretful and restless, and constantly runs about the room, cries and screams, and at last, under the influence of painful sensations, becomes maniacal.

This state of mind, lasting only for some hours, is followed by a quieter condition, which is accompanied only by hallucinations. These hallucinations are caused by all the sensual organs excepting the taste. They see birds of various colours, hear voices, feel as if sitting in the wet, and smell the most varied things.

Soon illusions of an hypochondriacal character supervene. The patient thinks he is dead, and has been present at his own funeral; the persons touching him, in his ideas, get taller and taller, etc., etc. Some of them will likewise talk to themselves, and carry on conversations with absent persons.

The trembling of the hands is increased, and is accompanied by muscular quivering, nystagmus, and tremor of the whole body.

At the commencement of the acute delirium, the voice and speech change in character.

This delirium tremens of morbid craving for morphia is not to be compared with a state of excitability also showing itself during the period of abstinence, which is caused by the administration of chloral.

If during the first two to four days a dose of 45 to 60 grains of chloral is given against the sleeplessness, some patients a few hours after its administration will become intensely excited. The patients cannot stop in bed, jump out of it, crying, laughing, singing, screaming, hammering at the doors and windows, knocking down the furniture, and at last begin to assault their attendants. Towards the morning they become quieter, and fall asleep for a short time, awaking generally with no recollection of the scenes of the night, so that the events which occurred can only be brought back to their memory with great difficulty.

The differential diagnosis of the delirium of morbid craving for morphia, from other delirious conditions, is only attended with difficulty if the original cause is kept back from the medical attendant, and if morbid craving for morphia comes under observation only in its latter stages, as then it is almost identical with chronic alcoholism in its principal symptoms, such as tremor, sleeplessness, slight impediment of speech, restlessness, mental anxiety, occasionally impaired sight, etc., etc.

The diagnosis also becomes more difficult if the patient suffering from morbid craving for morphia had lately taken large quantities of alcoholic drink, the latter fact only being mentioned to the medical attendant.

The difference between acute delirium tremens in consequence of morbid craving for morphia and the delirium tremens potatorum is as follows :

1. The delirium tremens of drunkards is of spontaneous origin, or shows itself after traumatic accidents, or in the course of acute ailments; the acute delirium caused by morphia becomes apparent only during the partial or complete deprivation of the drug.

2. In the acme of delirium potatorum the tremor mostly has gone, while it increases in the delirium of morbid craving for morphia.
3. Alcoholic beverages, often refused by the delirious person, increase the paroxysm, but never diminish or stop it; the patient delirious in consequence of the abuse of morphia asks for morphia, and becomes quieter for a short time after large doses of the drug have been administered.
4. The delirium potatorum lasts for several days or weeks. The duration of delirium tremens due to morbid craving for morphia lasts scarcely forty-eight hours.
5. The delirium potatorum ends in a collapse very often fatal, this collapse not being met with in delirium tremens of morphia poisoning.

A mistake with regard to delirium tremens resulting from lead poisoning[3] is hardly possible, as the gums show no greyish hue, and there is no paralysis of the extensor muscles in our disease; the change from excitable to a drowsy condition also excluding such poisoning.

### *Cases.*

#### *I. Delirium Tremens in consequence of Morbid Craving for Morphia. (Changeable Condition of the Pupils.)*

Mr. F. H., 30 years old, private gentleman. On account of severe headache, lasting day and night for a long time, patient was recommended to use injections of morphia, which he administered himself. He began to inject in 1872, stopped the drug for a time of his own accord, but began again to use it towards the end of the year, as the pains in the head were increasing, He gradually rose the daily dose of morphia to eight grains. When applying for admission to the Institution on October 29, 1875, he, according to his own statement, injected four grains daily. In consequence of the use of morphia he complains of the following symptoms: loss of sleep and appetite, constipation, diminished generative power verging on impotence, increased perspiration, attacks of fever (shivering, heat, sweating), showing no type, double vision, longing for alcoholic drinks, tremor of the hands.

**Present State.**—Patient is a tall, strongly built man, with powerful muscles and a moderate accumulation of fat. *Right pupil narrower than left*; auscultation and percussion do not show any abnormal condition of the lungs, heart, liver, and spleen. Urine contains neither albumen nor sugar, but much morphia, turns the polarised light to the left for more than two parts of the scale of the apparatus of Soleil-Ventzke.

*October 30, 1875.*—In the afternoon the treatment of deprivation was commenced. At 6 P.M. there was retching, restlessness, and craving for morphia. Patient took a great deal of wine. At 2 A.M. he jumps out of bed, says he cannot bear it any longer, if he was not better to-morrow he should kill himself; screams for morphia. *Breaks a door again rushes back to bed,* moves about, swears and curses. The tremor has increased; vomited once, one relaxed motion. At 5 A.M. *he talks quite incoherently.* He complains of severe epigastric pain, tearing pain in the limbs; there is yawning, sneezing, shivering; temperature normal; pulse 72, strong and powerful.

*October 31.*—Patient does not exactly remember the events of the night, moans and groans, asks for morphia, gets restless, moves about in the bed. Shivering, yawning, sneezing, severe epigastric pains—'A perfect rumbling in the stomach.' *He again talks nonsense in the course of the day*, does not know that the doctor has visited him, sees double; seven relaxed motions, and vomited twice. *Left pupil more dilated than the right.* In the evening tearing pains in the limbs, spasmodic contractions, very restless. At 9 P.M. 45 grains of chloral were given.

*November 1.*—Only one hour's rest in the night, very restless, craving for morphia, frequent yawning, sneezing, and thirst, complains of burning in the throat, violent pain in the limbs. In the morning one and a half hour's rest. At midday a warm bath with cold douche was given. At the least noise or touch, starts and feels a cold shiver pass all over him. In the afternoon a pain in the urinary passage when passing water. Towards the evening he becomes more restless. Severe pain in the epigastrium; temperature 38.1° C (100.58° F). Great prostration; he had five relaxed motions and had been twice sick in the last twenty-four hours. Pulse vacillates from 66 to 72, was hard and regular. At about 10 P.M. Patient had 45 grains of chloral, which greatly excited him; he jumped out of bed, ran about the room screaming and crying. At 11 P.M. another 30 grains of chloral were given; he then rested from 12 to 1 A.M. Afterwards continual intense excitement.

*November 2.*—Patient screamed and cried in the night, was very delirious, fancied himself persecuted and betrayed; towards the morning half an hour's rest. Seminal emission without erection took place. In daytime very restless, shivering, sneezing, yawning, head and stomach ache, great objection to light, violent pains in the legs. Craving for morphia. Temperature 38.1° C (100.58° F). Eleven relaxed motions, vomited once. In the course of the day two warm baths with the cold douche were given, the patient afterwards feeling a little better and quieter.

*November 3.*—During the whole of the day he was not very restless. There were periodic attacks of headache and pains in the stomach as well as cramp in the calves. Patient felt very weak, yawned and sneezed a good deal, but was able to spend an hour in the winter garden. Slept for several hours in the daytime with intervals. Pulse 60, full and strong, four relaxed motions, once vomiting.

*November 4.*—Slept for two and a half hours in the night with many breaks, suffered again from pains in the head, stomach, and calves, shivering and feeling of heat. Temperature normal. Pulse 64. Felt refreshed by the morning bath. Appetite moderate, eight relaxed motions, vomited once, frequent retching. The diplopia is now almost gone, but he finds difficulty in reading, 'the letters get blurred.'

*November 5.*—Has slept for three hours altogether, again very restless, languid pains in the legs, severe headache, increased lachrymal secretion, and very sensitive to the light of the lamp. Much sneezing. In the evening, patient feels comfortable.

*November 6.*—Hardly any sleep during the night, but not very restless during the first half of it. In the daytime the condition was tolerably good, excepting some pains in the epigastrium. Appetite good. Three relaxed motions. Frequent sneezing. In the evening 45 grains of chloral were given.

*November 7.*—Soon after the chloral was taken intense excitement came on. Patient throws himself on the ground, hammers at the door. Afterwards he slept for two and a half hours with intervals. During the day the condition is good. Appetite satisfactory.

*November 12.*—After having slept for nearly four hours in the night, he was in the morning in an excited state; speech hasty, quivering of the muscles of the face. Appetite good, bowels regular.

*November 14.*—Eight hours' sleep. In a very good frame of mind. Frequent sneezing, one relaxed motion.

*November 24.*—General condition satisfactory. Appetite, sleep, and digestion regular.

On December 6, 1875, patient leaves the Institution in perfect health. He has not had a relapse.

### *Case.*

### *Acute Morphia Poisoning.*

On June 11, 1875, a lady was by mistake subjected to an injection of 5 grains of morphia from a solution containing 25% of the drug. It at once caused severe pain at the place of injection and oppressive symptoms of the utmost gravity.

Twenty minutes later I found her with a dark red face and suffering from giddiness and drowsiness, the carotides beating intensely, the pupils being contracted to a minimum. Pulse 92, respiration 24. I made an injection of one-fortieth of a grain of atropia, repeating it twice at short intervals, as the pupils did not react. At last they began to dilate, the drowsiness and somnolence however increasing; the speech became slow, difficult, and unintelligible, the face of a dark red, the eyes bright.

Patient had some black coffee given, an ice-bag was applied to the head and leeches to both process, mastoid, and the nasal mucous membrane, but apparently without success. To keep her from falling asleep, a tepid bath with cold douche was given, and the patient made to walk about, supported by two persons. The respiration having sunk to four inspirations in the minute, I faradised the nerv. phrenicus. Patient neither noticed anyone talking to her, nor could be roused by stimulants; had to be put to bed, and sank into a deep sleep four hours after the poisoning had occurred. After the lapse of half an hour, the respiration having sunk to three per minute, it was again necessary to resort to Faradisation. The patient by this means woke up, smiling pleasantly; her face became paler, the pupils larger; she, however, immediately fell asleep again. The sleep this time was a short one, as she began to vomit severely every half-hour; a state of delirium followed, which allowed the patient to rest for a short time only. The respiration had increased to six per minute.

About twelve hours after the poisoning the severe bodily symptoms began to abate, patient again completely recovering her senses. Patient for a fortnight after the mishap remained in a weak condition, felt giddy, and was unable to walk or to think quickly.

On the second day the urine, drawn off in the night by the catheter, was examined; showing a light blue colour when mixed with a solution of caustic soda and sulfate of copper. After being heated the oxyhydrate of copper in solution was reduced to oxydulate of copper, the addition of alkali and bismuth producing a black colour when heated. The polarised light was turned towards the right for two or three fractional parts of the Soleil-Ventzke apparatus. Several days afterwards the pathological alterations of the urine had disappeared.

### *Experiments on Animals.*

*I.*

**A large rabbit** was given 4½ grains of morphia at 4 o'clock. Immediate somnolence. Reaction of the bulbi diminished; death at 6 o'clock.

**Post-mortem Examination three hours after.**—On pressing the abdomen 96 cubic centimetres of a light yellow urine passed out of the bladder, showing a slight flaky sediment. Specific gravity, 1.019. The urine shows the following condition:—

1. It precipitated a large quantity of red oxydulate of copper out of Fehling's solution.
2. It reduced pernitrate of bismuth.
3. With yeast active alcoholic fermentation was produced in it.
4. It turned the polarised light for four fractional parts of the Soleil-Ventzke apparatus.
5. It changed its colour when boiled with a solution of caustic soda.

6. On applying Trommer's test, it showed great reduction of colour without however precipitating red oxydulate of copper.
7. It contained traces of albumen.

*II.*

**A large rabbit** was given 7 grains of morphia at 5 P.M. It died in three quarters of an hour.

**Post-mortem Examination two hours afterwards.**—The urine forced out by pressure of the abdomen showed the following condition:—

1. It reduced alkaline solution of sulfate of copper, precipitating red oxydulate of copper.
2. The same with Fehling's solution.
3. After adding yeast and exposing it to a temperature of 40° C. (104° F.), it evolved carbonic acid gas after a short time.
4. It reduced pernitrate of bismuth.
5. Turns polarised light towards the right.
6. It contains albumen in clearly perceptible quantity.

On dissection, the corticalis of the kidneys is of a dark red colour. Substance of the liver flabby, can be crushed with a slight pressure of the finger. Stomach and intestines very full. The left ventricle feels extremely hard, the right is soft and flabby. Both contain coagulated blood.

### *III.*

**A large rabbit** is treated at 9.30 with an injection of 7 grains of morphia under the skin of the back. Died half an hour afterwards.

**Post-mortem Examination two hours afterwards.**—The urine evacuated from the bladder (quantity, about 106 cubic centimetres) did not contain any sugar, but slight quantities of albumen. The internal organs show no abnormal condition. The rigidity, showing itself at the moment of dying, was worthy of notice.

### *IV.*

**A middle-sized rabbit** had at 3 P.M. 5 grains of morphia injected under the skin of the back. The animal continued to live. The urine passed during the night (54 cubic centimetres).

# René Daumal, Carbon Tetrachloride, and Experiments in Near Death

*Jordan Jones*

THROUGHOUT THE HISTORY of psychoactive chemicals, substances from soma to crack cocaine have held a tripartite attraction: they have awakened our religious and philosophical sensibilities, leading us to a deeper understanding of cosmos and community; they have appealed to our pleasure instincts, offering recreation and a kind of psychic tourism; and they have appealed to Thanatos, our often denied death instinct. Examples of philosophical drug use include soma in Hinduism, wine in the Judeo-Christian tradition, peyote in the Native American southwest, and LSD in the hands of Aldous Huxley and other experimenters. Recreational or erotic drug use includes marijuana, what we call social drinking, and cocaine. The best known drugs of Thanatos are heroin, crack cocaine, nicotine, and PCP. Users who pick up a drug in the Thanatos category do so because their need exceeds the peril, or because they need peril.

People have often moved from one of these categories to another. In fact, one definition of addiction would be the transition from experimentation (Philosophia) or recreation (Eros) to a state in which the user is only in control to the extent that she or he insists on courting death (Thanatos). In addition, there are many users—Timothy Leary springs instantly to mind—who have been involved simultaneously in philosophical and hedonistic drug use.

* * *

Then, there is the special case of René Daumal, the French poet, translator, novelist, and essayist, who combined the deadly effects of the chemical carbon tetrachloride ($CCl_4$) with an intense desire to understand the au-delà, the beyond.

Although he did not have a death wish, Daumal had been intrigued by death since about the age of six when, without the canned interpretations of a religious upbringing, "the problem of death presented itself to me in all its nudity." His fascination with death led him to study the *Tibetan Book of the Dead (Bardo Thödol),* a guide to the realm where death and dream intersect. In a review of an English translation of the *Bardo Thödol,* Daumal wrote: "In its ritual usage, the *Bardo Thödol* is designed to guide a man through the decisive experience of death, to remind him of the teaching of the Tibetan Lamas, and to help him profit from this unique opportunity to wake up and escape the cycle of rebirth." One of the most important teachings in the *Bardo Thödol* is how the seeker may develop consciousness during the dream state. This 'dream yoga' has formed a significant part of the Tibetan Buddhist path to enlightenment since the eighth century CE. Understanding how to control the dream state is deemed essential for the navigation of the bardo, the transitional state between incarnations.

Daumal's experiments in sleep and near-death experience resemble the descriptions of Tibetan dream yoga one encounters in the *Bardo Thödol,* and led him to realize a similar conclusion: just as dreams are illusions, so is waking life. Daumal was interested in his own death, but could not study it except through the analogue of dream imagery: "Finding no means to experiment directly on death—on my death—I tried to study my sleep, supposing an analogy between the two. I tried, by various methods, to enter, fully conscious, into sleep." Eventually, he decided to confront death itself. "I would put my body into a state as close as possible to that of physiological death, but still use all my attention to remain conscious and to record everything that presented itself to me."

Daumal used carbon tetrachloride to induce these near-death experiences. Since he was a collector of beetles, he knew that the carbon tetrachloride that he used to kill specimens for his collection was chemically similar to the sedative chloroform, though more deadly. It would serve well as his passage to a dream state and then to the *au-delà.* He soaked a handkerchief in it and put the handkerchief in front of his face, figuring that as he approached death, his hand would fall and take the poison away from his nostrils.

In his essay "Le Souvenir Déterminant" ("The Decisive Memory"), Daumal describes his experiment. Under the deadly influence of the carbon tetrachloride, he began to experience the classic signs of asphyxiation: his heart began to beat wildly, and he felt the pulse in his temples; his head was buzzing, he was hyper-sensitive to sounds, and he began to see flashing lights. After seeing his life replayed before his eyes, Daumal realized that, while he was still in control of his body, and of his hand holding the handkerchief, and while he still understood words and felt he could use them sensibly, the world itself was slipping away. Words were comprehensible, but they had no correspondence to the exterior world, they no longer evoked real objects. In fact, the sensory world no longer had any meaning for him. He had entered a different world, one characterized by an "indescribable certainty … of the existence of another thing, a beyond, another world, or another sort of knowledge." This certainty was beyond the realm of language as it was beyond that of temporality.

He began to see a series of red and black circles and triangles transposed against one another. These geometrical objects moved around and transformed into one another in ways that did not make sense using any agreed-upon geometry. To sustain this new world, the progression of its new geometry, and himself in it, Daumal began, before he realized it, to chant: "Tern gwef tem gwef dr rr rr." All time and space were constructed in a non-Euclidean fashion, curved and turning in on themselves. Temporally, the experience was one of infinite repetition; spatially, it seemed that any line away from a point led back to that same point. Daumal was experiencing eternity first-hand. He himself was the flaw. For in this infinite world, he was finite, he was a being separate from pure existence, a temporally and spatially limited creature. His hand dropped the cloth, and he revived to a crushing headache that stayed with him the rest of the day. Daumal repeated his experiment—in the company of friends who might be able to revive him should things go awry—with similar results. Other friends performed it, with mixed results. None received the sense of certainty Daumal described except his close friend Roger Gilbert-Lecomte, with whom Daumal edited the journal *Le Grand Jeu*. Daumal felt that he had reached that source of visionary power and understanding that has been described in every age and culture.

* * *

Daumal's experimentation with carbon tetrachloride weakened his health. Even so, the same bravery in the face of death—a bravery that came from facing what he feared most—led Daumal to risk his life again. In 1944, with Paris still occupied by the Nazis, Daumal traveled from Vichy to Paris with his Jewish wife in order to see his master, Gurdjieff. Perhaps Daumal knew his days were numbered. Certainly it was no secret to him that his lung condition was tuberculosis, then as much a death sentence as the worst cancers are today. Until the end, though, Daumal was not the kind to take the hard realities of life and death lying down. He risked his life for serious matters, just as he had done with his experiments with carbon tetrachloride. He died shortly after his rigorous journey. Being a confirmed Vedantist, he felt that this life is not the end, but a middle passage through which we are bound to suffer, until our individual personalities are ready to be subsumed into the One. Far from this being a dry-as-dust theory or dogma, it was something he had already lived.

# Unglued

*Greg Boyd*

People say that I'm fortunate. After all, I've pursued my career as a sculptor without the constant struggle and financial strain with which most of my peers have had to contend. In college my studio art professors praised me highly and, as unlikely as it seems, I began exhibiting and selling my work even before I had completed my degree. In the years since, critics have written flattering articles about the ironic juxtapositions and the multiple worlds I present in miniature. Today patrons pay increasingly large sums of money for my creations, galleries in major cities exhibit and sell them, even a few small museums have added them to their permanent collections. Though I am certainly not among the top ranks of working sculptors, nevertheless my living (if one could call it that) is assured. Yet despite the appearance of success, I readily confess that I am a hopeless failure, a complete fraud, a pretender to my own talent, a vulture feeding on the eyes of a corpse.

As a child I was shy and sickly, largely ignored by other children. But unlike many with a delicate nature, I cared little for books. Instead, my genius manifested itself in a meticulous attention to detail and a keen interest in building. For hours I would sit by myself among my plastic blocks, creating fantastic palaces and imaginary cities. At the age of twelve I began building model airplanes, a task my patience rewarded with handsome results. I even won some contests sponsored by local hobby shops.

At first my parents were delighted. They saw how my successes helped my confidence and they encouraged me to continue. Soon my bedroom was filled with realistic-looking replicas of candy-colored hot-rods, gray battleships, red Folker tri-planes, and camouflage Spitfires. When I whined that I needed more space for my work, my parents obliged me by converting our detached two-car garage to a hobby room. They even gave me the key.

"I'm so happy you'll finally have room to spread out," my mother told me, though she really meant she was glad my paints and in-progress models would no longer be on constant view on a card table in the living room.

I quickly made the space my own. My father built me a large work bench and lined the walls with wooden shelves. I hung several dozen finished airplanes from the ceiling rafters and lined the shelves with plastic cars, ships, dinosaurs, military vehicles, monsters, animals and a series of anatomical models which I had special ordered from a medical supply company and of which I was particularly proud: a human heart with all its secret valves and chambers, a wonderfully realistic-looking eyeball. I set up my portable stereo in the room and played tapes of my favorite music while I worked, cutting molded plastic pieces from their stems with a sharp knife, sanding away the rough edges, painting in the tiniest details prior to assembling each model. I was fascinated by the properties of glue, how it seemed to eat away the plastic as it permanently fused the parts into a greater whole. Many times I witnessed this small miracle under my magnifying glass.

On weekends I ate lunch, and sometimes even dinner, at my workbench. I let it be known that I didn't like to be disturbed. By the time I was fifteen I became so protective of my little kingdom that I took to locking the door. No longer did I welcome anyone inside, not even my few friends from school. "I'm working on something really big," I told my parents. "It's going to be a surprise." By that time, of course, I'd stumbled onto the concept of synthesis and had already begun the slow, deliberate, inspired process—the mixing, the bringing together of opposites, the seamless joining of images, the fantastic coupling that would in time become my masterpiece.

Because I had no intellectual understanding of the work and relied purely on my intuition and inspiration to guide me, I developed a kind of primitive, quasi-religious ritual. First I would select one of several tapes to play—the specific music no longer seems important, only the fact that I was surrounded by sound. Then, seated on my high metal shop stool, amid my wooden toothpicks, pots of model paint, thinner and brushes, I would carefully squeeze a large mound of clear glue onto a pie tin (early on I realized the tubes themselves were difficult to control and messy) and place it directly in front of me on the bench. Then I leaned closely over the tin, my hands supporting my chin, and stared at the glue, meditating on its colorless consistency and strong odor until I could see exactly what needed to be done next.

During this time the music seemed to grow increasingly more distinct—not louder really, but focused, intense, hypnotic—and produced in me an effect similar to that of a nocturnal animal caught in the headlights of an on-coming car. My vision, too, seemed greatly enhanced. By vision I don't mean that I could read smaller characters at greater distance or any such nonsense. Rather, I could simultaneously see details set within their widest context and could thus reflect upon the specific and the general at once. I saw, through the same lens, a black cat slinking within an entire city, a lost ring upon the vastness of the ocean floor, a grasping hand among the killing fields of history, a woman's lips hovering in the sky above the world. This remarkable facility made it so each of my choices built upon what had come before in an ever-deepening aesthetic progression. Somehow I had stumbled onto a secret world and through it discovered how beauty and love were all-inclusive; they were what held the universe together, what helped us make sense of it all.

Over a single summer my sculpture blossomed, a huge flower reaching toward the sun. I sanded, painted and fit together thousands of plastic parts from many hundreds of models. As it grew, the work devoured some of my finished models whole; others I disassembled first and incorporated piece by piece. Slowly the sculpture expanded, spreading in every direction until it filled the garage from wall to wall. I had to borrow a step ladder from the tool shed to continue work amid the swirling mass of motorcycle engines, gothic spires, dismembered limbs, railroad tracks, trolls and soldiers, pirate ships' rigging, doll house decorations, decapitated heads, military paraphernalia, animal skeletons, brick facades, steam locomotives, historical panoramas, jesters and saints, painted genitalia and other hand-carved ornaments and flourishes.

The ladder, of course, was my undoing. It encouraged me to go higher than I should have gone, to cut away at the rafters until the roof began to sag, to begin hacking through the roof itself. That's when they came for me, with loud knocks, shouting and pleading, but I wouldn't let them in. In time my father grew impatient and broke down the door. Then my mother rushed inside and wrapped her arms around me like dark wings. She was crying as she led me outside into the fierce sunlight.

Later she told me I'd been laughing and crying at the same time when they found me atop the ladder. I don't remember what happened next, except that I somehow ended up at a clinic in the country, where I stayed several days. Then I went to live with my grandmother for a while. It was a period of whispering in other rooms and great concern for my health. I slept most of the time. Whenever I asked about the sculpture people became silent and changed the subject.

When my parents finally came to take me home again they picked me up in a new car, a Cadillac coupe de ville. I sniffed at the new vinyl in the back seat and remembered how I had used the right quarter panel from an earlier model of the same car as a crib for the baby Jesus I had placed within the bombed out French farmhouse next to the giant football helmet and the hinged rattlesnake jaw.

After he pulled the car into the driveway, my father stopped and told my mother and me to get out. "I'll park the car," he said, nodding toward the garage.

"No!" I cried, running toward the side entrance. I tested my hand on the knob and found it locked. Already I could hear the gears and a chain pulling the heavy double door. I rounded the corner and saw that the garage was empty.

It's taken me years to forgive my parents. I realize they had no idea what they were doing when they destroyed my sculpture. "We cleaned everything up," my mother explained. If only I had thought to take photos from different angles or to make detailed drawings—a schematic rendering—I might still have some hope of recreating it. Now, however, after so many futile attempts, I can only aspire to capture occasional parts of the vision, flat sections without scope or grandness, that return to me suddenly or in dreams.

This is the boneyard of scattered fragments from which I scavenge my fortune, gather my praise.

# Angel Rivera and the Sidewalk Jesus

*Jordan Jones*

Don drove up in his cherry red Chevelle convertible with dingle-balls hanging over the dash. For a gringo, he sure had pachuco tastes. I had been looking for him because he owed me a quarter of angel dust for helping him unload a jar of black beauties. It was getting harder and harder to sell black beauties and pink ladies, especially when you wanted to move a lot of them, like Mitch always did. There were just too many dealers. Speed was everywhere.

But angel dust was hard to find in the suburbs. I kept hearing about it from my friends in el barrio: how sweet it was, how it made you see stuff, and how it made everything funny. It made you macho and made women want to sleep with you. Those homies were nice to me. They forgave me, they said, for moving out of the barrio and into the white suburbs. They knew it wasn't my fault. My dad thought that just because his construction business started doing well, he could move into the 'burbs and become a gringo. But I was ok, because I was nothing like my dad. I told them I wanted to be a junky by the time I got out of high school.

They liked me because I had cojones and only wanted to do dangerous shit.

So I made that deal with Mitch: I would unload the beauties, if he would find me the dust. I sold the speed in the smoking area to other hard mestizos who like to trip. Sold 'em five at a time in baggies that I called party packs. Even though I said it was hard to sell, it's not really hard if you know a lot of people and which dudes like what.

"Hey! How's it hangin'?" Mitch said, sliding over to the passenger side. Still a white dork.

I gave him the shake through the open window. "Got the stuff?" I asked him. I could see he was nervous. He reached into his pocket then pulled out his fist with a baggie of dusted dope in it and handed it to me, looking around like a paranoid. I held the baggie up to see how much it was.

"Shit! Are you trying to get us busted?"

It was sift, not buds, but it was two whole fingers worth, twice what I thought it would be. It's always good to rag on your dealer though; it keeps him straight with you.

"It's sift, man. I thought we were talkin' buds."

"Hey, the sift was hard enough to get. It's not like I spray it myself."

"Yeah," I said, acting disappointed, feeling excited. "Next time: buds."

"Sure," Mitch said, "No problem. I think these guys will give me better stuff next time." I knew that was right.

Mitch drove away slowly, obeying all the traffic laws the way he always did right before or after making a sale. Even though he drove it like mi abuela, his ride was sweet. He had convinced his mother to buy it with some of the money she got because she was dying of cancer. The tires were bald and the top was ragged, but the car definitely had potential. Although it was supposed to be hers, she didn't go out much anymore. Just too plain sick, I guess. Mitch used it as a dealer's pussy wagon. He kept saying he was going to fix it up, but he never did. The girls didn't care, as long as he always had weed for them.

I CALLED MY homie Arturo and he met me at the corner of the field by the baseball diamond where we always smoked out. It's on campus, so you don't get picked up by the cops, and far enough from the school buildings so you can always hide the evidence if one of the yard duty ladies comes out to tell you to go to class.

We stuffed his pipe with the dusted weed and began toking. We laughed a lot, and I was just feeling high, nothing special. Then, my legs felt tight sitting there. I got up and started running around Arturo, who just looked up at me, laughing and rolling onto his back. On one of my circles around him, I felt myself pulled outward, like when you're swinging a rock in a sling, and it wants to fly. I ran to the fence, then hopped it in one movement. Wow! I never did that before. I ran down the street and around the corner, and down that street, about two miles. I knew I was in Mitch's neighborhood, near the lake, where the rich whities lived. I thought I'd go see him. I ran up Greenbrier, toward Mitch's place.

Just as I turned left onto Willow, I thought I saw something in the sidewalk in front of me. I stopped, and saw Jesus, like a chalk drawing, with his arms in the air over his shoulders. He looked just like he looks in that painting just to the right of the altar at St. Rose, only instead of his hands being nailed to the cross, he was holding his bloody hands up at me and saying, "Stop," although no sound came out. It was so weird. I just stood there looking at Jesus, alive in the sidewalk mouthing, "Stop," over and over.

Then he moved. He started coming out of the sidewalk. His head broke through the concrete first, and he flinched. Then his upraised hands came through with their nail holes, and his shoulders. He was coming up out of the sidewalk like his feet were on hinges, and I began to hear him walling, "No, Angel, mi hijo, no."

I freaked, and turned around and ran the other direction. Over my shoulder, I saw him running after me, arms outstretched like a mummy's, telling me no. When I got to the corner of Willow and Greenbrier, I ran across the street, looking back at the No Jesus. He was trailing bandages now, probably from the tomb.

When I hit the Chevelle, it was only going about 15 miles an hour, getting ready to turn on to Willow. I rolled over the hood and landed on the opposite sidewalk and grassy parkway. I looked behind me, and Jesus was getting out of the car, looking at me. Concerned, I guess. But I wanted nothing to do with that do-gooder who always says no. "Jesus, you're a dead man!" I yelled, getting up and running at him.

He saw that I was crazed and got back in the car and locked the doors. He was crying. I smashed my fist through the windshield. It wasn't Jesus anymore, it was Mitch, and he was saying, "I'm sick, don't hurt me, what are you doing?" I took my bloody right hand and tore through the convertible top and grabbed Mitch by the hair to tell him how cool dust is. I pulled him up but only got his hair. I looked down, and there was his bald mother, screaming and hiding her head. I screamed too, and ran home, screaming "Jesus! Madre!" halfway there. Somewhere around First Street I stopped running, stopped screaming, and began to limp. I noticed that I had a wig in my cut-up fist. I wiped the extra blood off my hand, then wrapped it in the wig. I told my parents I'd cut it in shop. My dad said I was a loser, that I'd never make it in construction if I can't keep my hands out of table saws.

Mitch says he ain't my homie no more.

# flag day

*m. i. blue*

I WAS THUMBING a ride to school and a new, blue vw bug pulled over, when i got in i saw this tall gink with wild eyes wearing an american flag around his neck like a cape.

"oh yeah...," i remembered, "it's flag day."

"yes," said the guy, looking directly at me for a full four seconds while he floored it through an intersection. he indicated the car around us with weedy eyebrows: "i stole it from my school..." then smiled, "i'm the flag boy ... i took a lot of pcp this morning ... this is the principal's car ... i stole it ... it's a horse tranquilizer..." that was all he felt i needed to know ... he headed into some sidestreets and put the pedal to the floor.

going around the first curve, i already knew what was going to happen when we went around the second. i got that weightless stomach-lifting feeling and we went over on two wheels like a circus act. the car tumbled, two-and-a-half somersaults right down the middle of the residential street, and the old red, white and blue was wrapping around and around both our heads like a puppy. when we stopped rolling and pulled old glory out of our faces, we were upside down in the capsized bug and neighbors were drifting across their wet green lawns toward us.

i was giggling. i think i was in shock. by the time the first neighbors started reaching us in their bathrobes and work drag, like angry villagers holding newspapers instead of torches, we'd already popped out of the crumpled vehicle and started to rock it back up onto its tires. it went over like a toy and as we climbed back in the flag boy was saying to the gathering townsfolk: "it's okay, it's my principal's car.... It's a volkswagen..." and at least a couple of them were nodding that they understood, looking at the caved-in roof.

i never made it to school that day. turns out flag day was the first day i ever shot drugs, go figure.

# Why Do Men Stupefy Themselves?

*Leo Tolstoy*

WHAT IS THE explanation of the fact that people use things that stupefy them: vodka, wine, beer, hashish, opium, tobacco, and other things less common: ether, morphia, fly agaric, etc.? Why did the practice begin? Why has it spread so rapidly, and why is it still spreading among all sorts of people, savage and civilized? How is it that where there is no vodka, wine or beer, we find opium, hashish, fly agaric, and the like, and that tobacco is used everywhere?

Why do people wish to stupefy themselves?

Ask anyone why he began drinking wine and why he now drinks it. He will reply, "Oh, I like it, and everybody drinks," and he may add, "it cheers me up." Some—those who have never once taken the trouble to consider whether they do well or ill to drink wine—may add that wine is good for the health and adds to one's strength; that is to say, will make a statement long since proved baseless.

Ask a smoker why he began to use tobacco and why he now smokes, and he also will reply: "To while away the time; everybody smokes."

Similar answers would probably be given by those who use opium, hashish, morphia, or fly-agaric.

"To while away time, to cheer oneself up; everybody does it." But it might be excusable to twiddle one's thumbs, to whistle, to hum tunes, to play a fife or to do something of that sort "to while away the time," "to cheer oneself up," or "because everybody does it"—that is to say, it might be excusable to do something which does not involve wasting Nature's wealth, or spending what has cost great labor to produce, or doing what brings evident harm to oneself and to others. But to produce tobacco, wine, hashish, and opium, the labor of millions of men is spent, and millions and millions of acres of the best land (often amid a population that is short of land) are employed to grow potatoes, hemp, poppies, vines, and tobacco.

Moreover, the use of these evidently harmful things produces terrible evils known and admitted by everyone, and destroys more people than all the wars and contagious diseases added together. And people know this, so that they cannot really use these things "to while away time," "to cheer themselves up," or because "everybody does it."

There must be some other reason.

Continually and everywhere one meets people who love their children and are ready to make all kinds of sacrifices for them, but who yet spend on vodka, wine and beer, or on opium, hashish, or even tobacco, as much as would quite suffice to feed their hungry and poverty-stricken children, or at least as much as would suffice to save them from misery.

Evidently if a man who has to choose between the want and sufferings of a family he loves on the one hand, and abstinence from stupefying things on the other, chooses the former—he must be induced thereto by something more potent than the consideration that everybody does it, or that it is pleasant. Evidently it is done not "to while away time," nor merely "to cheer himself up." He is actuated by some more powerful cause.

This cause—as far as I have detected it by reading about this subject and by observing other people, and particularly by observing my own case when I used to drink wine and smoke tobacco—this cause, I think, may be explained as follows:

When observing his own life, a man may often notice in himself two different beings: the one is blind and physical, the other sees and is spiritual. The blind animal being eats, drinks, rests, sleeps, propagates, and moves, like a wound-up machine. The seeing, spiritual being that is bound up with the animal does nothing of itself, but only appraises the activity of the animal being; coinciding with it when approving its activity, and diverging from it when disapproving.

This observing being may be compared to the needle of a compass, pointing with one end to the north and with the other to the south, but screened along its whole length by something not noticeable so long as it and the needle both point the same way; but which becomes obvious as soon as they point different ways.

In the same manner the seeing, spiritual being, whose manifestation we commonly call conscience, always points with one end towards right and with the other towards wrong, and we do not notice it while we follow the course it shows: the course from wrong to right. But one need only do something contrary to the indication of conscience to become aware of this spiritual being, which then shows how the animal activity has diverged from the direction indicated by conscience.

And as a navigator conscious that he is on the wrong track cannot continue to work the oars, engine, or sails, till he has adjusted his course to the indications of the compass, or has obliterated his consciousness of this divergence—each man who has felt the duality of his animal activity and his conscience can continue his activity only by adjusting that activity to the demands of conscience, or by hiding from himself the indications conscience gives him of the wrongness of his animal life.

All human life, we may say, consists solely of these two activities: (1) bringing one's activities into harmony with conscience, or (2) hiding from oneself the indications of conscience in order to be able to continue to live as before.

Some do the first, others the second. To attain the first there is but one means: moral enlightenment—the increase of light in oneself and attention to what it shows. To attain the second—to hide from oneself the indications of conscience—there are two means: one external and the other internal. The external means consists in occupations that divert one's attention from the indications given by conscience; the internal method consists in darkening conscience itself.

As a man has two ways of avoiding seeing an object that is before him: either by diverting his sight to other more striking objects, or by obstructing the sight of his own eyes—just so a man can hide from himself the indications of conscience in two ways: either by the external method of diverting his attention to various occupations, cares, amusements, or games; or by the internal method of obstructing the organ of attention itself.

For people of dull, limited moral feeling, the external diversions are often quite sufficient to enable them not to perceive the indications conscience gives of the wrong-ness of their lives. But for morally sensitive people those means are often insufficient.

The external means do not quite divert attention from the consciousness of discord between one's life and the demands of conscience. This consciousness hampers one's life: and in order to be able to go on living as before people have recourse to the reliable, internal method, which is that of darkening conscience itself by poisoning the brain with stupefying substances.

One is not living as conscience demands, yet lacks the strength to reshape one's life in accord with its demands. The diversions which might distract attention from the consciousness of this discord are insufficient, or have become stale, and so—in order to be able to live on, disregarding the indications conscience gives of the wrongness of their life—people (by poisoning it temporarily) stop the activity of the organ through which conscience manifests itself, as a man by covering his eyes hides from himself what he does not wish to see.

The cause of the world-wide consumption of hashish, opium, wine, and tobacco, lies not in the taste, nor in any pleasure, recreation, or mirth they afford, but simply in man's need to hide from himself the demands of conscience.

I was going along the street one day, and passing some cabmen who were talking, I heard one of them say: "Of course when a man's sober he's ashamed to do it!"

When a man is sober he is ashamed of what seems all right when he is drunk. In these words we have the essential underlying cause prompting men to resort to stupefiers. People resort to them either to escape feeling ashamed after having done something contrary to their consciences, or to bring themselves beforehand into a state in which they can commit actions contrary to conscience, but to which their animal nature prompts them.

A man when sober is ashamed to go after a prostitute, ashamed to steal, ashamed to kill. A drunken man is ashamed of none of these things, and therefore if a man wishes to do something his conscience condemns he stupefies himself.

I remember being struck by the evidence of a cook who was tried for murdering a relation of mine, an old lady in whose service he lived. He related that when he had sent away his paramour, the servant-girl, and the time had come to act, he wished to go into the bedroom with a knife, but felt that while sober he could not commit the deed he had planned ... "when a man's sober he's ashamed." He turned back, drank two tumblers of vodka he had prepared beforehand, and only then felt himself ready, and committed the crime.

Nine-tenths of the crimes are committed in that way: "Drink to keep up your courage."

Half the women who fall do so under the influence of wine. Nearly all visits to disorderly houses are paid by men who are intoxicated. People know this capacity of wine to stifle the voice of conscience, and intentionally use it for that purpose.

Not only do people stupefy themselves to stifle their own consciences, but, knowing how wine acts, they intentionally stupefy others when they wish to make them commit actions contrary to conscience—that is, they arrange to stupefy people in order to deprive them of conscience. In war, soldiers are usually intoxicated before a hand-to-hand fight. All the French soldiers in the assaults on Sevastopol were drunk.

When a fortified place has been captured but the soldiers do not sack it and slay the defenseless old men and children, orders are often given to make them drunk and then they do what is expected of them.

Everyone knows people who have taken to drink in consequence of some wrong-doing that has tormented their conscience. Anyone can notice that those who lead immoral lives are more attracted than others by stupefying substances. Bands of robbers or thieves, and prostitutes, cannot live without intoxicants.

Everyone knows and admits that the use of stupefying substances is a consequence of the pangs of conscience, and that in certain immoral ways of life stupefying substances are employed to stifle conscience. Everyone knows and admits also that the use of stupefiers does stifle conscience: that a drunken man is capable of deeds of which when sober he would not think for a moment.

Everyone agrees to this, but strange to say when the use of stupefiers does not result in such deeds as thefts, murders, violations, and so forth—when stupefiers are taken not after some terrible crimes, but by men following professions which we do not consider criminal, and when the substances are consumed not in large quantities at once but continually in moderate doses—then (for some reason) it is assumed that stupefying substances have no tendency to stifle conscience.

Thus it is supposed that a well-to-do Russian's glass of vodka before each meal and tumbler of wine with the meal, or a Frenchman's absinthe, or an Englishman's port wine and porter, or a German's lager-beer, or a well-to-do Chinaman's moderate dose of opium, and the smoking of tobacco with them—is done only for pleasure and has no effect whatever on these people's consciences.

It is supposed that if after this customary stupefaction no crime is committed—no theft or murder, but only customary bad and stupid actions—then these actions have occurred of themselves and are not evoked by the stupefaction. It is supposed that if these people have not committed offences against the criminal law they have no need to stifle the voice of conscience, and that the life led by people who habitually stupefy themselves is quite a good life, and would be precisely the same if they did not stupefy themselves. It is supposed that the constant use of stupefiers does not in the least darken their consciences.

Though everybody knows by experience that a man's frame of mind is altered by the use of wine or tobacco, that he is not ashamed of things which but for the stimulant he would be ashamed of, that after each twinge of conscience, however slight, he is inclined to have recourse to some stupefier, and that under the influence of stupefiers it is difficult to reflect on his life and position, and that the constant and regular use of stupefiers produces the same physiological effect as its occasional immoderate use does—yet in spite of all this it seems to men who drink and smoke moderately that they use stupefiers not at all to stifle conscience, but only for the flavor or for pleasure.

But one need only think of the matter seriously and impartially—not trying to excuse oneself—to understand, first, that if the use of stupefiers in large occasional doses stifles man's conscience, their regular use must have a like effect (always first intensifying and then dulling the activity of the brain) whether they are taken in large or small doses; secondly, that all stupefiers have the quality of stifling conscience, and have this always—both when under their influence murders, robberies, and violations are committed, and when under their influence words are spoken which would not have been spoken, or things are thought and felt which but for them would not have been thought and felt; and, thirdly, that if the use of stupefiers is needed to pacify and stifle the consciences of thieves, robbers, and prostitutes, it is also wanted by people engaged in occupations condemned by their own consciences, even though these occupations may be considered proper and honorable by other people.

In a word, it is impossible to avoid understanding that the use of stupefiers, in large or small amounts, occasionally or regularly, in the higher or lower circles of society, is evoked by one and the same cause, the need to stifle the voice of conscience in order not to be aware of the discord existing between one's way of life and the demands of one's conscience.

In that alone lies the reason of the widespread use of all stupefying substances, and among the rest of tobacco—probably the most generally used and most harmful.

It is supposed that tobacco cheers one up, clears the thoughts, and attracts one merely like any other habit—without at all producing the deadening of conscience produced by wine.

But you need only observe attentively the conditions under which a special desire to smoke arises, and you will be convinced that stupefying with tobacco acts on the conscience as wine does, and that people consciously have recourse to this method of stupefaction just when they require it for that purpose. If tobacco merely cleared the thoughts and cheered one up there would not be such a passionate craving for it, a craving showing itself just on certain definite occasions. People would not say, as they do, that they would rather go without bread than without tobacco, and would not often actually prefer tobacco to food.

That cook who murdered his mistress said that when he entered the bedroom and had gashed her throat with his knife and she had fallen with a rattle in her throat and the blood had gushed out in a torrent—he lost his courage. "I could not finish her off," he said, "but I went back from the bedroom to the sitting-room and sat down there and smoked a cigarette." Only after stupefying himself with tobacco was he able to return to the bedroom, finish cutting the old lady's throat, and begin examining her things.

Evidently the desire to smoke at that moment was evoked in him, not by a wish to clear his thoughts or be merry, but by the need to stifle something that prevented him from completing what he had planned to do.

Any smoker may detect in himself the same definite desire to stupefy himself with tobacco at certain specially difficult moments. I look back at the days when I used to smoke: when was it that I felt a special need of tobacco? It was always at moments when I did not wish to remember certain things that presented themselves to my recollection, when I wished to forget—not to think.

I sit by myself doing nothing and know I ought to set to work, but I don't feel inclined to, so I smoke and go on sitting. I have promised to be at someone's house by five o'clock, but I have stayed too long somewhere else. I remember that I have missed the appointment, but I do not like to remember it, so I smoke. I get vexed and say unpleasant things to someone, and know I am doing wrong and see that I ought to stop, but I want to give vent to my irritability—so I smoke and continue to be irritable. I play at cards and lose more than I intended to risk—so I smoke. I have placed myself in an awkward position, have acted badly, have made a mistake, and ought to acknowledge the mess I am in and thus escape from it, but I do not like to acknowledge it, so I accuse others—and smoke. I write something and am not quite satisfied with what I have written. I ought to abandon it, but I wish to finish what I have planned to do—so I smoke. I dispute, and see that my opponent and I do not understand and cannot understand one another, but I wish to express my opinion, so I continue to talk—and I smoke.

What distinguishes tobacco from most other stupefiers, besides the ease with which one can stupefy oneself with it and its apparent harmlessness, is its portability and the possibility of applying it to meet small, isolated occurrences that disturb one.

Not to mention that the use of opium, wine, and hashish involves the use of certain appliances not always at hand, while one can always carry tobacco and paper with one; and that the opium-smoker and the drunkard evoke horror while a tobacco-smoker does not seem at all repulsive—the advantage of tobacco over other stupefiers is, that the stupefaction of opium, hashish, or wine extends to all the sensations and acts received or produced during a certain somewhat extended period of time—while the stupefaction from tobacco can be directed to any separate occurrence.

You wish to do what you ought not to, so you smoke a cigarette and stupefy yourself sufficiently to enable you to do what should not be done, and then you are all right again, and can think and speak clearly; or you feel you have done what you should not—again you smoke a cigarette and the unpleasant consciousness of the wrong or awkward action is obliterated, and you can occupy yourself with other things and forget it.

But apart from individual cases in which every smoker has recourse to smoking, not to satisfy a habit or while away time but as a means of stifling his conscience with reference to acts he is about to commit or has already committed, is it not quite evident that there is a strict and definite relation between men's way of life and their passion for smoking?

When do lads begin to smoke? Usually when they lose their childish innocence. How is it that smokers can abandon smoking when they come among more moral conditions of life, and again start smoking as soon as they fall among a depraved set? Why do gamblers almost all smoke? Why among women do those who lead a regular life smoke least? Why do prostitutes and madmen all smoke?

Habit is habit, but evidently smoking stands in some definite connection with the craving to stifle conscience, and achieves the end required of it.

One may observe in the case of almost every smoker to what an extent smoking drowns the voice of conscience. Every smoker when yielding to his desire forgets, or sets at naught, the very first demands of social life—demands he expects others to observe, and which he observes in all other cases until his conscience is stifled by tobacco. Everyone of average education considers it inadmissible, ill-bred, and inhumane to infringe the peace, comfort, and still more the health of others for his own pleasure. No one would allow himself to wet a room in which people are sitting, or to make a noise, shout, let in cold, hot, or ill-smelling air, or commit acts that incommode or harm others. But out of a thousand smokers not one will shrink from producing unwholesome smoke in a room where the air is breathed by non-smoking women and children.

If smokers do usually say to those present: "You don't object?" everyone knows that the customary answer is: "Not at all" (although it cannot be pleasant to a non-smoker to breathe tainted air, and to find stinking cigar ends in glasses and cups or on plates and candlesticks, or even in ashpans). But even if non-smoking adults did not object to tobacco smoke, it could not be pleasant or good for the children whose consent no one asks. Yet people who are honorable and humane in all other respects smoke in the presence of children at dinner in small rooms, vitiating the air with tobacco smoke, without feeling the slightest twinge of conscience.

It is usually said (and I used to say) that smoking facilitates mental work. And that is undoubtedly true if one considers only the quantity of one's mental output. To a man who smokes, and who consequently ceases strictly to appraise and weigh his thoughts, it seems as if he suddenly had many thoughts. But this is not because he really has many thoughts, but only because he has lost control of his thoughts.

When a man works he is always conscious of two beings in himself: the one works, the other appraises the work. The stricter the appraisement the slower and the better is the work; and vice versa, when the appraiser is under the influence of something that stupefies him, more work gets done, but its quality is poorer.

"If I do not smoke I cannot write. I cannot get on; I begin and cannot continue," is what is usually said, and what I used to say. What does it really mean? It means either that you have nothing to write, or that what you wish to write has not yet matured in your consciousness but is only beginning dimly to present itself to you, and the appraising critic within, when not stupefied with tobacco, tells you so. If you did not smoke you would either abandon what you have begun, or you would wait until your thought has cleared itself in your mind; you would try to penetrate into what presents itself dimly to you, would consider the objections that offer themselves, and would turn all your attention to the elucidation of the thought.

But you smoke, the critic within you is stupefied, and the hindrance to your work is removed. What seemed insignificant to you when not inebriated by tobacco, again seems important; what seemed obscure no longer seems so; the objections that presented themselves vanish and you continue to write, and write much and rapidly.

But can such a small—such a trifling—alteration as the slight intoxication produced by the moderate use of wine or tobacco produce important consequences?

"If a man smokes opium or hashish, or intoxicates himself with wine till he falls down and loses his senses, of course the consequences may be very serious; but it surely cannot have any serious consequences if a man merely comes slightly under the influence of hops or tobacco," is what is usually said.

It seems to people that a slight stupefaction, a little darkening of the judgment, cannot have any important influence. But to think so is like supposing that it may harm a watch to be struck against a stone, but that a little dirt introduced into it cannot be harmful.

Remember, however, that the chief work actuating man's whole life is not done by his hands, his feet, or his back, but by his consciousness. Before a man can do anything with his feet or hands, a certain alteration has first to take place in his consciousness. And this alteration defines all the subsequent movements of the man. Yet these alterations are always minute and almost imperceptible.

Bryullov [a celebrated Russian painter] one day corrected a pupil's study. The pupil, having glanced at the altered drawing, exclaimed: "Why, you only touched it a tiny bit, but it is quite another thing." Bryullov replied: "Art begins where the tiny bit begins."

That saying is strikingly true not only of art but of all life. One may say that true life begins where the tiny bit begins—where what seem to us minute and infinitely small alterations take place. True life is not lived where great external changes take place—where people move about, clash, fight, and slay one another—it is lived only where these tiny, tiny, infinitesimally small changes occur.

Let each man remember himself as he has been during the years of his drinking or smoking, and let him test the matter in his experience of other people, and everyone will see a definite constant line dividing those who are addicted to stupefiers from those who are free from them. The more a man stupefies himself the more he is morally immovable.

Terrible, as they are described to us, are the consequences of opium and hashish on individuals; terrible, as we know them, are the consequences of alcohol to flagrant drunkards; but incomparably more terrible to our whole society are the consequences of what is considered the harmless, moderate use of spirits, wine, beer, and tobacco, to which the majority of men, and especially our so-called cultured classes, are addicted.

The consequences must naturally be terrible, admitting the fact, which must be admitted, that the guiding activities of society—political, official, scientific, literary, and artistic—are carried on for the most part by people in an abnormal state: by people who are drunk.

It is generally supposed that a man who, like most people of our well-to-do-classes, takes alcoholic drink almost every time he eats, is in a perfectly normal and sober condition next day, during working hours. But this is quite an error. A man who drank a bottle of wine, a glass of spirits, or two glasses of ale, yesterday, is now in the usual state of drowsiness or depression which follows excitement, and is therefore in a condition of mental prostration, which is increased by smoking. For a man who habitually smokes and drinks in moderation, to bring his brain into a normal condition would require at least a week or more of abstinence from wine and tobacco. But that hardly ever occurs.

So that most of what goes on among us, whether done by people who rule and teach others, or by those who are ruled and taught, is done when the doers are not sober.[4]

And let not this be taken as a joke or an exaggeration. The confusion, and above all the imbecility, of our lives, arises chiefly from the constant state of intoxication in which most people live. Could people who are not drunk possibly do all that is being done around us—from building the Eiffel Tower to accepting military service?

Without any need whatever, a company is formed, capital collected, men labor, make calculations, and draw plans; millions of working days and thousands of tons of iron are spent to build a tower; and millions of people consider it their duty to climb up it, stop awhile on it, and then climb down again; and the building and visiting of this tower evoke no other reflection than a wish and intention to build other towers, in other places, still bigger. Could sober people act like that?

Or take another case. For dozens of years past, all the European peoples have been busy devising the very best ways of killing people, and teaching as many young men as possible, as soon as they reach manhood, how to murder. Everyone knows that there can be no invasion by barbarians, but that these preparations made by the different civilized and Christian nations are directed against one another; everyone knows that this is burdensome, painful, inconvenient, ruinous, immoral, impious, and irrational—but everyone continues to prepare for mutual murder. Some devise political combinations to decide who is to kill whom and with what allies, others direct those who are being taught to murder, and others again yield—against their will, against their conscience, against their reason—to these preparations for murder.

Could sober people do these things? Only drunkards who never reach a state of sobriety could do them and live on in the horrible state of discord between life and conscience in which, not only in this but in all other respects, the people of our society are now living.

Never before, I suppose, have people lived with the demands of their conscience so evidently in contradiction to their actions.

Humanity today has as it were stuck fast. It is as though some external cause hindered it from occupying a position in natural accord with its perceptions. And the cause—if not the only one, then certainly the greatest—is this physical condition of stupefaction induced by wine and tobacco to which the great majority of people in our society reduce themselves.

Emancipation from this terrible evil will be an epoch in the life of humanity; and that epoch seems to be at hand. The evil is recognized. An alteration has already taken place in our perception concerning the use of stupefying substances. People have understood the terrible harm of these things and are beginning to point them out, and this almost unnoticed alteration in perception will inevitably bring about the emancipation of men from the use of stupefying things—will enable them to open their eyes to the demands of their consciences, and they will begin to order their lives in accord with their perceptions.

And this seems to be already beginning. But as always it is beginning among the upper classes only after all the lower classes have already been infected.

*—Translated from the Russian*
*by Aylmer Maude*

# Circle Game

*Michael Stephans*

He inhaled five sprays of Alupent to calm the asthma. It made him so jumpy that he couldn't sit still for longer than a minute without changing positions. Electricity raced through his veins and arteries. He downed four glasses of white zinfandel in an attempt to relax his nerve endings, but the wine made him so woozy that functioning optimally was out of the question. To counteract this situation, he snorted four hefty lines of cocaine and began to regain some of his composure; however, this caused his heart to palpitate wildly. He opened his shirt and watched the center of his chest rise and fall to the tune of its own organic montuno. He reached into his briefcase and retrieved two valium tabs, and chased these with a shot of Dewar's. The pounding in his chest and ears stopped, but was replaced by an oppressive lethargy. He was losing his equilibrium. It took enormous effort to rise from his chair and stumble into the kitchen. His wife had hidden the desoxyn in the cookie tin, and of course he knew this, since he was well acquainted with all of her secret drug caches around the house. He dry-swallowed the desoxyn and in a few moments, became perfectly still. An enormous reservoir of energy surged through his body. He began to shake slightly as he reached under the stereo receiver for the joint. Good old cannabis indica. Mellows you out just fine. He barely had time to sink back into the recliner when he was overcome by a new sensation: hunger. Rising tentatively from the chair, he returned to the kitchen where an unfortunate banana cream pie (with real Graham-cracker crust just like Mom used to make) fell victim to his voracious and slightly-left-of-center appetite. Fifteen minutes went by, leaving only a bent pie tin and whatever few crumbs he did not shovel into the gaping maw of his mouth. The hunger gave way to thirst, and he eyed the coffeemaker and its two-day-old contents. Adding a handful of ice cubes and three packets of sugar substitute (he was, after all, on a diet), he drank the muddy java straight from the glass pot. The caffeine cleared his head, but wreaked havoc upon his upper intestines, causing him to double up with cramps. He dragged himself to the medicine chest and took a swig out of the Mylanta bottle and chewed the rest of the antacid tablets. The chalky liquid and the tablets caused him to choke violently, his entire windpipe constricting itself, as though it were being squeezed by an invisible hand. He reached into his pocket and retrieved the nearly-forgotten inhalator. The asthma was coming back.

He inhaled five sprays of Alupent to calm the asthma. It made him so jumpy that he couldn't sit still for longer than a minute without changing positions. Electricity raced through his veins and arteries. He downed four glasses of white zinfandel in an attempt to relax his nerve endings, but the wine made him so woozy that functioning optimally was out of the question. To counteract this situation, he snorted four hefty lines of cocaine and began to regain some of his composure; however, this caused his heart to palpitate wildly. He opened his shirt and watched the center of his chest rise and fall to the tune of its own organic montuno. He reached into his briefcase ...

# About the Authors

**Charles Baudelaire (1821–1867).** Major post-romantic and proto-symbolist French poet best known for his daringly innovative volume of verse, *Flowers of Evil,* which created a scandal upon its debut. An important art critic, literary impresario, and translator of Edgar Allan Poe who, prior to being rediscovered in France by Baudelaire, had already lapsed into semi-obscurity in the United States. Like Maupassant, died from syphilitic infection.

**William James (1842–1920).** American medical psychologist and philosopher. His father Henry was a Swedenborgian clergyman, and his brother Henry was the noted novelist. He overcame crippling neurasthenia to become a leading proponent of the philosophical school of pragmatism, and of "functionalism" in consciousness theory. He was a pal of Charles Peirce and Oliver Wendell Holmes. Wrote *The Principles of Psychology; The Will to Believe;* and *The Varieties of Religious Experience,* from which this selection is excerpted.

**Marie Corelli (1855–1924).** Pen name of Mary Mackay. English. Educated in a French convent, Corelli began writing after a psychic experience convinced her she should take up literature. She eventually authored more than thirty novels—all of them moralistic, sentimental romances. Achieved immense popular success, and was said to be Queen Victoria's favorite novelist. The fortune she made from book sales enabled her to retire to Stratford-on-Avon, where she apparently fancied herself Shakespeare's successor. She fought encroaching development of the area, and died alone and neglected. Her books include *Ardath; The Soul of Lilith;* and *The Sorrows of Satan.*

**Ernest Dowson (1867–1900).** English poet; part of the coterie of *fin-de-siècle* English Decadents. A chum of Oscar Wilde, Arthur Symons, Aubrey Beardsley, and Richard Le Gallienne. Conceived a violent infatuation for the twelve-year-old daughter of a Soho tavern-keeper—the inspiration for the Cynara of his well-known poem "Non Sum Qualis Eram Bonae Sub Regno Cynarae." Dowson, along with W. B. Yeats, was exposed to mescaline by Havelock Ellis. Born the child of wealthy parents, he dropped out of Oxford University and took up residence in a tumbledown dockside shack in the seedy Limehouse district. Haunted by his father's death and by his mother's suicide six months later, he became self-destructive and dissolute, and used opium, absinthe, and hashish. His health was destroyed by alcoholism. A friend found him dying in a Parisian wine cellar, and brought him back to London, where he expired from tuberculosis at the age of thirty-two. A master of elegiac verse, he was the author of *Dilemmas* and *Decorations:* bitter products of a poet who had passed through the dark night of the soul.

**Jean Richepin (1849–1926).** Popular French poet and dramatist who produced several collections of short fiction dealing with innumerable imaginative theses often set at the extremes of human experience, including this one which features his character Harry Sloughby, the fictitious Englishman who figures in several of his stories. In terms of themes, if not of treatment, Richepin was well ahead of his time; a sort of Rod Serling of gaslamp France.

**(Pierre Jules) Théophile Gautier (1811–1872)** was a French poet, dramatist, novelist, and art, drama, ballet and literary critic. At first an aspiring painter, Gautier was famous for the carefree Bohemian lifestyle he shared with many of his artist cronies. He maintained lifelong friendships with prominent romanticist authors and artists of his day and was a much beloved and esteemed figure on the contemporary cultural scene. Gérard de Nerval was one of many close literary comrades with whom he associated from an early age. At the so-called "Battle of Hernani" accompanying the debut of Victor Hugo's groundbreaking play, Gautier is still remembered for the bright red sash he sported as a member of the pro-romantic faction during the clash. Credited as the first to formally expound the theory of art for art's sake, Gautier made his living as a journalist, an occupation he found distasteful. He was a popular travel writer and found employment as personal librarian to Mathilde Bonaparte, cousin of Napoleon III. Eventually, he was elected chairman of the National Society of Fine Arts and served as director of the *Revue de Paris.* In his youth, along with fellow poet

Charles Baudelaire and others, he regularly indulged in the use of drugs such as hashish and opium.

**Fitz Hugh Ludlow (1836–1870).** A Presbyterian minister's son raised in Poughkeepsie, New York, the youthful Ludlow coaxed the local apothecary into allowing him to experiment with opium, chloroform, ether, and tincture of cannabis (the patent medicine "Tilden's Extract", available over-the-counter at six cents a dose). In 1857, he published *The Hasheesh Eater,* which created a sensation, and became a best-seller. Practiced anesthesiology as a student at the Union College Medical School and was admitted to the bar, but abandoned law for literature. Edited *Vanity Fair* and was active as a theater, art, and music critic. Authored another drug-themed book, *The Opium Habit,* which was published in 1868. He died in Switzerland, where he had gone in search of a cure for a pulmonary disorder. Walt Whitman was one of his chums at Raffs Beer Cellar in New York, and Mark Twain, an ardent admirer, is said to have released nothing for publication without Ludlow's review and approval. Nature painter Albert Bierstadt accompanied Ludlow on an epic trip through the largely unexplored American West.

**J. C. O'Day.** This confessional anecdote (1899) by an American physician regards his misadventures with a locomotive after taking an overdose of cannabis extract. Written for *Plexus* magazine in 1891.

**Hendrik DeLeeuw (1891–1977).** Dutch explorer, lecturer and ethnologist who wrote exposées of prostitution and drug addiction such as *Fallen Angels* and *Flower of Joy*, and studies in social anthropology such as *Java Jungle Trails; Cities of Sin; The Story of Rubber*; and *The Romance of Spice.* He specialized in the sort of exotic travel and adventure literature typically featured in men's magazines of the 1950s such as *Esquire, Stag, Argosy*, and *True.*

**Thomas de Quincey (1785–1859).** Running away from school at age seventeen, English author-to-be Thomas de Quincey tramped throughout Wales and became a beggar in London, until he was rescued from utter destitution by a streetwalker. Later he enrolled at Oxford University, but left without taking a degree. There, he had begun using opium for relief from a chronic facial ailment, and became habituated. He formed fast friendships with fellow Lake Poets Samuel Taylor Coleridge and William Wordsworth, whose cottage, at Grasmere, in the Lake District, he rented. He is also known for his elegant and insightful essays such as *On Knocking at the Gate in Macbeth.* His *Confessions of an English Opium-Eater* was published in 1822. At the height of his addiction he was consuming a daily dose sufficient to kill a man several times over.

**Harry Hubbell Kane (1854–?).** American journalist and social historian who authored the comprehensive treatise *Opium Smoking in America and China* at a time when this problem was just becoming a major phenomenon in American cities, especially in major ports such as San Francisco and New

York. A work of social anthropology which stands out by virtue of its detailed observation and scientific analysis.

**Stephen Crane (1871–1900).** American author whose style of robust naturalism influenced succeeding generations of writers from Frank Norris and Theodore Dreiser to Sherwood Anderson and Ernest Hemingway. A frequenter of New York's Bowery and Hell's Kitchen slums, he was an impressionistic journalist who covered not only the Gotham beat, but the Greco-Turkish War of 1897 and the Spanish American War. During his stint as a correspondent in the latter he was rumored, probably falsely, to have used drugs. He survived shipwreck and both wars only to be cut down by tuberculosis at age twenty-eight. Like another famous consumptive, Doc Holliday, he had a reckless disregard for his health. Author of *The Red Badge of Courage; The Black Riders and Other Lines*; and *Maggie: A Girl of the Streets.* A friend of the American literati Hamlin Garland and William Dean Howells and of their English counterparts Joseph Conrad, Ford Madox Ford, and H. G. Wells.

**Anonymous** reportage such as "An 'Opium Joint' Raided ..." was typical of the yellow journalism of the American press of the 1890s. This article, which appeared in the September 28, 1891 edition of the *New York Times,* plays up the danger of the corruption of a twelve-year-old girl who was enticed "to buy ten cents worth of opium" for a neighbor.

**Charles (John Huffam) Dickens (1812–1870).** Victorian novelist, probably the most popular and successful of his day.

Creator of many memorable fictional characters in numerous established classics including *Great Expectations*; *David Copperfield*; *A Tale of Two Cities*; *The Pickwick Papers*; and *Oliver Twist*. The excerpt reprinted here forms the opening chapter of *The Mystery of Edwin Drood*, Dickens's last and, perhaps, moodiest novel, left unfinished at his death.

**Claude Farrère (1876–1957),** pseudonym of Frédéric-Charles Bargone. French naval officer and literary exoticist in the tradition of Pierre Loti, Rudyard Kipling, and Joseph Conrad. Having, by 1918, attained the rank of *capitaine de corvette*, Farrere passed his naval career putting into remote and colorful ports around the world and spent several years in the Far East. He won the Goncourt Prize in 1906, and was elected to the French Academy in 1935. Author of *Opium Smoke*; *Battle*; and *My Travels*.

**Santiago Dabove (1899–1951).** Argentine author of *Death and All Its Trappings*, an odd assortment of occult fantasy, science fiction, cruel tales, and metaphysical minitexts with morbid preoccupations. The same volume also contains apocalyptic meditations, accounts of doomed narcissi, and two drug-themed compositions: "Magic Treatment," which concerns peyote, and the item presented here. When a detractor faulted Dabove because the sum total of his lifelong literary output consisted of the single title mentioned above, Dabove's friend Jorge Luis Borges defended him with the observation that not many people manage to produce so much as one book.

**Ahmad Mahmood (1941–2002).** Born in Ahvaz, Iran. Engaged in illegal political activities during his youth, was arrested, jailed, and exiled, and was never able to finish school. He learned to write outside academic circles, holding twenty different jobs while steeping himself in the study of literature and polishing his craft. By the mid-1980s, following publication of his long novel *Zero Degree,* he had achieved sound recognition, and became a familiar face on the contemporary Persian literary scene. Known for his depiction of the miserable lives of the inhabitants of the harsh desert regions of southern Iran, one of his best-known stories deals with people who sell their blood out of indigence and desperation. "Junkie Monkey," his tale of a pathetic animal exploited by all-too-human relatives is reminiscent of those made famous a generation earlier by Sadegh Hedayat.

**Sampurnanand (1891–1969)** was an Indian social philosopher, a friend of Jawaharlal Nehru, and author of *The Individual and the State* and *Memories and Reflections.* An apologist for and explicator of Indian and Hindu thought, he was involved with the mediation of policy issues during the post-independence period in India (1948).

**(Henry) Havelock Ellis (1859–1939).** British physician and pioneering experimental psychologist noted for his ground-breaking *Studies in the Psychology of Sex* in seven volumes, which was banned in England as obscene, and whose availability in the United States was restricted to members of the medical profession until the mid-1930s. A leader in this field, like Kinsey and Krafft-Ebbing, and a champion of sex education. Authored books on a variety of scientific and literary subjects. Convinced the poets Ernest Dowson and William Butler Yeats, both of whom had had prior experience with opium and hashish, to try mescaline, which he imported to England from North America in the late 1890s. The results were published in his 1911 book *The World of Dreams.*

Peruvian **Eugenio Buona,** whose real name is Francisco Vallebuona Cardenas, has published various volumes of poetry and, in 1966, the collection of stories *Mercedes Rueda,* which has been said to be characterized by a "direct prose, almost blood-curdling for its rawness; heterodox and insolent." Buona, along with the poet Marco Antonio Corcuera, published between 1967 and 1969 a beautiful review dedicated to verse. Since 1968, he has written the weekly column "At the Earth's Roof" for the *Daily Express* of Lima. "Ayahuasca" derives from his book *3 Stories and 60 Chronicles.*

**H(erbert) G(eorge) Wells (1866–1946).** British historian, social philosopher, and gaslamp era writer of speculative fiction; founder, with Jules Verne, of modern science fiction. Wrote *The Time Machine; The Invisible Man; The War of the Worlds; The Shape of Things to Come; The Mind at the End of its Tether;* and *The Island of Dr. Moreau.* Grew increasingly pessimistic as he aged. A social crusader, he became, in later years, a sort of secular prophet and public advisor on the ills of the world, and a self-appointed voice of scientific thought and rationalist futurism.

**Nathaniel Hawthorne (1804–1864).** Scion of old Puritan stock, Hawthorne was born in Salem, Massachusetts, and spent most of his life in the state, from the Berkshires to Boston. All his life, he was plagued by guilt over the part played by his ancestors in the Salem witch trials, and other acts of religious intolerance. He spent several months at the Brook Farm Utopian commune, and was acquainted not only with Herman Melville but with the principals of the Transcendentalist circle including Ralph Waldo Emerson, Margaret Fuller, Henry Thoreau, and Bronson Alcott. He took a job as surveyor for the port of Salem, and worked for awhile at the Boston customs house. He wrote a biography of his Bowdoin College classmate and later U. S. president Franklin Pierce, and died while sojourning in the White Mountains with this old confrère. About two years before his death, he aged very suddenly; his hair turned white, he suffered nosebleeds, and inexplicably became obsessed with scrawling the figure "64" on slips of paper. A profound moral allegorist renowned for such books as *The Scarlet Letter*; *The House of Seven Gables*; and *Twice-Told Tales*, Hawthorne was an inimitably insightful psychologist and masterful proponent of the symbolic romance.

**Gaston Danville (1870–?)** was the pseudonym of a certain A. Blocq, a Frenchman about whom little else is known, except that he authored *Infinities of Flesh*, which appeared in 1892, followed by *Stories* (1893); *Psychology of Love* (1894); *Towards Death* (1897); *Magician Lover* (1902); *Perfumes of the Voluptuous* (1905); and *Magnetism and Spiritism* (1908).

**(Henri René Albert) Guy de Maupassant (1850–1893).** De Maupassant's mother, while pregnant, was convinced she was about to give birth to a genius. During his early teens, he saved eccentric English poet Algernon Charles Swinburne from drowning and was rewarded with the gift of a mummified hand. A protégé of Gustave Flaubert, he was expelled from school for writing obscene verse. Always a lady-killer, he maintained a lifetime of dalliances with women; a propensity possibly inherited from his playboy father. During his early adulthood, he used to pick up girls at a favorite Parisian dive, La Grenouillere, for one-night-stands, and from one of these he contracted the venereal disease which eventually led to his derangement. A languidly handsome yachtsman and man about town, he eventually attempted suicide, was interned in a sanitarium, and died insane from the advanced stages of tertiary syphilis. Called by Hippolyte Taine "the sad bull," he was addicted to ether, like Jean Lorrain.

**Jean Lorrain (1855–1906).** Nom de plume of Paul Duval, flamboyant homosexual and social butterfly of Belle Époque France. Addicted to ether, Duval was the author of *Affidavits of an Ether-Drinker*; *Masks*; and *Imbiber of Souls*, collections of fantastic tales, and of the decadent novel *Monsieur de Phocas*. Like Gautier, he was a celebrity journalist of prodigious output but, unlike Gautier, he offended just about everyone. He fought a pistol duel with Marcel Proust, and was challenged at one time or another by Guy de Maupassant, the journalist René Maizeroy, and Paul Verlaine. He was once sued for defamation of character and, on another occasion, for outraging public morals. He was an etheromane and an aesthetic upstart, and cultivated about himself a legend of amorality, provocation, and decadence. He had a childhood crush on Judith Gautier, daughter of the famous Romantic writer and wife of Catulle Mendès, and he never outgrew this infatuation. He also doted on Sarah Bernhardt, who put up with his adoration but kept him at arm's length, refusing to act in any of the several plays he wrote for her. He hung around with the Hydropaths, a clique of literateurs in bohemian Montmartre and, later, at a salon, met Barbey d'Aurevilly, under the sway of whose ideology of "dandyism" he enthusiastically fell. He knew everyone who was anyone in *fin de siècle* Paris, where he did the rounds with the likes of Rothschilde and Colette. He "wrote vicious reviews ... in which he cultivated a scathing rhetoric," as one scholar has put it. At various spas he took water cures for his tuberculosis and degenerated digestive system (ulcerated by ether), and died from a perforated colon after giving himself an enema.

**Peter Mark Roget (1779–1869).** English physician and lexicographer who spent 50 years compiling his *Thesaurus of English Words and Phrases,* first published in 1852. This opus went through 28 editions by the time of his death, and has been regularly reprinted ever since. Roget was an erudite and decorous philologist and inventor who practiced medicine in London and kept thorough, blow-by-blow records of his experiments with laughing gas.

**Benjamin Paul Blood (1832–1919).** American poet and socialist thinker. Author of *Pluriverse* and of the curious tract *The Anesthetic Revelation and the Gist of Philosophy* (1874), in which the state of consciousness induced by the inhalation of nitrous oxide is described as one of "primal prestige and appalling solemnity" leading to an "initiation into the secret of life."

**Maurice Level (1875–1926).** French sportsman, bon vivant, and knight of the Legion of Honor, Level was a writer of the Human Document school, many of whose stories, with their ironic twists and "shocker" endings, were adapted by the Grand Guignol Theater in Paris. A trained surgeon and brain specialist, he was condemned by a skating accident in Switzerland in 1910 to a life of limited physical exertion, and he gave up medicine for literature, eventually authoring more than 700 stories, some of which are collected in English translation in *Tales of Mystery and Horror* (1920).

**Horacio Quiroga (1878–1937).** Like Edgar Allan Poe, his illustrious forebear and idol, Uruguayan author Horacio Quiroga was a negative romantic. He spent most of his maturity in Misiones, a jungle district at the corners of Paraguay, Uruguay, Argentina, and Brazil, where he tried to establish a small plantation of cotton while composing his darkly pessimistic tales of modern gothicism, and periodically dabbling in drugs, clinically noting the effects in detailed personal journals.

**Aleister Crowley (1875–1947).** Bisexual English occultist who called himself 'Master Therion,' 'Great Beast 666,' and 'The Mage.' Variously a pornographer, alpinist, great white hunter, poetaster, cult-leader, necromancer, self-styled prophet, yogi, and fakir, he climbed Kangchenjunga (K2) in the Himalayas, and scaled volcanic peaks in Mexico, atop one of which he lived for three weeks on champagne. One of his homosexual followers committed suicide, and he was known to drive his female consorts insane: three of his wives were institutionalized. He was a chess champion, a spy, is supposed to have shot two Indians in Calcutta, masqueraded as an Egyptian sultan, a Scottish laird, A Free Irish, and a Russian count. One of his mistresses, whom he called "scarlet women," stabbed him with a carving knife. He set up the Abbey of Thelema in Sicily, from which he was expelled by Mussolini when one of his acolytes died from enteric fever after drinking the blood of a sacrificed cat during a Black Mass. He became *persona non grata* in Italy and France. He was a votive, along with leading members of the Irish literary renaissance, of the Hermetic Order of the Golden Dawn, and used drugs—opium, hashish, morphine, ether, and cocaine in prodigious quantities. Was a guru to L. Ron Hubbard, the founder of Scientology, staged his own suicide in Hell's Mouth, Sicily, and later turned up in Berlin for an exhibition of his paintings. He promoted "elixir of life" pills which contained his own semen. He filed his incisors to points, and defecated on carpets because he considered his feces holy. All in all, a huckster nonpareil in the mystico-occult humbug tradition of Cheiro, Mesmer, Blavatsky, and Gurdjieff. In 1910 Crowley went to the

Detroit headquarters of the Parke-Davis pharmaceutical company to secure their newly developed extract of peyote, which he brought back to England and used to turn on the audiences at his lectures. He sampled every drug available as a vehicle for transcendence. He designed a new Tarot deck, and abridged the *I Ching*; he claimed to communicate telepathically with a Higher Intelligence … etc., etc.…

**Fred V. Williams.** San Francisco crime reporter circa 1920. Author of *The Hop-Heads: Personal Experiences Among the Users of Dope in the San Francisco Underworld*—"Police Gazette"–style portraits of the daily lives of junkies.

**Edward Levinstein (1831–1882).** German medical historian who was one of the first to make a systematic examination, in *Die Morphiumsucht* (1878), of the emerging problem of morphine addiction.

**Jordan Jones.** American poet, essayist, translator, and publisher; the author of *Sand & Coal* and *The Wheel* and editor of the lauded but alas now defunct avant-garde journal *Bakunin*. His translations from René Daumal's *The Anti-Heaven* have appeared in a variety of magazines and in chapbook form. "Angel Rivera and the Sidewalk Jesus" is an excerpt from a picaresque novel-in-progress. He is the editor of Coyote Arts Press.

**Greg Boyd** is an American novelist, translator, and belle lettrist who created the celebrated but now-defunct *Asylum* magazine and founded Asylum Arts Publications. A publisher and gifted factotum of the book arts, Boyd also makes woodcuts, and illustrates, edits and designs fine limited editions. Among his own books are *Carnival Aptitude; The Nambuli Papers;* and *Horny* (all from Asylum Arts).

San Francisco litterateur **m. i. blue** is a regular participant in area poetry readings and spoken word events, and has published sporadically in a rich variety of literary journals. He has said that he "longs to live as an old dog sleeps: deeply, twitching with dreams."

**Count Leo Tolstoy (1828–1910)** was a landed Russian nobleman who primarily wrote novels and short stories. Following a mid-life spiritual crisis, he adopted a posture of asceticism, rejecting private property, renouncing material possessions and instituting schools for the education of his serfs. He became increasingly known as a social philosopher and reformer, and espoused severely moralistic views in accordance with his beliefs as a born-again Christian. Prior to this transformation, Tolstoy had been a rather profligate youth, given to gambling and carousing and, when his professors wrote him off as ineducable, he left university and embarked on a brief military career. Like fellow Russian aristocrats-turned-anarchists Prince Kropotkin and Mikhail Bakunin, Tolstoy's political philosophy was influenced by the ideas of radical French philosopher Pierre-Joseph Proudhon, and he fervently advocated non-violence, rejected government authority and official church doctrine, championed oppressed peasants against the entrenched feudal system which still prevailed in Russia during his lifetime, and embraced pacifism and vegetarianism. Best known as the author of the novels *Anna Karenina; The Death of Ivan Ilyich;* and *War and Peace,* Tolstoy also penned morally prescriptive texts intended to cure social ills. Some of these are *The Kingdom of God is Within You; What is to be Done?; The Dream Shattered Sixty Years Ago;* and *Why do Men Stupefy Themselves?* The latter is a sympathetic document compassionately treating the general subject of intoxication as an avenue of hedonism and personal escape, as well as a metaphysical problem brought about by the inner emptiness men feel as a result of spiritual poverty and affliction.

**Michael Stephans** is an American author of such works of poetry and prose as *Bright Size Life; Mythematics;* and *The Color of Stones.* In addition to his literary endeavors, he has pursued a career as a composer and musician, having performed with such jazz and pop greats as Cal Tjader, Charlie Byrd, David Bowie, and The Rolling Stones.

# Other Notable Authors

**Alain Bosquet (1919–1998).** French poet and diplomat, born Anatole Bisk in Odessa, Ukraine, Russia. Variously a Belgian and an American citizen, and resident of Bulgaria, and occupation-era Germany, who is said to have evolved artistically from surrealism to satire, which he called the practice of "fervent derision." Won the Apollinaire Prize and authored novels, criticism, and a massive autobiography.

**William S(eward) Burroughs (1914–1997).** Descendant of the inventor of the adding machine, world-traveler, devotee of global drug culture, heroin addict, and American underground author of *Junkie; Naked Lunch; The Soft Machine; The Ticket That Exploded;* and *Nova Express,* who spent much of his life abroad. A friend of Allen Ginsberg, with whom he corresponded for many years, Burroughs was identified with the Beat scene. At one time or another he worked as an exterminator, bartender, and private investigator. Accidentally shot and killed his wife in Mexico City while playing a game of William Tell. Created the fictional realm of Interzone, where life is based on the "Algebra of Need," and in which, according to one critic, "all humanity suffers from some form of addiction, because the body is a biological trap and society is run by control addicts who use the needs of the body to satisfy their obsession with power."

**William Burroughs, Jr. (1947–1981).** Son of Beat icon William S. Burroughs. Author of *Speed* and *Kentucky Ham*, autobiographical chronicles of a life of reckless excess, and the personal hell of stimulant addiction and alcoholism. Estranged from his father most of his life, Burroughs, Jr. was raised in St. Louis and Palm Beach by his paternal grandparents. Addicted to methedrine and arrested for forging a prescription, he underwent compulsory treatment at the Federal Narcotics Farm in Lexington. He died from liver failure at the age of thirty-three.

**Albert Cossery (1913–2008).** Born in Cairo, Egypt. Was schooled by a religious order and very early came under the spell of Baudelaire and developed a taste for the macabre. Published the collection of stories *God-Forsaken.* After World War II, he established himself in France. Cossery's short fiction is predicated on a brutish, larval world of extreme social marginals who, unable to find happiness even in their dreams, frequently resort to drugs out of sheer existential despair.

**Geza Csath (1887–1919).** Hungarian neurologist who was addicted to opium, and injected morphine and pantopon. After service during World War I, according to his biographer, he "showed definite signs of insanity, carried knives and had his family followed by detectives. Finally, in the presence of their infant daughter, he shot his wife with a revolver. He was moved to an insane asylum where he tried, unsuccessfully, to commit suicide. Months later he was able to escape, and made a last, desperate effort to reach Budapest, possibly the clinic of Moravcik, his psychiatrist. At the new demarcation line he was stopped by Serbian border guards. After a short struggle he gave up, but suddenly swallowed poison and died amidst the bewildered soldiers." Author of *The Magician's Garden and Other Stories.*

**Isabelle Eberhardt (1877–1904).** Raised in Switzerland by exiles from the Russian court of Tzar Alexander II, and treated as a boy by her anarchist-nihilist stepfather, Eberhardt, by the age of sixteen, spoke six languages, including Arabic. When, in her later teens, she proclaimed to her stepfather her wish to commit suicide, he promptly offered her his revolver. After the deaths of her parents, she traveled to Algeria and Morocco where, dressed as a man, she engaged in all sorts of exotic adventures, including political intrigue on behalf of the French government. In North Africa she eventually became a member of a Sufi sect, the Qadiriya Brotherhood and, at one point, took refuge in a Moroccan religious retreat. She married a sergeant in the Foreign Legion, was the object of an assassination attempt, and drowned in a Saharan flash flood at the age of twenty-seven. Her books include *The Oblivion Seekers* and *Vagabond.*

**(Irwin) Allen Ginsberg (1926–1997)** was an American poet and a legendary kingpin of the Beat Movement noted for his seminal 1950s poem *Howl* which lamented materialism and conformity in American society. A lifelong spiritual seeker and Buddhist, Ginsberg led a humble existence in New York's Greenwich Village and took part in scores of political protest marches, anti-war sit-ins, drug legalization rallies and other activities aimed at calling attention to persistent social problems and changing ossified government policies. In the 1970s, he co-founded the Jack Kerouac School of Disembodied Poetics in Boulder, Colorado. An intimate of Kerouac, Ginsberg maintained close ties with Gregory Corso, Lawrence Ferlinghetti, and other beat writers throughout his life. Many years before undertaking a much sensationalized public program of psychedelic drug advocacy, Ginsberg experienced two significant mystical experiences—the first, a spontaneous vision of early nineteenth century English poet William Blake; and the second, experienced during the throes of a peyote session, a vision of San Francisco's Francis Drake Hotel as the maw of the Ammonite child-devouring god Moloch. In 1965, Allen Ginsberg headlined the epochal International Poetry Incarnation at London's Royal Albert Hall, an event that showcased cutting-edge contemporary poets and was commemorated in the documentary film *Wholly Communion.* Ginsberg traveled widely and was expelled from several countries where he attempted to practice free speech, including China, Cuba, and Czechoslovakia, where he was crowned King of May by an enthusiastic populace, but branded an "immoral menace" by government officials who indignantly gave him the boot. Ginsberg, who has been called "as much a social force as a literary phenomenon," openly promoted drug use. He sponsored legalization of marijuana and endorsed a program of demystification and responsible investigation of psychedelics. The 1963 City Lights book *The Yage Letters* consists of correspondence between himself and fellow beat William S. Burroughs chronicling their respective experiences in the depths of the Amazon jungle, with yage, or ayahuasca, the most powerful psychedelic substance known.

**Aldous Leonard Huxley (1894–1963).** English author educated at Eton and Oxford who, after extensive travels, came to settle in California. Scion of a family of famous British scientists, he forsook his early intentions to study medicine after an eye problem almost blinded him at age sixteen. Celebrated for his novels, particularly those of a speculative cast such as Brave New World and Island, Huxley also published *The Doors of Perception* and *Heaven and Hell*, studies of psychedelic states induced by mescaline. He died on November 22, 1963, the same day John F. Kennedy was assassinated, after being administered an intramuscular injection of 100 micrograms of LSD.

**Ernst Jünger (1895–1998)** was a German writer of fiction, nonfiction, essays, diaries and memoirs, as well as an entomologist, soldier and battlefield photographer who was awarded the military citation known as the "Blue Max." In his youth, he participated in the Wandervogel Movement, then served as a lieutenant during World War I. Jünger regarded war and its personal challenges to combatants as a test of human capacities and an impetus to inner potential and exaltation of the individual. In a twisted chicane of political intrigue during the rise of Nazism and the brief tenure of the Third Reich, Jünger declined an invitation to head the German Academy of Literature, was assigned to an administrative post in Paris where he hobnobbed with cultural icons Jean Cocteau and Pablo Picasso, and was implicated in the von Stauffenberg plot to assassinate Adolf Hitler. A friend of Martin Heidegger, Jünger eventually cranked out more than fifty books during the course of a long life. Jünger's literary artistry engendered such well-known titles as *Storm of Steel*; *Fire and Blood*; and the anthology *War and Warriors*; as well as the allegorical *On the Marble Cliffs*; and the early example of magical realism *The Glass Bees*. Jünger explored the effects of ether, hashish, cocaine, mescaline and LSD, which he took on more than one occasion in the company of Albert Hofmann, the chemist who originally synthesized it. He coined the term "psychonautics" in reference to the neural adventures facilitated by the ingestion of psychedelics.

**Timothy Francis Leary (1920–1996)** was an American psychologist and writer, christened by the press during the 1960s as the "High Priest of LSD" and famed for the provocative phrase "turn on, tune in, drop out." Because of his popularization of psychedelic drugs and avid proselytizing for their use, he was characterized as a Pied Piper enthralling misguided youth and President Richard Nixon named him "the most dangerous man in America." Leary came to national prominence while conducting experiments with LSD and psilocybin as a professor at Harvard University before these substances were outlawed. After being discharged under a cloud of controversy, Leary embarked on a spectacular career of LSD advocacy, indefatigably championing "acid" as a chemical key to consciousness expansion and spiritual liberation. With co-professor Richard Alpert, he authored

*The Psychedelic Experience*, a step-by-step navigation manual for LSD trips based on the *Tibetan Book of the Dead.* Leary was so feared by uncomprehending civic authorities that he was jailed all over the world thirty times during a twenty year period and, at one point, was sentenced to ninety-five years' imprisonment for possession of a small quantity of drugs which may have been planted by government agents in order to incriminate him. Leary created the Castalia Foundation in Millbrook, New York and a new religion—the League for Spiritual Discovery—which proclaimed LSD as its sacrament, and was a gubernatorial candidate in California during the late 1960s. Leary authored a variety of books including an autobiography titled *Flashbacks.*

**Terence McKenna (1946–2000).** Author of *The Invisible Landscape; True Hallucinations;* and *Food of the Gods: the Search for the Original Tree of Knowledge: a Radical History of Plants, Drugs, and Human Evolution.* Lecturer, lay anthropologist, and social commentator who advanced the interesting supposition that human intelligence was sparked by the ingestion of psychedelic mushrooms by nomadic bands of early men, and that the evolution of consciousness dates from these foraging activities of proto-humans.

**Robert Gordon Wasson (1898–1986)** was an American author, financier, and mycologist specializing in the properties and lore of "magic mushrooms." Wasson undertook expeditions to Mexico to collect specimens and study the religious use of mushrooms by indigenes. He was one of the first outsiders to take part in related rituals. Wasson's findings during these outings fueled the concept among modern scientists of the ability of entheogenic substances to act as gateways to ulterior realities impinging on our own, and laid the foundation, in the popular mind, for the mystical, metaphysical aura surrounding these drugs. The torch lit by Wasson was taken up later by fellow travelers Terence McKenna and brother Dennis, an ethnobotanist who, although particularly fascinated by DMT, systematically explored the potential of a whole spectrum of entheogens, convinced that the implications of psychedelics have been far from exhausted and that, as neuroscience and psychopharmacology continue their inexorable march towards higher knowledge, the nature and magnitude of future discoveries are matters that defy speculation. Wasson suggested that the euphoriant called soma in the ancient Hindu Vedas was, in fact, a distillate of the fly agaric mushroom, and that the active ingredient of the inebriant kykeon which figured in the ceremonies of the ancient Greek Eleusinian mystery cult was an alkaloid derived from ergot, the organic source of LSD. Among Wasson's noted works are *The Wondrous Mushroom*; *The Road to Eleusis*; and *Soma: Divine Mushroom of Immortality*.

**Irvine Welsh.** Scottish author of splenetic drug-themed novels with contemporary settings such as *The Acid House*; *Ecstasy: Three Tales of Chemical Romance*; and the graphic, hard-edged *Trainspotting*, made into a controversial motion picture.

# Notes

1. Rue de la Gaïté = Gaity Street, Paris.
2. More exact directions for treatment may be found in "Drugs That Enslave," etc., Philadelphia, 1881.
3. Wunderlich, 'Pathol, und Therapie,' tom. iv., p. 17. Griesinger, 'Pathol, und Therapie der psychischen Krankheken,' 1871, p. 177.
4. But how is it that people who do not drink or smoke are often morally on an incomparably lower plane than others who drink and smoke? And why do people who drink and smoke often manifest very high qualities both mentally and morally?

   The answer is, first, that we do not know the height that those who drink and smoke would have attained had they not drunk and smoked.

   And secondly, from the fact that morally gifted people achieve great things in spite of the deteriorating effect of stupefying substances, we can but conclude that they would have produced yet greater things had they not stupefied themselves. It is very probable, as a friend remarked to me, that Kant's works would not have been written in such a curious and bad style had he not smoked so much.

   Lastly, the lower a man's mental and moral plane the less does he feel the discord between his conscience and his life, and therefore the less does he feel a craving to stupefy himself; and on the other hand a parallel reason explains why the most sensitive natures—those which immediately and morbidly feel the discord between life and conscience—so often indulge in narcotics and perish by them.

www.ingramcontent.com/pod-product-compliance
Lightning Source LLC
Chambersburg PA
CBHW060304100726
47907CB00002B/281
* 9 7 8 1 5 8 7 7 5 0 2 6 7 *